Governance Entrepreneurs

Global partnerships have transformed international institutions by creating platforms for direct collaboration with nongovernmental organizations, foundations, companies, and local actors. They introduce a model of governance that is decentralized, networked, and voluntary and which melds public purpose with private practice. How can we account for such substantial institutional change in a system made by states and for states?

Governance Entrepreneurs examines the rise and outcomes of global partnerships across multiple policy domains: human rights, health, environment, sustainable development, and children. It argues that international organizations have played a central role as entrepreneurs of such governance innovation in coalition with proactive states and non-state actors, yet this entrepreneurship is risky, and success is not assured. This is the first study to leverage comprehensive quantitative and qualitative analysis that illuminates the variable politics and outcomes of public–private partnerships across multilateral institutions, including the UN Secretariat, the World Bank, UNEP, the WHO, and UNICEF.

LILIANA B. ANDONOVA is Professor of International Relations and Political Science and Academic Co-Director of the Center for International Environmental Studies at the Graduate Institute of International and Development Studies, Geneva. She is the author of *Transnational Politics of the Environment* (2003), co-author of *Transnational Climate Change Governance* (2014), and co-editor of a special issue on the Comparative Politics of Transnational Climate Governance of the *International Interactions* journal (2017).

BUSINESS AND PUBLIC POLICY

This series aims to play a pioneering role in shaping the emerging field of business and public policy. *Business and Public Policy* focuses on two central questions. First, how does public policy influence business strategy, operations, organization, and governance, and with what consequences for both business and society? Second, how do businesses themselves influence policy institutions, policy processes, and other policy actors and with what outcomes?

Other Books in the Series
Timothy Werner, *Public Forces and Private Politics in American Big Business*
Hevina S. Dashwood, *The Rise of Global Corporate Social Responsibility: Mining and the Spread of Global Norms*
Llewelyn Hughes, *Globalizing Oil: Firms and Oil Market Governance in France, Japan, and the United States*
Edward T. Walker, *Grassroots for Hire: Public Affairs Consultants in American Democracy*
Christian R. Thauer, *The Managerial Sources of Corporate Social Responsibility: The Spread of Global Standards*
Kiyoteru Tsutsui & Alwyn Lim (Editors), *Corporate Social Responsibility in a Globalizing World*
Aseema Sinha, *Globalizing India: How Global Rules and Markets are Shaping India's Rise to Power*
Victor Menaldo, *The Institutions Curse: Natural Resources, Politics, and Development*
Jeroen van der Heijden, *Innovations in Environmental Governance: Governing for Less in East and West*

Governance Entrepreneurs

International Organizations and the Rise of Global Public–Private Partnerships

LILIANA B. ANDONOVA
Graduate Institute for International and Development Studies, Geneva

CAMBRIDGE
UNIVERSITY PRESS

CAMBRIDGE
UNIVERSITY PRESS

University Printing House, Cambridge CB2 8BS, United Kingdom

One Liberty Plaza, 20th Floor, New York, NY 10006, USA

477 Williamstown Road, Port Melbourne, VIC 3207, Australia

314-321, 3rd Floor, Plot 3, Splendor Forum, Jasola District Centre, New Delhi - 110025, India

79 Anson Road, #06-04/06, Singapore 079906

Cambridge University Press is part of the University of Cambridge.

It furthers the University's mission by disseminating knowledge in the pursuit of
education, learning and research at the highest international levels of excellence.

www.cambridge.org
Information on this title: www.cambridge.org/9781316617038
DOI: 10.1017/9781316694015

© Liliana B. Andonova 2017

First published 2017
First paperback edition 2019

A catalogue record for this publication is available from the British Library

Library of Congress Cataloging in Publication data
Names: Andonova, Liliana B., author.
Title: Governance entrepreneurs : international organizations and the rise of global
public-private partnerships / Liliana Andonova.
Description: New York : Cambridge University Press, 2017. | Series: Business and
public policy | Includes bibliographical references and index.
Identifiers: LCCN 2017016928| ISBN 9781107165663 (hardback) |
ISBN 9781316617038 (paperback)
Subjects: LCSH: Social service–International cooperation. | Public-private sector
cooperation. | BISAC: POLITICAL SCIENCE / International Relations / General.
Classification: LCC HV544.5 .A54 2017 | DDC 361.2/6–dc23 LC record available
at https://lccn.loc.gov/2017016928

ISBN 978-1-107-16566-3 Hardback
ISBN 978-1-316-61703-8 Paperback

Contents

Figures

Tables

Acknowledgments

How do institutions change in response to complex challenges to human security and planetary sustainability? The exploration of large and enduring questions often starts from a focal image or an event that captures imagination. This book began with the observation of important organizational transformation – the rise of global public–private partnerships to tackle pressing problems of health, human rights, environment, and development more broadly. Global partnerships straddle traditional divisions between the public and the private spheres and between international cooperation, domestic politics, and local concerns. These arrangements are incredibly diverse in terms of structure, objectives, and participation. How can we account for such layering of different forms of governance? What are the roles of private actors and public institutions? How do global partnerships govern? This book takes on the challenge to conceptualize institutional transformation and examine in broad strokes partnership governance across the international system. The focal idea that emerged is that of entrepreneurship – a concerted effort by coalitions of actors that straddles scales and sources of authority to experiment with new mechanisms of governance and justify their institutionalization. International organizations have played a central role in these processes both as entrepreneurs and enablers of the cycle of change. The analysis and documentation of the rise of global partnerships relied on multi-method research across issue domains of international governance. Fortunately, I found tremendous support in this endeavor for which I will be always grateful. The scale of the research and analysis would not have been possible without the generous support of academic funding, the insights of many interviews, and the feedback and deliberation with colleagues, friends, and family.

The research was supported by the Swiss National Science Foundation (SNF grant numbers 2054 and 2067), including the data collection and a large part of the qualitative research that informs this book.

This funding made possible the broad and comparative perspective on institutional change and global partnerships offered by the analysis. The Giorgio Ruffolo Fellowship at the Sustainability Science Program of the Harvard Kennedy School, in turn, provided the basis for the intellectual development of the initial stages of the project, methodology, and research, for which I am much obliged. As a Fernand Braudel Fellow at the Department of Political and Social Sciences of the European University Institute (EUI), I undertook the final revisions of the book. It has been a true privilege to interact with and learn from colleagues at the Centre for International Environmental Studies (CIES) of the Graduate Institute, at the Sustainability Science Program at the Harvard Kennedy School, and at the EUI.

I gratefully acknowledge the research assistance of Manoela Assayag, who supported the creation of the Global Partnership Database; to Defne Gonenc, who worked in the final stages of completing the database, both under the SNF projects; as well as to Alain Schaub, Zuzana Hudáková, Kathryn Chelminski, Elena Zheglova, and Diana Jack, all of whom contributed important elements to assembling the research, figures, and other elements of the book. As part of the SNF project, Kate Mann and Heather Lima supported the endeavor with invaluable editing input and advice, as well as with good humor.

I am much indebted to colleagues who have graciously read and offered comments on different chapters of the book, contributing to the debate that it pursues, including Bob Keohane, Bill Clark, Tom Biersteker, John Ruggie, Nancy Dickson, Andrew Clapham, Gian Luca Burci, Ron Mitchell, Julia Marton-Lefèvre, Jessica Green, Tom Hale, Charlie Roger, Bernhard Fuhrer, Judith Kelley, and Tana Johnson. I have enjoyed discussing the project with many colleagues and friends who care deeply about issues of institutions, rights, and advancing sustainability and well-being, including László Bruszt, Jacqueline Coté, Adrienne Héritier, Calestous Juma, Annabelle Littoz-Monnet, Stephanie Hofmann, Lisa Prügl, Suerie Moon, Anna Grzymala-Busse, Hanspeter Kriesi, Jennifer Welsh, Amanda Dawson, Susan McCrory, Alessandra Vellucci, Eugenia Marinova, Gergana Yankova, Ani Yankova, Moira Faul, Grainne Ward, Clare McGurk Sheridan, Gerasim Dochev, Victoria Docheva, Matt Gershoff, Petio Andonov, and Ganka Andonova.

I am grateful to the experts in various organizations that agreed to discuss different aspects of partnership governance and thus provided important reality checks and extraordinary insights on the processes of institutional change and partnerships governance. References to these interviews are included and acknowledged across the book. Special thanks to William Kennedy, Tim Swanson, Steven Stone, Garrette Clark, Derek Eaton, Gian Luca Burci, Susan Bissell, Pascal Villeneuve, Marilena Viviani, Sally Burnheim, Sophia Drewnowski, and Chris Gerrard for their broad perspective on partnerships and important suggestions and contacts on the practice of partnering. Clearly, a research undertaking of such breadth and ambition could not have been accomplished without open doors, exchange of ideas, and learning. Needless to say, the author is solely responsible for any claims that the book makes or interpretation of events, data, and interviews.

Aseem Prakash and John Haslam have made the realization of this book possible with their interest in subject, support, and outstanding professional guidance. Thank you! The review process at Cambridge University Press has been remarkable in speed and quality. I am grateful to the two anonymous reviewers for the detailed attention and suggestions on the manuscript, which have contributed to casting more broadly and critically the net of the analysis. The work of the production team at Cambridge University Press is much appreciated, including the support from Daniel George Brown, Ishwarya Mathavan, Kim Husband and many others.

As always, I am the most indebted to my family – my husband Tiho and daughters Daniela and Nicolena, to my mom Saba and dad Nikolai, and to my brother George. Thank you for unwavering support and interest in the book, counting the months, days, and pages to its publication! Please read on.

1 | *Introduction – Global Partnerships*

I propose that you, the business leaders gathered here in Davos, and we, the United Nations, initiate a Global Compact of shared values and principles, which will give a human face to the global market.[1]

Kofi Annan, UN Secretary General, speaking at the
World Economic Forum Annual Meeting 1999

Introduction

"Kill seven diseases, save 1.2m lives a year" – a punchy headline describes the sharp fall in deaths since the millennium, thanks to concerted cooperation on some of the world's deadliest diseases (*Economist* 2015). The news concerning diseases such as malaria, HIV/AIDS, measles, polio, and tuberculosis makes the front cover of the *Economist* magazine and signals the successful impact of well-orchestrated and determined medical campaigns. However, these striking advances would not have been possible without the emergence of global partnerships and a new type of collective action to tackle global problems. The Global Fund to Fight Aids, Tuberculosis and Malaria (The Global Fund), the Stop TB partnership, the Global Polio Eradication Initiative, and tens of other related partnerships have allowed the mobilization of resources, collective commitments, innovation, and advocacy on a scale necessary to combat such scourges. The emergence of global public–private partnerships created as new hybrid governance to complement state-driven multilateralism and their impact on global problems cannot be underestimated.

This book examines the rise of global partnerships and how they are changing the face of international governance.[2] If the twentieth century

---

[1] Annan 1999, www.un.org/press/en/1999/19990201.sgsm6881.html, accessed September 2012.

[2] The term "global partnerships" is used throughout the book as a shorthand for "global public–private partnerships."

1

was marked by the rise of multilateralism, the twenty-first century has been characterized by its transformation. Following the turbulence of the Great Depression and two world wars, nation-states constructed in 1945 a complex architecture of intergovernmental institutions. Multilateralism rested on a set of shared principles, norms, and rules built by and for states, reflecting the interests and ideas of the victorious powers. This web of institutions rapidly expanded, alongside the complexity of issues on the international agenda. By the turn of the century, however, state-centric multilateralism was undergoing turbulence and metamorphosis driven by growing discontent.

Globalization, understood as the proliferation of networks of global connectedness and interdependence,[3] was amplifying transboundary problems, while intergovernmental interest in cooperation was stagnating. Emerging powers and developing countries felt that their priorities were not being adequately represented in the institutional constellation of decision making. Societal actors were demanding greater accountability of international organizations (IOs). Important global objectives such as poverty reduction, access to health, education, and human rights were being woefully underachieved. As states debated but perpetually fell short of achieving major reforms of international institutions, the multilateral system began to open up to direct collaboration with the private sector and other nonstate actors through partnerships.

Global public–private partnerships are voluntary agreements between public actors (IOs, states, or substate public authorities) and nonstate actors (nongovernmental organizations [NGOs], companies, foundations, etc.) on a set of governance objectives and norms, rules, practices, or implementation procedures and their attainment across multiple jurisdictions and levels of governance.[4]

The objective of this study is to theorize the process of institutional change, which has produced new hybrid governance, and to document

---

[3] Castells 1996; Keohane and Nye 2000; Held and McGrew 2002.

[4] The term "private" refers here to a variety of nonstate actors (companies, NGOs, foundations, and other groups), as commonly used in international relations literature. The term "public–private partnerships" is used more restrictively in the business administration literature, where it signifies cooperation between public institutions and private-sector entities, which are distinct from social partnerships between nonprofit organizations and business (Austin and Seitanidi 2014; Waddock 1988; Stadtler and Probst 2012).

its impact on international relations. The argument posits that IOs have played a central role as entrepreneurs of significant institutional change, enabling unprecedented level of collaboration on global issues across the public and private spheres. Driven by organizational interests and empowered by their expertise and selective support from member states, international agencies have actively mobilized or brokered transnational coalitions with entrepreneurial states and nonstate actors. Transnational business, advocates, and philanthropists for their part are increasingly reaching out to the multilateral sphere for institutional platforms, normative framing, and political risk management through voluntary governance programs.

The agency of both private and public entrepreneurs is essential for the rise of partnerships. However, it is IOs that often lead or provide the forum and normative glue for such collaboration, crafting a political space for the interface between public purpose and private practice in international relations. The institutional capital of the multilateral system has in effect enabled it to reinvent itself and to engage the agency, resources, expertise, and norms of diverse global actors from business to advocacy organizations and from local communities to transnational associations. The change is endogenous in the way that it has been engineered from *within* the multilateral system, in response to a broad range of external stimuli associated with globalization and internal political incentives of IOs and member states. Such an activist role by IOs with respect to the private sphere is surprising from the perspective of much of the international relations literature, which has traditionally focused on the steering role of states and attributed to IOs limited capacity for endogenous change.

Global partnerships have tackled many seemingly intractable problems, but their rise is not without controversy. A series of carbon funds, facilitated by the World Bank and its partners, increased substantially the financing for climate change by leveraging new resources. While intergovernmental negations remained deadlocked from 2000 to 2011, this financial push integrated the climate change issue into the development agenda. Global partnerships have also changed how the multilateral system governs. They have introduced a model of governance that is decentralized, networked, and voluntary and that melds the public purpose of formal organizations with private practice. These features can enable some actors to engage in collective action before a broad consensus is achieved, to experiment with innovative solutions, and, in some instances but not all, to make significant contribution to the production of public goods. They constitute a significant departure from the hierarchical organizational structure of multilateral institutions and from the strict interpretation of their authority as granted by and for states.[5] It is precisely the interface between the public mandates of international institutions and the exercise of private authority in collaborative initiatives that inevitably generates contention.

The World Bank partnerships for climate finance have drawn scrutiny for creating a parallel structure with asymmetric influence of donor countries, compared to the more broadly representative process under the United Nations Framework Convention for Climate Change (UNFCCC). Similarly, critics question the very disease-focused and technology-based approach of many health partnerships whose human and development gains are celebrated by many observers because of concerns that such vertical approaches may divert attention and resources from public health systems. An early article by Kent Buse and Andrew Harmer (2004, p. 50) asks: "[D]o those who govern partnerships constitute unrepresentative and unaccountable elite?" Critics are concerned whether the influx of private resources could shift the international agenda toward certain priorities while crowding out other, equally important ones. Can direct participation by nonstate actors undermine the very intergovernmental foundations of IOs by reducing the relative role of states as principals and channels of state-based accountability?

The unresolved debates on the nature of global partnerships and the evolving structure of international relations require us to step back and provide a more in-depth analysis on the politics of institutional change and its outcomes. We need to inquire what kinds of actors engage in

---

[5] The terms "international institution" and "multilateral institution" are used here in a broad sense to encompass the institutional features of international regimes, specified in a collaborative volume by Steven Krasner and his colleagues as "implicit or explicit principles, norms, rules, and decision making procedures around which actors' expectations converge in a given area of international relations" (Krasner 1983, p. 2). International organizations (IOs) are understood to be the formal organizational infrastructure and an element of international institutions; they operate according to specific hierarchies, missions, rules, procedures, and resources (Ruggie 1992). The features of institutions can take multiple forms other than bureaucratic hierarchies (Keohane 1984; Ostrom 1990). The new set of organizational forms introduced by global partnerships, as elaborated in this chapter, thus amount to an important change in the organizational features of multilateral institutions.

the establishment of new mechanisms of governance across public and private domains – what are the drivers of such entrepreneurship and what political conditions facilitate or limit the scope of public–private collaboration. We also need more systematic empirical evidence on the outcomes of global partnerships in terms of the governance priorities and instruments they bring to the multilateral system in order to start addressing contentious policy debates.

Therefore, three analytic questions underpin this inquiry into the process that has generated new hybrid governance and examines its impact: (1) Why and under what conditions do states and IOs increasingly share decision-making and implementation authority with nonstate actors? (2) What are the governance instruments and outcomes of global partnerships and how has the agency of IOs and nonstate actors shaped these outcomes? (3) How does collaboration across the public and private spheres diffuse across the multilateral system to become institutionalized as part of its structure?

To address these questions, this book develops a theory of endogenous institutional change. The theoretical framework draws on a dynamic interpretation of the principal–agent (PA) model of delegation of public authority from states as principals to IOs as agents and bureaucratic managers of cooperation. It inquires why and under what conditions both agents and a subset of principals would engage external, nonstate actors in new governance mechanisms and thus implicitly change the institutional status quo. This is unlike most applications of PA models, which view IOs as agents prone to agency drift and states as principals seeking to control such tendencies. Instead, the theory stipulates the possibility of forging entrepreneurial coalitions *between* agents and like-minded principals, seeking to spur dynamic processes of change from within and in collaboration with external actors. Such change is nonlinear, as we shall see in subsequent chapters. It involves a three-step cycle of organizational entrepreneurship – from agenda setting and experimental adoption of partnership initiatives to replication and diffusion of partnership practices and finally to the attainment of more permanent institutionalization of the hybrid model within the multilateral system.

This study thus advances the understanding of global partnerships as institutional innovation that has emerged in response to globalization through a process of experimentation, contestation, and subsequent institutionalization, which has been overlooked by theories of cooperation and IOs. By examining the endogenous dynamics of institutional change and the entrepreneurship of global partnerships, the book contributes to the broader inquiry on the structure of global governance in several distinct ways. It sheds light on global partnerships as a specific new organizational form that entails an interface between networks and hierarchies and between intergovernmentalism and transnationalism, leading us to better understand how such partnerships have changed the face of multilateral governance. It also elaborates an organizational theory of dynamic institutional change *within* the multilateral system. Partnerships are neither a product of intergovernmental design nor a bureaucratic progeny of mission extensions; they are driven by entrepreneurial coalitions and iterative processes that cut across organizational lines.[6] Finally, the book makes an important empirical contribution. It paints a comparative and theoretically informed canvas of the politics, patterns, and outcomes of collaborative governance across multiple organizational spheres including the United Nations Secretariat, the World Bank, the United Nations Environment Program (UNEP), the United Nations Children's Fund (UNICEF), and the World Health Organization (WHO). The chapters analyze diverse areas of governance such as the UN partnership engagement with business and human rights, environment and sustainable development, and children's health. This canvas sheds concrete light on contested debates about the sources of authority embedded in global partnerships. It documents the leading role of public organizations, illuminating a much more dynamic and dialectic picture of institutional experimentation and change than what is implicitly assumed by either partnership enthusiasts or partnership skeptics.

The rest of this chapter elaborates the main organizational features of global partnerships and how they constitute an important departure from the traditional structure of the multilateral system. It proceeds to argue why we need a more explicit focus on governance entrepreneurs and endogenous organizational change to understand global partnerships and evolving institutions more broadly. The

---

[6] This book contributes most directly to the literature examining the role of IOs in facilitating informal governance and access by nonstate actors (Abbott *et al.* 2015; Andonova 2010; Hale and Roger 2014; Tallberg *et al.* 2013; Johnson 2014). It brings in a new theoretical perspective and data, which stipulates an endogenous process of institutional change that is entrepreneurial and iterative and cuts across the assumed divide between state principals and agencies.

structure of the book and the empirical inquiry are outlined in the conclusion of this chapter.

Global Partnerships as New Governance

In 2001, the Global Fund to Fight HIV/AIDS, Tuberculosis, and Malaria was jointly established by states, IOs, and nonstate actors as the largest global institution for health financing. Two years later, in 2002, the World Summit on Sustainable Development in Johannesburg, South Africa, became the first intergovernmental meeting to adopt public–private partnerships as an official outcome. By 2014, coordinated actions of several partnerships had elicited substantial policy and financial commitment by governments to reduce unacceptable and preventable levels of maternal and childhood mortality at birth and infancy, which have persisted among the poorest regions of the world. In all these instances, IOs, nonstate actors, and states or local authorities have come together to tackle problems that cross boundaries and scales from local to global.

Global partnerships constitute an innovation in the sphere of multilateral governance in several important ways. Partnerships introduce *new actors* from both the private and substate sectors into the formulation and implementation of governance objectives in an international system that has been designed by and for nation-states. Furthermore, they involve *collaboration* between state and nonstate actors, which implies joint decision making with respect to commonly identified or agreed-on objectives, to which partners contribute different sorts of resources, knowledge, or claims of legitimacy. Public–private collaborations in the international sphere thus involve the explicit rearticulation of the scope of public and private authority across governance jurisdictions and scales in the advancement of public purpose.[7] It is the agreement on a public purpose, meaning a steering toward shared and publicly recognized objectives, that qualifies partnerships as a form of governance.[8] Partnerships are therefore qualitatively different arrangements compared to the more traditional interactions between state and nonstate actors, such as lobbying, shaming, consultation, subcontracting, or providing formal access such

---

[7] Andonova 2006, 2010; Bull and McNeill 2007; Elsig and Amalric 2008; Schäferhoff, Campe and Kaan 2009.
[8] Andonova, Betsill, and Bulkeley 2009; Biersteker 2009; Rosenau 1992.

Table 1.1 *Global partnerships as organizational innovation in the multilateral system*

Multilateral Institutions	Global Partnerships
Centralized bureaucracies	Decentralized networks
Delegated authority	Multiple sources of authority
Sphere of competence	Pooling of competencies
Legalization	No or soft legalization
Stability & continuity	Flexibility
Inclusiveness	Self-selection

as observer or consultative status.[9] Global partnerships involve collaboration that is *global* in reach rather than bilateral or domestic. They operate within the broad framework of the multilateral system, connecting diverse sets of actors across jurisdictions in response to problems with transnational dimensions.[10]

Although embedded in the multilateral system, global partnerships also represent a significant organizational change in several distinct ways (see Table 1.1). They are configured as *network-based organizational structures* that involve horizontal, nonuniversal, and reciprocal interactions around a common purpose. Such a structure is distinct from the legalized, bureaucratic organization of the multilateral system, which has traditionally relied largely on intergovernmental agreements

[9] On the variety of such interactions between nonstate actors and IOs, see, among others, Bulkeley *et al.* 2014; Keck and Sikkink 1998; Bernauer, Böhmelt and Koubi 2013; Betsill and Corell 2008; Fox and Brown 1998; Keohane and Nye 2000; Willetts 1996; Weiss and Gordenker 1996; Princen and Finger 1994; Raustiala 1997; Tallberg *et al.* 2013. The emphasis on joint decision making also differentiates global partnerships from uses of the term "public–private partnerships" in domestic contexts, where it frequently signifies the subcontracting of functions (such as provision or management of utilities, infrastructure construction, etc.) to private actors.

[10] A plethora of concepts have been used to capture the diverse manifestations of transnational governance that may include public and private actors, among them "public policy networks," "multisectoral networks," "hybrid networks," "learning networks," and other terminology (Reinicke 1999; Benner, Streck and Witte 2003; Reinicke and Deng 2000; Ruggie 2002.) The focus here is on global partnerships as one specific type of transnational governance, which is significant in itself and transformative of the multilateral system.

and a vertical scheme of domestic implementation.[11] As managers of multilateral regimes, IOs operate as hierarchically organized bureaucracies with formal public authority delegated from member states. Global partnerships, for the most part, operate as networks that link actors horizontally across jurisdictions, as well as across levels of governance, from local to global. A global partnership network can thus involve a variable mix of agreements and responsibilities for implementation among supranational, national, subnational, state, and nonstate actors.

Furthermore, while the multilateral system is organized around public bureaucracies with delineated spheres of competence, standard procedures, and solutions,[12] partnerships deliberately pool sources of expertise and resources from the public and private spheres. They combine public mandates with market- and norm-based mechanisms of steering.[13] Some of the advantages of global partnerships are their lower levels of bureaucratization and ability to bring together diverse competencies, expertise, and resources. Most global partnerships have relatively small or no independent secretariats and involve a variable mix of expertise that can include that of several IOs, as well as of NGOs, private-sector entities, and national or subnational agencies.

A related line of organizational differentiation between multilateral institutions and global partnerships has to do with their legalization and universality (Table 1.1). Partnerships depart from the contemporary model of multilateral governance in that they are *voluntary* in the sense of being largely nonbinding under international public law. Multilateral institutions and managing IOs, on the other hand, are established by and embedded in a system of international hard and soft laws.[14] Partnerships typically rest on voluntary agreements such as memoranda of understanding or in certain cases simply on public announcements without a necessarily formalized agreement that carries the force of international

---

[11] Kahler 2009; Abbott and Snidal 2009.
[12] Cohen, March and Olsen 1972; Barnett and Finnemore 2004; Weber 1964; Ruggie 1992.
[13] Andonova 2010; Bull and McNeill 2007; Kaul 2005; Nelson 2002. By deliberately pooling public and private authority, partnerships thus present a different modality of governance innovation compared to private regulations made largely by nonstate actors (Hall and Biersteker 2002) or informal intergovernmental organizations and transgovernmental networks that rest largely on public authority (Vabulas and Snidal 2013; Raustiala 2002; Slaughter 2004)
[14] Chayes and Chayes 1995; Goldstein *et al.* 2001; Pauwelyn *et al.* 2012.

public law. Global partnerships are connected, however, even if indirectly, to international normative or regulatory documents from which they frequently derive or justify their governance objectives.[15]

Finally, global partnerships differ substantially from multilateral institutions in the degree of universality and stability they bring to cooperation (Table 1.1). Multilateral institutions are bureaucratically structured and legalized to bring continuity, predictability, and inclusiveness within functional or geographical areas of cooperation. They are intended to facilitate cooperation by fostering more stable expectations among member states through reciprocity, credible commitments, normative consensus, and information sharing.[16] Public–private partnerships, by contrast, emerge as largely nonlegalized coalitions of like-minded actors. They emphasize flexibility and willing self-selectiveness rather than universal or comprehensive membership for the purposes of achieving a set of specific governance objectives rather than inducing broader continuity in the system.

Understanding these stylized characteristics of global partnerships as a form of governance is necessary to appreciate the puzzle of the rise of new public–private arrangements within multilateral institutions intended to be controlled by states. Importantly, these characteristics also lie at the heart of unresolved public and academic debates on the worth and effects of partnerships in global governance. On the one hand, the organizational characteristics of global partnerships – network-based structure, pooling of authority and competencies, voluntarism, self-selection, and flexibility – can in principle help circumvent some classic problems of large-scale collective action that have plagued many aspects of intergovernmental cooperation. Partnerships can facilitate collective action, for example, by engaging smaller groups of actors, whose voluntary participation in such governance ventures may be informed by expected overlaps between private or local and global benefits of cooperation.[17] This was precisely the case in the creation of multiple targeted funds for climate finance, while global cooperation on climate change stagnated. The voluntary, nonlegalized nature of the agreements also reduces the political cost of entry and exit to global partnerships

---

[15] Andonova and Carbonnier 2014; Ruggie 2004; Boisson de Chazournes and Mazuyer 2011.

[16] Keohane 1984; Krasner 1983; Ruggie 1998.

[17] Olson 1971; Keohane and Ostrom 1995; Oye and Maxwell 1995; Andonova 2009, 2010; Potoski and Prakash 2005.

and thus enhances the likelihood of engagement.[18] Willing, self-selective participation in partnerships can be based on a set of commonly shared norms, which are then further amplified and exported through the network of the partnership by processes of learning, trust building, social monitoring, or implementation.[19] Thus, partnerships can spur incremental collective action toward global objectives in parallel to or in lieu of more encompassing but slower intergovernmental efforts. Indeed, the stagnation of intergovernmental cooperation on a number of fronts since the late 1990s has contributed to greater demand for and initiative toward experimenting with softer forms of governance.[20]

Proponents and architects of partnership governance point to the complementarities between the multilateral and partnership models of governance. They emphasize the potential contribution of collaborative networks to uncovering new areas of congruence between local and global benefits and unlocking new resource streams toward the provision of global public goods.[21] Indeed, it is hard to imagine that the humanitarian and development crisis associated with the HIV/AIDS pandemic of the late 1990s could have been addressed without partnerships that leveraged public objectives, streams of public and private financing, and technology and institutional innovations.[22] Similar approaches have been used to increase the ground-level and lateral support to humanitarian missions[23] or to leverage scientific research, technology, and extension services to dramatically improve food production and reduce hunger through the Consultative Group for Integrated Agricultural Research.[24]

On the other hand, the very collective action advantages of global partnerships imply that their contribution to global problem solving is likely to be partial and uneven precisely because their organizational structure relies on a high degree of congruence of interests, norms and overlapping private and public benefits. Critics charge

---

[18] Hirschman 1970; Andonova 2006, 2014.
[19] Ostrom 1990; Ruggie 2002.
[20] Hale and Held 2011; Keohane and Victor 2011; Hoffmann 2011; Morse and Keohane 2014; Mitchell 2003; Andonova and Mitchell 2010; Viñuales 2013.
[21] Kaul and Conceicao 2005; Kaul, Grunberg, and Stern 1999; Ruggie 2002.
[22] Szlezák *et al.* 2010.
[23] Andonova and Carbonnier 2014.
[24] Clark *et al.* 2016.

that such partial action through voluntary coalitions can serve to preempt more ambitious efforts for comprehensive and legalized collaboration and can skew the governance agenda toward the preferences of powerful corporate and advocacy interests.[25] The proliferation of global partnerships as venues for governance can thus stun the multilateral agenda rather than advance it; or steer it toward a narrower set of objectives that are in line with the interests of partners. For instance, the slow response to the 2014 Ebola crisis prompted a critique of the WHO for limited support for public health systems, arguably as a consequence of prioritizing vertical, technology-based interventions. Equally, the proliferation of partnerships for clean energy has been interpreted as a strategy to undermine the regulatory relevance of the UNFCCC Kyoto Protocol. Legal scholars question more broadly how the inflow of significant private resources can shape public agendas or introduce tension of differential accountability by IOs to states as formal principals and to multistakeholder partnership boards.[26]

In sum, the features of global partnerships make them both a novel mechanism for potentially important collective action and a form of governance contested for its voluntarism, fragmentation, and asymmetric influence. The perspective elaborated in this book moves the debate beyond the polarization between partnership skeptics and enthusiasts. By theorizing and documenting the agency behind new governance, the analysis shows that public actors and particularly IOs and government finance have remained at the core of new partnership governance. Public institutions thus actively engage nonstate actors in response to some form of turbulence in international relations associated with stagnation of intergovernmental support of IOs, legitimacy pressures for improved performance, or structural imbalances between public and private resources in development. Partnering is not a linear process, therefore, but one that involves a struggle for proving the concept with concrete results, learning, and some degree of institutionalization, without which new forms of governance cannot take root within the edifice of the multilateral system.

---

[25] Bäckstrand 2006; Bexell and Mörth 2010; Bendell *et al.* 2010; Bull and McNeill 2007; Weissbrodt 2008; Utting and Zammit 2006; Ottaway 2001; Newell 2012.
[26] Burci 2009.

Rise and Diversity of Global Partnerships

Global partnerships are an important phenomenon with which international relations theory needs to grapple not only because they represent a new form of organizing cooperation, but also because of their rapid rise and ubiquity in global governance. When the contemporary multilateral system was crafted, direct collaboration with nonstate actors was rare and confined to organizations with historical ties to civil society or business. The International Red Cross, for example, was founded in 1859 in Switzerland by Henry Dunant and his collaborators as a civic movement. Subsequently, the International Committee of the Red Cross, which has the status of an independent humanitarian organization, was vested with authority by the intergovernmental Geneva Conventions (1949) to promote humanitarian norms and principles and implement activities in the spirit of the Conventions. The International Labor Organization (ILO) is another example of a body with hybrid public and private representation. Created in 1919 in the aftermath of World War I, the ILO statute envisages tri-partite participation and decision making by states, labor organizations, and business organizations to promote peace based on social dialogue and justice.

A small number of intergovernmental institutions have historically collaborated with nongovernmental organizations in the implementation of specific functional objectives. Shortly after its creation in the post–World War II period, UNICEF established special relations with nongovernmental organizations for the purposes of timely delivery of assistance, implementation of programs on the ground, and fundraising. The intergovernmental Ramsar Convention on Wetlands chose as its secretariat the International Union for Conservation of Nature and Natural Resources (IUCN), the oldest conservation network of associations, with hybrid membership composed of governmental and nongovernmental organizations as well as scientists.

Beyond several unique and historically shaped institutions, however, public–private collaboration remained relatively rare in the multilateral sphere until the 1990s. In one of the first surveys of trends in public–private collaboration, Inge Kaul and her colleagues reviewed some 400 partnerships, revealing a sharp increase in this mode of collaboration since the 1980s and particularly after the mid-1990s.[27]

---

[27] Kaul 2005; see also Bull and McNeill 2007.

Today, most agencies within the UN family have some partnership activities with designated staff and focal points for collaborative work with the private sector. The Sustainable Development Goals (SDGs) adopted by the UN General Assembly in 2015 included SDG 17 on strengthening means of implementation, including through "global partnership for sustainable development."[28] Global partnerships have become recognized as an integral part of international governance.

Figure 1.1 pools data of the partnership portfolios of UNEP, the World Bank, WHO, and UNICEF, which are examined in detail later on, to illustrate the dramatic rise of public–private collaboration in the multilateral system. As Chapter 2 explains in greater detail, the research design of this study and systematic collection of data allows us to examine institutional change over time as well as comparatively – across issues and across organizations with substantial partnership activity but with very different approaches to engaging nonstate actors. The data show a clear trend toward a substantial increase in collaborative governance since the 1990s, with a particularly strong tendency around the turn of the millennium, as illustrated by the bars in Figure 1.1, which reflect the number of partnerships created in a given year. Although the figure captures only a snapshot of the larger collaborative governance landscape, it reveals that while partnerships were a relatively marginal activity for IOs until the 1990s, since then these organizations have become involved in hundreds of global partnerships. Moreover, global partnerships have facilitated collaboration not only between public and private actors in the international sphere but also across IOs. A number of partnerships, particularly those related to health, entail a considerable degree of coordination among international agencies and domestic counterparts.

Existing studies indicate a tendency toward variable public–private collaboration across IOs and areas of governance, with considerable clustering of such initiatives in the areas of global health and the environment, as well as disaster response, nutrition and education.[29] In Kaul's survey, for example, more than 50 of the 400 global public–private partnerships reviewed relate to health or environmental

---

[28] United Nations 2016, accessed via http://sustainabledevelopment.un.org/, July 2016.

[29] Stadtler 2011; Andonova and Carbonnier 2014; Martens 2007; Thomas and Fritz 2006; Beisheim and Liese 2014.

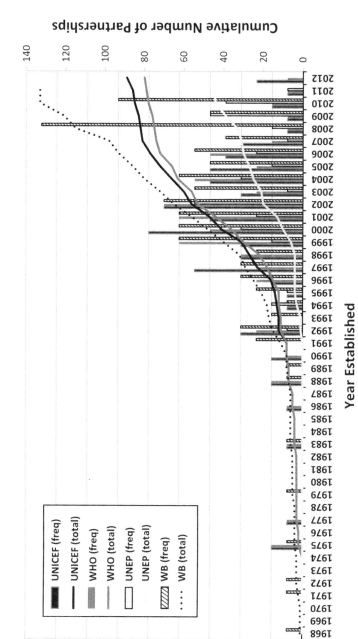

Figure 1.1 Rise of global public–private partnerships in the multilateral system

Source: Global Partnerships Database (see Annex on methodology)

problems.[30] The thematic contribution of the United Nations Foundations (UNF) and the portfolio of the United Nations Fund for International Partnerships (UNFIP), created in 2000 as related platforms to facilitate public–private partnerships across UN agencies, reflect a similar emphasis on clustering of partnership projects around certain governance priorities such as children's health (63% of all UNF financing for 1998–2010), the environment (14%), as well as population and women (12%).[31] These trends beg questions about the underlying reasons for variations in collaborative activity across time, across IOs, and across and within issue areas. What are the dynamics and broad patterns of partnership entrepreneurship and their implications for the problem-solving capacity of the multilateral system?

Capturing and analyzing the universe of global partnerships is a challenging endeavor. As a result of their flexible, networked, and voluntary organization, partnerships are in some ways a moving target. They are decentralized, rapidly evolving, and variable in terms of scope, size, governance structure, purpose, and degree to which their governance structure is embedded in multilateral institutions. The Global Fund, for example, which by 2015 had mobilized some US $33 billion across 144 countries for preventing and treating malaria, HIV/AIDS, and tuberculosis, is one incarnation of a global partnership.[32] The ten thousand partnership projects between local communities, NGOs, and governments facilitated by the Small Grants Programme partnership platform represent another facet of the phenomenon, operating at a very different scale and level of governance. The Global Fund is one of the few partnerships with an independent secretariat and mobilizes millions of dollars, including a substantial share from the private sector, in the fight against three of the deadliest health pandemics. The Small Grants Programme is a program under the Global Environmental Facility (GEF); it mobilizes grants of up to US$50,000 to sprinkle the globe with partnerships that produce community and environmental cobenefits through innovative technologies or services such as solar stoves, retrofitting of municipal buildings, conserving biodiversity to enhance local livelihoods, and hundreds of other approaches that link global sustainability and community

---

[30] Kaul 2005.
[31] UNGA 2011a A/66/188, p. 21.
[32] http://www.theglobalfund.org/, accessed April 2015 and August 2016.

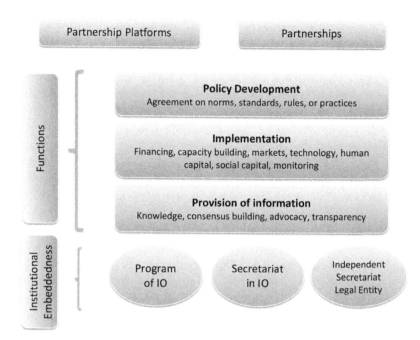

Figure 1.2 Diversity of global partnerships

development.[33] As these two examples illustrate, global partnerships are diverse in form and function, as well as layered across institutions and levels of governance.

Existing literature on global partnerships has contributed greatly to understanding the variability in form and particularly the variety of functions that partnerships are set to provide in global governance.[34] At the broadest level of aggregation and for the purposes of this study, it is useful to distinguish between partnerships and partnership platforms as two ways of organizing collaborative initiatives in the multilateral system (Figure 1.2).

---

[33] Andonova 2010.
[34] Andonova and Levy 2003; Andonova 2014; Hale and Mauzerall 2004; Bäckstrand 2008; Beisheim, Campe and Schäferhoff 2010; Beisheim *et al.* 2014; Börzel and Risse 2005; Bull and McNeill 2007; Glasbergen, Biermann and Mol 2007; Pattberg *et al.* 2012; Pattberg and Stipple 2008; Prügl and True 2014; Reinicke 1999; Kaul 2005; Nelson 2002; Benner, Streck and Witte 2003; Beisheim and Liese 2014; Bexell and Mörth 2010.

Partnership platforms consist of two layers of collaborative agreements. At the global level, public and private partners conclude an agreement on a broad set of goals and means to pursue them. These platforms then provide a framework, typically in the form of institutional support (information, networks, contracting), and often funding to enable a multiplicity of actors to contribute to these goals through a second layer of partnership projects, implemented across multiple governance scales and jurisdictions. The United Nations Fund for International Partnerships, which is analyzed in Chapter 3, is an example of a prominent partnership platform that has facilitated the opening of UN agencies to collaboration with nonstate actors by brokering and supporting hundreds of partnerships. The partnership process established at the 2002 World Summit on Sustainable Development is another partnership platform, which, however, has had highly variable success in enabling partnerships for sustainability.[35]

The Partnerships category in Figure 1.2 is reserved for freestanding, individual partnerships organized by public, private, and/or substate actors around a set of governance objectives, which partnership participants *contribute to or pursue themselves*. Such partnerships are not oriented primarily toward enabling partnership activity by others, as in the case of partnership platforms. Each individual partnership establishes a layer of agreements, norms, and practices to which participants commit. The Global Compact, for example, is a partnership that involves agreement between companies, UN organizations, states, and societal organizations to promote ten principles on human rights, environment, social rights, and anti-corruption. The signatories of the Global Compact undertake to advance the implementation of the ten principles themselves as well as to promote these principles among other actors. While freestanding partnerships can also disburse financing and design specific projects to advance their governance objectives, there is no distinct layering of programmatic and project-based activities as with partnership platforms. As with all ideal types, there are certainly overlaps and grey areas between the two categories of partnership platforms and partnerships, which only reinforce the multilayered and overlapping nature of the partnership phenomena. The

---

[35] Pattberg, Biermann and Chan 2012; Andonova and Levy 2003; Andonova 2014; Bäckstrand 2006.

distinction between partnership platforms and freestanding partnerships also helps us to better grasp the cycle of endogenous change in the empirical chapters, including processes of entrepreneurship, diffusion, and gradually formal institutionalization of partnerships within the multilateral system, in which partnership platforms have often played a central role.

Global partnerships also vary in the governance functions they seek to provide. I divide these functions into three categories: policy development, implementation, and provision of information (see Figure 1.2). Listed in Figure 1.2 are examples of the governance instruments and means, which global partnerships can leverage both from nonstate and public sources to contribute to the provision of specific functions.[36]

Global partnerships engage in *policy development* when they establish new agreements on norms, rules, or standards among a broader set of governmental and nongovernmental actors. Examples include the Flexible Framework Initiative for Chemical Accident Prevention and Preparedness, facilitated by UNEP and discussed in Chapter 4, or the World Commission on Dams, which is a collaborative initiative between governments, NGOs, the private sector, and IOs that established a set of voluntary norms for socially and environmentally sustainable dam development.[37] Partnerships are expected to enable new means of *implementation* by combining the resources, comparative advantages, and mandates of public organizations with the resources, market instruments, societal expertise, and reach of commercial entities and societal actors.[38] As Chapters 3 through 5 show, partnerships engaging in implementation range from World Bank climate finance initiatives to health partnerships seeking to enable access to particular medical technologies to UNICEF–private-sector partnerships on the logistics of delivering disaster relief or implementing programs for improved nutrition. Finally, several prominent partnerships, among them the UNEP Finance Initiative, the Global Reporting

---

[36] A number of policy and academic studies provide wide-ranging classifications of possible and actual governance functions, toward which global partnerships can contribute new resources and instruments. See Andonova, Betsill and Bulkeley 2009; Biermann *et al.* 2007; Bull and McNeill 2007; Kaul 2005; Nelson 2002; Witte and Reinicke 2005; Andonova and Levy 2003.

[37] Bissel 2001; Reinicke and Deng 2000; Dingwerth 2005.

[38] Kaul 2005. On the relevance and variable performance of global partnerships with respect to supporting capacity and means of implementations in areas of limited statehood, see Beisheim *et al.* 2014; Risse 2011.

Initiative, and Renewable Energy Network 21, perform governance functions largely by *producing and disseminating information* related to sustainability, corporate social responsibility practices, and the evolution of relevant public policies.[39] The provision of information often complements initiatives seeking to advance policy development or implementation.

While some global partnerships can involve all three governance functions, many tend to be created with a predominant focus on a very specific function and specific instruments for achieving it. The Global Fund, for example, emphasizes means of implementation through the pooling of financial resources and medical technology, although its activities indirectly influence global policy objectives for health. The Global Compact engages in policy development through norm interpretation and agreement with the business community. It also emphasizes dissemination of information as the main tool for implementing and increasing the reach of the normative agreements established.

Global partnerships also vary in their governance structures and the extent to which they are embedded in multilateral institutions. It is possible to distinguish three types of arrangements: (i) partnerships functioning without secretariats and managed as programs of an IO or a partner organization, which is the case for the majority of the partnerships in the multilateral system; (ii) partnerships with small secretariats hosted by IOs such as the Global Compact or Renewable Energy Network 21; and (iii) partnerships that are separate legal entities with independent secretariats such as the Global Fund, although they do involve collaboration with IOs. A number of examples, such as the Global Alliance for Vaccines and Immunization (GAVI) or the Global Water Partnership, have evolved from IO–managed programs into partnerships with independent secretariats. The conceptualization of the variable structures and functions of partnerships allows us to appreciate the complexity of the phenomenon and to examine critically what types of instruments they bring to support international objectives. One important aim of this book is to advance the understanding of partnership governance and to shed light on contentious debates by presenting new systematic data on the clustering of governance functions and instruments they have deployed across multiple institutional arenas.

---

[39] Dingwerth and Eichinger 2010; Brown, de Jong and Lissidrenska 2009; Brown, de Jong and Levy 2009.

Entrepreneurs of New Governance

Global partnerships have become an essential feature of the contemporary organizational diversification of international governance. How can international relations theory account for this substantial institutional change within the multilateral system? This book points to governance entrepreneurs and political coalitions as the driving forces behind an iterative cycle of change.

Governance entrepreneurs are defined here as *political actors actively seeking institutional change*.[40] These actors operate across the international and domestic domains and use a variety of strategies to explain, justify, and promote the adoption as well as the uptake and institutionalization of new governance instruments. Policy entrepreneurs are not assumed to necessarily have the strong ethical drive of norm entrepreneurs (although they can also be informed by moral principles); instead, their essential characteristics are specified as "expertise and persistence," which they use to advance personal, agency, or interest group agendas.[41]

Ultimately, the basic political dynamics of governance entrepreneurship are similar to other forms of policy entrepreneurship despite the different outcomes such actors may pursue in the public space. Actors with strong incentives and motivation to spur institutional change engage in identifying and placing on the governance agenda a set of problems and ideas for new institutional solutions. The strategies by which they present their ideas and advance the agenda for institutional change will necessarily involve building supporting political coalitions, as well as some degree of consensus between public and private entrepreneurs on the ends and means of new governance. Finally, to advance institutional change, the coalition of governance entrepreneurs has to master capacity to identify "windows of opportunity" and to package resources such as knowledge, information, financing, norms, and political leverage to promote specific institutional solutions.[42] Such strategies typically unfold in a cycle of steps, which can be propelled but also blocked by external events and alternative coalitions.

---

[40] The concept builds on work on norm and policy entrepreneurs. See Finnemore and Sikkink 2001; Fakuda-Parr and Hulme 2011; Price 1998; Waddock 2008; Mintrom 1997; Kingdon 1984.

[41] Weissert 1991.

[42] Mintrom 1997; Sabatier and Jenkins-Smith 1993; Kingdon 1984; Polsby 1984; Weissert 1991.

Governance entrepreneurs, like entrepreneurs more generally, take risks in experimenting with new ideas and governance arrangements, and success is not necessarily guaranteed. Michael Mintrom draws an eloquent parallel between entrepreneurs in the economic and policy spheres:

Policy entrepreneurs can be thought of as being to the policy-making process what economic entrepreneurs are to the marketplace ... Policy entrepreneurs are able to spot problems, they are prepared to take risks to promote innovative approaches to problem solving, and they have the ability to organize others to help turn policy ideas into government policies.[43]

A theoretical perspective on governance entrepreneurs and their role in spearheading dynamic institutional change is essential for understanding the emergence, patterns, and outcomes of global partnerships for several reasons. First, the analysis starts with the premise that while institutions are typically created to perform a set of functions, structural turbulence associated with globalization and functional imperatives on the multilateral system to cope with global challenges are not sufficient to explain institutional change and form. Institutional theorists observe that efficiency-enhancing institutions themselves have the characteristics of a public good and are thus likely to be undersupplied unless actors have asymmetric incentives and the political clout to spearhead change and collective institutions.[44] As Robert O. Keohane reflects in a lecture on the challenges of globalization and governance: "Functional solutions to the problem of institutional existence are ... incomplete. There must be political entrepreneurs with both the capacity and the incentives to invest in the creation of institutions and the monitoring and enforcement of rules."[45]

Second, for any broad governance problem, multiple institutions could provide equilibrium solutions.[46] The incentives and power of the actors to shape the conditions for institutional innovation and choices need, therefore, to be theorized rather than assumed.[47] The focus of this study is thus on explaining the source of governance entrepreneurship and the iterative cycle of change in the multilateral system that such entrepreneurship entails. It examines the motivation and strategies of diverse sets of entrepreneurs and the central role of

---

[43] Mintrom 1997, p. 70.
[44] Keohane 2001; North 1990; Olson 1971.
[45] Keohane 2001, p. 4.
[46] Krasner 1991; Morrow 1994; Martin 1992.
[47] Hurrell 2007; Keohane 1984; 2001; Mattli and Woods 2009; Faul 2016.

IOs in the political processes that enable or constrain collaborative interface between transnational actors and multilateral institutions.[48]

The analysis does not assume that such change is inevitable in the context of globalization or necessarily successful. On the contrary, it develops a governance entrepreneurship framework of institutional change to address the *puzzle* of risk taking and organizational innovation in an institutional system designed to be relatively inert and heavily controlled by states.[49] So while the marketplace may reward innovation and successful risk taking and domestic policy entrepreneurship can bring about specific political benefits for winning coalitions,[50] the multilateral system's default setting is continuity and standard procedure rather than governance innovation beyond the state. Green (2013) distinguishes, for example, between delegation to private authority by intergovernmental decision and "entrepreneurial" private governance that is convened by nonstate actors. The theoretical argument and extensive empirical material presented in this book demonstrate that public–private partnerships represent neither a radical "power shift" from established institutions nor a marginal governance aberration from traditional state-centered power politics. These new organizational forms are to a great extent a product of the contemporary density of multilateral institutions and reflect the variable incentives, expertise, and autonomy of IOs to respond to external pressures and engage both internal and external entrepreneurs in institutional experimentation and new governance.

Alternative Perspectives

Partnerships as Transnational Governance

Current perspectives examine public–private partnerships as part of a thickening layer of transnational governance beyond the formal

---

[48] By emphasizing the agency of IOs in the entrepreneurship of dynamic institutional change in the multilateral system, this book contributes to recent literature that looks more closely at the roles of these agencies in facilitating interactions with transnational actors and soft governance (Abbott *et al.* 2015; Green 2013; Hale and Roger 2014; Jönsson and Tallberg 2010; Tallberg *et al.* 2013). This study theorizes more specifically the organizational processes and coalitions building across IOs, their principals, and external actors to account for dynamic institutional change from within.

[49] Krasner 1983.

[50] Kingdon 1984; Majone 1996.

edifice of state-based institutions. Transnational relations, which are interactions and associations among actors across jurisdictions without the intermediation of a central foreign policy establishment, are as old as international relations.[51] Such interactions, however, have become thicker, faster, and more institutionalized as a result of contemporary advances in communication, democratization, and multidimensional interdependence.[52] Transnational networks bring to the global agenda issues that were formerly considered largely within the sphere of state authority and domestic politics. At the same time, problems that are global in nature and formally included on the intergovernmental agenda such as climate change, forestry, development, or global public health are being acted on directly by a variety of nonstate, substate, and bureaucratic actors through transnational networks. Transnational actors not only have agency in seeking to influence the state and intergovernmental policy; they increasingly assume authority to act directly and steer behavior on specific global problems. In other words, they engage in governance.[53] As Keohane and Nye anticipated at the turn of the millennium in their reflection on globalization and governance, "... not only the geography of governance is more complex, but so are its modalities. Such arrangements will ... involve a heterogeneous array of agents – from private sector and the third sector as well as from government."[54] Grande and Pauly note the search for governance innovation through transnational networks: "... [W]e are living through a remarkable period of experimentation aimed at creating collective problem-solving capacity that is beyond and below the contours ... territorial and functional boundaries of the nation state."[55]

Partnerships are thus understood as a particular type of transnational governance on a continuum from largely private regulations to public networks that link subnational authorities and domestic agencies across borders.[56] The present study contributes to the literature

---

[51] Keohane and Nye 1971.
[52] Keohane and Nye 2000; Held and McGrew 2002.
[53] Andonova, Betsill and Bulkeley 2009; Andonova and Hale 2017; Hale and Held 2011; Avant, Finnemore and Sell 2010; Avant and Westerwinter 2016; Roger and Dauvergne 2016; Selin and VanDeveer 2009 .
[54] Keohane and Nye 2000, pp. 12–14.
[55] Grande and Pauly 2005, p. 285.
[56] Andonova 2010; Bulkeley *et al.* 2014; Pattberg *et al.* 2012; Beisheim and Liese 2014.

on the diversification of contemporary systems of global governance by examining how transnational governance interplays with intergovernmental institutions. It focuses on the political origins of collaborative initiatives that straddle the traditional distinction between private and public authority, revealing a closer interplay between network-based and hierarchical organizational structures than previously recognized.[57] Transnational partnerships are not simply a parallel system of network-based governance. They have emerged in close interaction with the organizational imperatives faced by international institutions and have in turn become an institutional feature of the multilateral system.

Response to Globalization and Structural Change

A second perspective on the nature of global partnerships presents such initiatives as a marriage of necessity between an intergovernmental system in stress and a potent transnational sector in order to deliver neglected public goods and to tame globalization.[58] Partnerships and other public policy networks emerge, in the words of Reinicke (1999), to correct "market and intergovernmental failures" as well as to address "the participatory gap" and "democratic deficit" in global governance. They are intended to boost the effectiveness and output-based legitimacy of the multilateral system through improved problem solving. A series of case studies and partnership "best practices" illustrates the provision of specific global public goods such as access to medical technology to tackle global pandemics, the financing of nutrition and education programs, or attempts at global management of problems associated with water, climate, or disaster relief.[59]

The emphasis in this literature is thus on external stress factors and structural changes associated with globalization, as well as on functional failures of multilateral institutions. These structural changes have to do with the exponential increase of private investment flows

[57] For supporting line of argumentation in other governance arenas, see Andonova, Hale and Roger 2017; Slaughter 2004; Raustiala 2002; Green 2013.
[58] Ruggie 2003b; Kaul 2005; Bissel 2001; Castells 2005; Held and McGrew 2002; Reinicke 1999; Reinicke and Deng 2000.
[59] Nelson 2002; Witte and Reinicke 2005; World Bank Operations Evaluation Department 2001.

since the 1990s and the parallel stagnation of official development assistance. They have to do with the visible growth and reach of corporations as well as the influence of other private actors such as NGOs, foundations, and markets. Such structural changes in the international political economy have increased the turbulence in the organizational environment of IOs, which faced increasing advocacy pressure to counterbalance market failures and social risks while being hamstrung for resources by the very governments they represent. In his essay "Taking Embedded Liberalism Global," John G. Ruggie eloquently draws a parallel between the stabilizing functions of domestic Keynesian institutions in the post–World War II era of economic liberalization and the intended role of partnerships such as the Global Compact in managing the risks of contemporary globalization:

The combination of global governance gaps and governance failures ... created an organization niche that civil society actors began to occupy, and from which they have been engaging the global business community in the attempt to combine their newly acquired rights with new social responsibilities. Now we are slowly beginning to come to a full circle: business wants to help to channel some of the pressure it faces into the construction of at least minimally functioning public sectors, including at the global level.[60]

The globalization perspective on the rise of partnerships thus underscores the impact of rising policy pressures as a consequence of greater and more complex transnational spillovers. While these are important insights on which the present study builds, structural perspectives are insufficient to explain the uneven patterns of public–private collaboration and its outcomes. Empirical investigations of larger sets of partnership activities reveal highly uneven distribution of partnership governance both across issues and across states and geographies that cannot be accounted for simply by imperatives to provide global public goods or address market and policy failures.[61] The theoretical focus on the political entrepreneurs of institutional change, as discussed earlier, challenges the notion that functional failure and structural turbulence can themselves account for the nature of change and institutional form. It asks, precisely: who are the entrepreneurs of such change, what are their motivations, and what kinds of political conditions must they put in place to convene new mechanisms of governance? In other words,

---

[60] Ruggie 2003b, p. 20; Ruggie 1982.
[61] Andonova and Levy 2003; Glasbergen, Biermann and Mol 2007; Biermann *et al.* 2007; Andonova 2010; Richter 2004; Widdus 2001; Compagnon 2012.

the theoretical perspective introduces political agency to the account of institutional change, which may be triggered at least in part by organizational turbulence associated with globalization but cannot be explained by structural variables alone in its variation and modalities.

Corporate Takeover versus Public Good

A third set of perspectives views partnerships as an extension of private authority to the multilateral sphere and a power shift away from formal public institutions.[62] Indeed, the rise of private regulations appears to be the dominant and best-documented mode of nonstate actor participation in global governance. Private transnational governance takes a variety of forms including self-regulation through corporate social responsibility (CSR) practices, voluntary certification schemes such as Responsible Care, the ISO14000 series, and the Forest Stewardship Council (FSC), or industry codes and standards. These initiatives are managed primarily by and for nonstate actors without direct intermediation by the state. By inquiring about the sources of authority of such initiatives, the literature illuminates how markets, norms, standards, and practices are employed by a variety of nonstate actors to steer or constrain behavior.[63]

While private regulation operates in the "shadow" of the state, global partnerships differ importantly in that they actively straddle the public–private divide in the international sphere. They involve deliberate codecision by public and private actors and a pooling of competencies and resources (Table 1.1.) As a consequence, partnerships have attracted much debate as to the nature of private influence on public institutions. As discussed earlier, advocacy critics characterize partnerships as capture of international institutions by transnational corporate interests and the neoliberal ideology that backs them. Advocacy movements in global health have questioned the strong engagement of the Bill and Melinda Gates Foundation and the very concept of partnership as masking undue influence of corporate power. Corporate accountability critics have characterized initiatives

---

[62] Mathews 1997; Martens 2007; Bull and McNeill 2007; Bendell *et al.* 2010; Mert 2015.

[63] See among others, Clapp 2005; Cashore *et al.* 2004; Haufler 2001; Garcia-Johnson 2000; Prakash and Potoski 2006a, 2006b; Pattberg 2007; Vogel 2005, 2008; Büthe and Mattli 2011; Hall and Biersteker 2002; Cutler, Haufler and Porter 1999; Héritier 2002; Green 2013; Newell and Paterson 2011.

such as the Global Compact as bluewashing of large business. Beyond advocacy discourse, scholars pick up on the uneven participation in and clustering of partnerships as evidence of the disproportionate influence by large transnational actors – be they NGOs, companies, or foundations. Such influence entails worrisome consequences of overcrowding alternative policy objectives and skewing the governance agenda toward corporate priorities. This may put into question the equity and democratic accountability of participation by nonstate actors, which is intended to expand the openness and societal reach of multilateral institutions.[64]

For international institutions, therefore, the tension between their public mandates and private participation through partnerships is real. However, the central role of IOs, stipulated and documented in this book, in steering the creation and activities of global partnerships suggests a more complex interaction between the public and the private spheres than implied by the corporate takeover thesis. Equating partnerships with the privatization of governance or abdication of authority to nonstate actors ignores the foundational process of the rearticulation of public and private objectives around collaborative initiatives. By focusing on governance entrepreneurs and the iterative cycle of creating partnerships as new governance instruments embedded in the norms of the multilateral system, the analytical framework of the book challenges linear notions on the nature of change as either capture by transnational interests or response to functional imperatives. The entrepreneurs of new governance, among whom are many prominent public figures such as the former UN Secretary General Kofi Annan or the former Director General of the WHO Gro Harlmen Brundtland take risks in proposing direct collaboration with nonstate actors. They also adopt strategies to ensure that organizational objectives, mandates, and normative roles take center-stage in hybrid governance. They craft political space in which such strategies can be deliberated. Since the success of new experimental governance is far from assured, partnerships that survive to become institutional features of multilateralism have to gain

---

[64] Andonova 2010; Dingwerth and Eichinger 2010; Bexell and Mörth 2010; Steets 2010; Börzel and Risse 2005; Bäckstrand 2006; Ottaway 2001; Utting and Zammit 2006; Utting 2002; Bull and McNeill 2007; Newell 2012; Mert 2015; Prügl and True 2014.

broader political vetting beyond initiating coalitions. Contestation is part of the process, but so is the need to establish a normative fit with the public mandate.

Current perspectives thus propose alternative interpretations of global partnerships: as *modality of transnational governance*, as *functional innovation* in the context of globalization, or as *potential corporate and ideological capture* of international institutions. This book attempts to resolve, for the first time, many of the underlying questions obstructing our view of the way in which global partnerships emerge. It introduces the concept of governance entrepreneurs and considers the pivotal role of political coalitions in finding open space for new mechanisms of collaboration. In so doing, the book aims to advance the study of global partnerships by constructing a theory about the agency and conditions for institutional change and to provide a clear method to better understand the many public–private collaborations, bridging gaps across organizational domains and issue areas.

Approach and Structure of the Book

Research on global partnerships has so far focused largely on prominent cases: the Global Compact, the Johannesburg partnerships for sustainable development, the Global Reporting Initiative, the Global Fund for HIV/AIDS, Malaria and Tuberculosis, GAVI, and so forth. While such an approach has illuminated important features of partnership governance, it is hardly sufficient to grasp the larger dynamics of change in which individual partnerships play a part. This study seeks to contribute to a broader understanding of global partnership as an example of institutional innovation, by undertaking the first systematic examination of the entrepreneurship, politics, and outcomes of global partnerships across several issue areas and organizational fields. The structure of the book follows these objectives.

Chapter 2 elaborates a theory of iterative and endogenous institutional change. It advances a *dynamic* conceptualization of the principal–agent model of IOs to consider the central role of international agencies in brokering the interface between their member states and a turbulent external environment that includes a growing number of private governors. The theory specifies five propositions on the politics likely to shape the cycle of governance entrepreneurship of global partnerships. These propositions highlight a set of conditions – related to agency autonomy and epistemic capacity, turbulence in the organizational environment of IOs, and entrepreneurial coalitions between IOs, proactive states, and external actors that have shaped the experimentation with global partnerships, their outcomes, and incremental institutionalization. The theory thus sheds light on a process of institutional change that is endogenous and dynamic – enabled from within the organizational structure of the multilateral system under a set of external and internal stimuli.

The research design of the empirical chapters intends to capture important variation in the explanatory factors specified by the theory of institutional change. It examines the relevance of agency autonomy and expert capacity across organizational fields and the impact of intertemporal changes in resource and legitimacy pressures on processes of governance entrepreneurship and change. The book provides a detailed empirical account on the rise of public–private collaborations over time and across five institutional domains of the multilateral system: the UN Secretariat, UNEP, the World Bank, UNICEF, and the WHO. These organizations have become important arenas of partnership collaboration, providing an empirical laboratory to examine the hypothesized political dynamics of institutional change over time and their generalizability across different settings. At the same time, the comparative analysis of partnership outcomes across different agencies allows us to assess the relevance of organizational expertise, circumstances, and priorities in shaping the entrepreneurship of new governance and its variable manifestations in international affairs.

Chapter 3 begins the empirical inquiry by focusing on the UN Secretariat and the somewhat counterintuitive role of the Office of the Secretary General under the leadership of Kofi Annan, and later of Ban-Ki Moon, in spearheading closer collaboration between the UN and the private sector. While the permanent members of the UN Security Council can and do exert substantial political control over the Secretary General, the broad mandate and moral authority of the Office have historically provided a degree of discretion for activist leadership and change when windows of opportunity arise. This organizational study allows us to examine the conditions under which agencies and their leadership might be able to carve out greater autonomy for institutional innovation than formal institutional rules might imply, and the relevance of entrepreneurial coalitions among the IOs, a subset of principals, and external actors in spearheading change.

Chapter 4 analyzes the rise and outcomes of global partnerships for environmental sustainability within the organizational domains of UNEP and of the World Bank. Problems of environmental protection and sustainability are traditionally characterized by a variable degree of divergence of positions among states. This policy field is also increasingly populated with diverse transnational actors and private initiatives. Given the substantial managerial autonomy and epistemic specialization of the two organizations, the theoretical framework leads us to expect highly variable opportunities for the entrepreneurship of global partnerships over time and across specific environmental issues and organizational fields. The comparative approach allows us to assess the argument that the characteristics of these two very different IOs are likely to have a visible imprint on their approach to engaging with nonstate actors and on the makeup and outcomes of global partnerships. The cases are also interesting because much of the conventional wisdom presents UNEP and the World Bank as unlikely arenas of organizational innovation.

Chapter 5 follows the entrepreneurial cycles through which global partnerships have become a major institutional feature in global health governance and children's issues. The WHO and UNICEF, as the two leading agencies in this field, enjoy a substantial degree of autonomy related to their specific expertise. This arena presents in many ways the most likely case for the organizational theory of institutional change and global partnership. There has been relatively high intergovernmental consensus on policy objectives related to children's well-being, and global health pandemics but persistent failures of implementation and growing pressure by advocacy actors. The two organizations, however, have faced organizational pressures to a different degree and have historically very different relations with the private sector. The theoretical framework leads us to expect a visible lift in partnership activity in this issue area following the mobilization of advocacy concern in the late 1990s. The comparative analysis across institutions inquires how specific organizational circumstances and expertise have influenced governance outcomes for global health and children given the substantial cross-organizational coordination in this policy arena.

The empirical chapters draw on extensive qualitative and quantitative research, which includes semistructured interviews, text analysis of primary documents, secondary literature, and descriptive statistical analysis based on the Global Partnerships Database. The Global Partnerships Database is a new source of data, constructed for the purposes of this study, on the partnership portfolios of the four specialized agencies examined here (UNEP, the World Bank, the WHO, and UNICEF).[65] The statistical analysis for Chapter 3 draws on data provided by the Global Compact Office and by the United Nations Fund for International Partnerships, both managed by the UN Secretariat. For the first time, the Global Partnerships Database provides an opportunity to present a systematic view of partnership governance across time and organizational fields of the multilateral system, as well as to study specific patterns of their emergence, clustering, and outcomes.

The empirical narrative in each chapter is structured around three levels of aggregation. The analysis first examines the political motivations and dynamic policy coalitions among IOs, state principals, and external actors, which drive cycles of governance entrepreneurship of global partnerships. Drawing on extensive primary research, the qualitative analysis allows us to document and distinguish the observable implications of the theory of dynamic institutional change from those of alternative arguments. Each chapter also examines quantitatively how organizational features affect partnership outcomes in terms of partners engaged, issues tackled, and types of governance instruments used. Finally, cases of specific partnership initiatives shed more fine-grained light on the strategies of governance entrepreneurs and the life cycle of governance experimentation, which have contributed to the broader institutionalization of global partnerships. This multilayered empirical story attempts to reconstruct the puzzle of the partnership phenomenon from its many pieces and to illuminate its characteristics of outcomes across multilateral institutions.

[65] See Annex for further detail on the Global Partnerships Database.

2 | *Theory of Dynamic Institutional Change*

Introduction

The world is constantly changing as humanity grapples with seemingly intractable and ever more complex problems: climate change, security threats, and humanitarian crises that may quickly take on a global scale and transcend international and domestic plains of action. This chapter will argue that multilateral institutions have driven through dynamic changes to their structures to keep on top of increasingly exigent situations that daily threaten to overwhelm them. Traditional theories of international institutions have focused on a need for stability, centered on inducing and sustaining cooperation among states. However, in elaborating a theory of dynamic institutional change, this chapter will show that such an equilibrium viewpoint has been challenged by contemporary structuring of international governance. The rescaling of international politics has demanded a closer interplay between transnational forces and formal institutions. These supranational challenges have inspired IOs to embrace public–private partnerships in seeking solutions.

The theoretical framework is in dialogue with two broad perspectives on change in the multilateral system. The first retains an emphasis on states as the main principals behind international regimes, relying on sufficient convergence or overlap of interest among power holders for institutions to be reformed or new mechanisms created. The path is one of punctuated equilibrium, in which periods of stability are followed by crises or substantial dissatisfaction with the status quo by major powers willing to act.[1] Powerful states created the UN in the wake of World War II. They led to the adoption of the Montreal Protocol to regulate ozone-depleting substances after the discovery of

---

[1] Colgan, Keohane and Van de Graaf 2011; Nielson and Tierney 2003; Krasner 1983.

the ozone hole over Antarctica and, more recently, spearheaded the establishment of the International Renewable Energy Agency.

Another set of perspectives focuses on international bureaucracies. Change can take different forms and directions. According to the "garbage can" metaphor elaborated in sociology, bureaucracies have a tendency to pick from a pool of existing solutions and apply them to parallel streams of old and new policy problems.[2] The result is institutional adaptation of standard procedure rather than substantive change or innovation. Such behavior may even counter the reforms intended by states or undermine the normative core of the institutions, resulting in organizational pathologies.[3] The World Bank's environmental reforms of the 1990s, adopted under pressure from advocacy groups and state principals, looked like the "emperor's new clothes," according to some observers.[4] New sustainability policies were seen as a façade behind which World Bank managers conspired to pursue traditional large infrastructure projects with environmental trimmings attached or the extension of market-based solutions. Rational-choice theories on bureaucratic organizations, in turn, stipulate that international agencies act opportunistically to orchestrate new initiatives and shape the design of institutions.[5] Such models rest on assumptions of interest divergence between bureaucracies and member states and the ability of bureaucrats to act in relative isolation and thus influence outcomes by other means. The specter of unaccountable bureaucracies defining new institutional spin-offs or regulations finds a ready hearing in debates on political accountability and sovereignty in the European Union or on the workings of the International Monetary Fund and the World Trade Organization.

This book challenges the apparent dichotomy between state-centric and bureaucracy-focused perspectives on change and stagnation of international institutions. It proposes a dynamic organizational theory of change, which emphasizes the role of entrepreneurial actors in identifying innovative institutional solutions and their ability to forge supportive political coalitions for their adoption. The theory stipulates that IOs are likely to drive such entrepreneurship when they have epistemic capacity for initiative and because of their centrality as operational agencies between intergovernmental mandates, policy imperatives, and

[2] Cohen, March and Olsen 1972.
[3] Barnett and Finnemore 2004; Weaver 2009.
[4] Rich 1994; Wade 1997.
[5] Abbott *et al.* 2015; Johnson 2014.

a growing sphere of transnational actors and private regulations. Such processes are thus endogenous in the sense that they are not imposed by actors external to the organization and rely critically on political entrepreneurs to spearhead new institutional features from within.

Global partnerships represent such a dynamic reconfiguration of international institutions creating, as they do, new platforms for direct collaboration with the transnational sphere. Institutional innovation, enabled through the structure of the multilateral system, has similarly made a dramatic mark in international relations on a broader scale.

Consider the creation of peacekeeping. The first peacekeeping force did not emerge by intergovernmental design and negotiation. In 1956, UN Secretary General Dag Hammarskjold interpreted the provisions of the UN Charter to propose the insertion of a neutral force in the context of the Suez Crisis, which had placed the allies of the U.S. and the Soviet Union in a face-to-face confrontation at the height of the Cold War. The first UN Emergency Force was thus put in place with UN leadership and ability to interpret the nexus between peace and sovereignty, with the backing of large and medium powers. In 2005, the UN interpreted further sovereignty and security with the formulation of the three pillars of the Responsibility to Protect in the General Assembly Resolution 60/1 on the 2005 World Summit Outcome. The Responsibility to Protect framework establishes the presumption of sovereignty "as responsibility to protect" populations from mass atrocities, including the responsibility of the international community to take collective action under the UN Charter to protect populations if a state is failing to do so.[6] These historical initiatives have introduced substantially new normative pillars in security and humanitarian affairs,[7] through leadership coalitions involving IOs, states, and external epistemic communities rather than through intergovernmental fiat or bureaucratic opportunism. Via similar political processes, international development institutions have evolved from almost exclusive focus on poverty reduction through economic growth and expansion of infrastructure to greater emphasis on human development and sustainability.[8]

The study of global partnerships provides an opportunity to theorize how and through what political processes multilateral agencies

---

[6] UNGA 2005c.
[7] Welsh and Banda 2010.
[8] Jolly, Emmerij and Weiss 2009; Matson, Clark and Andersson 2016.

have contributed to the adoption of new forms of governance. The theoretical argument stipulates that the organizational makeup of the contemporary multilateral sphere has enabled entrepreneurship of new governance mechanisms from within. IOs, under conditions of external turbulence and facilitated by their agency autonomy and expertise, have played a central role as both entrepreneurs and brokers of partnerships through supportive alliances. Global partnerships are thus best understood as institutional change that is partially endogenous to the multilateral system but is also dynamic. It involves leadership coalitions among international agencies, like-minded states, and external actors, as well as willingness to engage in experimentation and gain broader political backing and legitimation of new governance instruments. Such governance entrepreneurship is counterintuitive from the point of view of theoretic perspectives that conceptualize international agencies as arenas for powerful states or as bureaucracies prone to inertia and opportunistic behavior outside the control of states.

This chapter spells out the theory of governance entrepreneurship and institutional change to guide the comparative analysis of the intertemporal rise of global partnerships, as well as their variable outcomes across issues and institutions. It elaborates a dynamic interpretation of the principal–agent perspective of organizations to illuminate the central role of IOs as mediators between intergovernmental politics, public expectations, and the turbulence associated with globalization and the rise of transnational nonstate actors. On the basis of such conceptualization, the theoretical framework advances a set of propositions on the variation in the motivations, capacity and political opportunities for IOs to engage in the development of public–private partnership across time and institutional contexts. The theory furthermore anticipates an iterative life cycle of governance entrepreneurship through which global partnerships are conceived and adopted as endogenous change. The chapter concludes with a discussion of the observable implications of the theory and the research methodology to assess these implications and alternative perspectives.

IOs and Change: Conceptual Foundations

The central role of IOs in the entrepreneurship of global partnerships cannot be neatly separated from an understanding of their characteristics both as agencies with delegated authority by states and as visible public bureaucracies embedded in the global sphere. Principal–agent models of delegation and sociological perspectives on bureaucracies are often framed as competing or alternative.[9] While such juxtaposition stems from differential ontological and epistemological bases, the analysis joins a growing body of scholarship that views such theoretic bifurcation as unnecessarily limiting for addressing political puzzles.[10]

The principal–agent perspective is a core element of the theory of endogenous institutional change elaborated here, because it formalizes the foundational relationship of granting authority by states to IOs and their state-based accountability and constraints. However, unlike existing applications, the theory elaborates a more *dynamic* interpretation of the delegation model in order to account for the complex interactions between states, organizations, and their external environment through which the entrepreneurship of global partnership takes place.

Principal–agent models conceptualize states as collective principals, which delegate authority to IOs to manage a set of intergovernmental rules, norms, and agreements. States derive benefits from delegation in the form of agency specialization and expertise, monitoring of cooperation outcomes, dissemination of information, dispute resolution, and other functions that advance the purposes of cooperation. Similar to other delegation contexts, be it in economics or domestic politics, the agents are assumed to have a degree of agency autonomy to exert influence on international outcomes.[11] Such autonomy stems from imperfect and variable degrees of control by member states due to specialization and asymmetric information in favor of the agent, as well as from the incomplete nature of agency contracts that could

---

[9] Barnett and Finnemore 2004; Hawkins *et al.* 2006.

[10] Biermann and Siebenhüner 2009; Sil and Katzenstein 2010; Weaver 2009; Johnson 2014.

[11] The principal–agent model developed first in economics to illuminate the organization and contractual relations of the firm, whereby shareholders as principals delegate authority and provide some degree of autonomy to the management as the agent (Alchian and Demsetz 1972; Williamson 1985). It was subsequently applied to the study of U.S. political institutions such as executive agencies, Congressional committees, and the policy processes (McCubbins, Noll and Weingast 1987, 1989; McCubbins and Schwartz 1984; Moe 1984, 1990; Schepsle and Weingast 1987, 1994; Kiewiet and McCubbins 1991). See Pollack 1997, 2003; Nielson and Tierney 2003; Grant and Keohane 2005; Hawkins *et al.* 2006 as seminal early applications to the study of IOs.

become subject to interpretation.[12] The assumption of disconnect between the interests of principals and the agents and the autonomous capacity of agents to act opportunistically and pursue their own ends drives much of the classic principal–agent analysis. A central preoccupation of delegation models is how principals can minimize the potential losses from opportunistic behavior while optimizing the benefits of specialization. Such considerations often translate in public discourse under the rubrics of "inefficient, runaway bureaucracies," "mission creep," and overstepping the scope of their delegated functions. They reflect concerns about political control and accountability of distant international agencies, especially to domestic constituencies from which political authority ultimately stems.

The theory of endogenous institutional change offers a more dynamic interpretation of delegation models by problematizing the strict assumption of differential preferences between principals and agents. It considers under what conditions the incentives of international agencies and those of a subset of states may align in entrepreneurial coalitions for change. The dichotomy between agents and principals is thus challenged, while the name of the game becomes politics and coalition building beyond agency slack and principal control, which inevitably also occur.

While the principal–agent perspective attributes greater scope for organizational influence compared to classic realist or institutional theories of international relations, it has nonetheless drawn critique for relatively thin conceptualization of IOs as agents with assumed preferences.[13] As Hawkins and Jacoby point out: "...[I]f scholars are to successfully analyze the interaction between principals and agents, they need to understand agents in greater detail."[14] The theoretical framework developed in this book draws on sociological theories of organizations to substantiate how the nature, norms, and expertise of these agencies can influence their engagement in the entrepreneurship of public–private partnerships. Sociological perspectives lead us to take a more detailed account of internal organizational politics and countervailing tendencies between bureaucratic inertia, innovation, and normative contestation. It draws our attention to concerns about

---

[12] Pollack 1997; Bradley and Kelley 2008; Hawkins *et al.* 2006; Abbott and Snidal 1998; Vaubel 2006.
[13] Barnett and Finnemore 2004; Hawkins and Jacoby 2006.
[14] Hawkins and Jacoby 2006, p. 200.

agency resources and legitimacy and their resonance with political principals and the external environment of organizations.[15]

Figure 2.1 illustrates the dynamic interpretation of international delegation to IOs, which provides the conceptual foundation of the theoretical framework. Traditional applications of the principal–agent model focus on different preferences between agents and principals. The theoretical framework advanced here looks at how coalitions of agents and principals engage in joint entrepreneurship of institutional change. It furthermore situates the interactions between states and agencies in an organizational environment that is increasingly influenced by growing numbers of transnational actors.

The solid arrows in Figure 2.1 represent the chain of formal delegation of authority on which traditional accounts of delegation focus; the dotted arrows reflect the possibility that IOs may have incentives to engage like-minded principals and in, some instances, domestic constituencies or transnational actors to advance a strategy for institutional reform. Similarly, dotted lines in the direction of IOs indicate that some governments or substate actors may have incentives to reach out to international institutions in order to advance policy agendas and institutional change through informal coalitions. This model of interactions captures also the sensitivity of IOs to pressures and legitimacy concerns in their organizational environment from the continuing rise of nonstate actors such as NGOs, private companies, foundations, or epistemic communities.[16] International agencies are the most likely entrepreneurs of new collaborative governance as existing mediators between a turbulent global domain and interstate politics. As Ernst B. Haas anticipated in his work on knowledge and IO influence, these agencies are "...part of everybody's experience because they are mediators of policy. They are a part of the international repertoire of fora that talk about and authorize innovation. Hence, we can see them as agents of innovation."[17] Drawing on the assumptions of the dynamic organizational model elaborated here and illustrated by Figure 2.1, the following sections ask under what

---

[15] See, among others, Allison 1969; Barnett and Finnemore 2004; Chorev 2012; Cohen, March and Olsen 1972; Haas, E. 1990; March 1965; March and Olsen 1983; DiMaggio and Powell 1983; Hannan and Freeman 1989; Weber 1964.

[16] Fox and Brown 1998; Tallberg *et al.* 2013; Tarrow 2001; Sikkink 2005. See also earlier work by Simmons (1993) on dynamic contracting and institutional innovation.

[17] Haas E. 1990, p. 14.

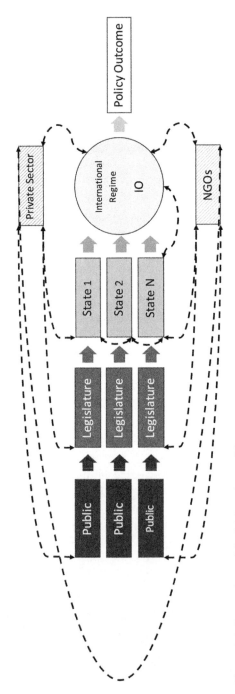

Figure 2.1 Dynamic model of delegation to IOs

conditions and through what processes governance entrepreneurs initiate effort to change institutional structures and develop global partnerships.

Conditions for Entrepreneurial Change

IOs are public bureaucracies with delegated authority from nation states. This then begs the question: under what conditions would states be willing to share authority with nonstate actors or leave sufficient space for governance entrepreneurs to facilitate global public–private partnerships? Furthermore, it is necessary to identify what motivates these organizations to initiate new forms of govern-ance and what kinds of organizational capacities are likely to be conducive for such change. Therefore, the first two propositions of the theoretical framework focus on the state-dominated structure of the multilateral system to stipulate when IOs would have sufficient scope for initiative to create coalitions for new governance. Propo-sition 3 examines organizational motivations to engage in global partnerships, emphasizing the relevance of organizational turbulence associated with budgetary threats and legitimacy pressures. Finally, propositions 4 and 5 focus on the differential capabilities of IOs to pursue public–private alliances, drawing on their expertise and on external resources associated with the rise of transnational actors and voluntary governance. Together these theoretical arguments provide analytic lenses to explain the processes of the intertemporal rise in global partnerships and their variable clustering and outcomes across multilateral institutions.

Agency Autonomy and Agent-Principal Coalitions

Agency autonomy, understood as the scope for independent action that organizations can master from their principals, delimits in import-ant ways their influence in international life. IOs can set agendas for policy change but largely within their delegated authority.[18] Further-more, tacit or explicit backing by principals, or at least by a sufficient subset of influential principals, is necessary for the adoption and insti-tutionalization of agency initiatives.[19] Propositions 1 and 2 therefore

[18] McCubbins, Noll and Weingast 1989; Pollack 1997.
[19] Farrell and Héritier 2007; McCubbins *et al.* 1989; Pollack 1997.

anticipate that the variable degree of agency autonomy across IOs and the political position of states are baseline conditions likely to shape the emergence of global partnerships and their variation across issue areas. They anticipate that, beyond the contractual design of any given IO, there is a spectrum of *political* constellations – from broad intergovernmental consensus to moderate preference divergence among states – which may provide space and even incentives for international agencies to engage in entrepreneurial coalitions for global partnerships. These political constellations are elaborated in turn.

> *Proposition 1: IOs are more likely to engage in the development of global partnerships when they have greater agency autonomy. Such autonomy to enable coalitions for change is most likely when governments are in broad agreement on objectives and norms of cooperation.*

The logic of Proposition 1 stems from the fundamental premise of delegation theory that political principals delegate authority to the extent that they anticipate benefits from agency specialization, while seeking to minimize the political risks of agency activism or slack. IOs with a constitutional structure that grants them greater autonomy therefore will have greater scope for collaboration with nonstate actors within the domain of their mandate. However, as IOs open the doors to greater interaction with advocacy or business entities, they can inadvertently or deliberately augment their autonomy by bringing in external resources and reducing financial dependence on the principals or by increasing their informational advantage.[20] Such collaboration can shift the focal point of policy trajectories toward a more activist direction that is favored by the agency or toward the preferences of some principals compared to others.[21] For instance, an alliance between a development bank and transnational environmental organizations may partially shift the focus of development cooperation toward greater emphasis on conservation or other global problems compared to domestic economic or environmental priorities of developing countries as state principals. If China and India, let us say, prefer to keep development aid focused on infrastructure or local pollution, World Bank partnerships such as the Tiger Initiative, the

---

[20] Hawkins and Jacoby 2006; Tallberg *et al.* 2013.
[21] Krehbiel 1992; McCubbins, Noll and Weingast 1989; Weingast and Moran 1983; Haas, P. 1989.

Climate Finance partnerships, or its collaboration with the Nature Conservancy may be stacking the deck toward global concerns.

This discussion implies that even when agencies have formal autonomy, state support for partnerships with external actors is likely to be cautious and variable, balancing the risk of increased agency activism against the global benefits from leveraging external knowledge and resources toward the implementation of international mandates. This may help explain some of the variation in the uneven clustering of global partnerships across international institutions and issue areas, as discussed in Chapter 1. In arenas where states are concerned about relative gains and sovereign control or where states have considerable divergence of preferences, agency autonomy is typically highly constrained.[22] The risks of incremental shifts in the status quo resulting from new experimental governance are likely to be perceived as considerable, since they may entail high distributional consequences. Indeed, a study by Tallberg and his colleagues anticipates very limited formal opening of IOs to access by nonstate actors under such conditions,[23] making the prospects of public–private partnerships very slim on issues such as security, peacekeeping, or trade.

By contrast, policy arenas characterized by relatively broad intergovernmental consensus on the objectives of cooperation but limited headways in terms of their practical implementation are likely to present greater political leeway for agency entrepreneurship of new collaborative governance. Examples of such issues include the advancement of children's well-being, improved coordination of disaster relief, the containment of global health pandemics, or even global environmental and human development issues that are included under the commonly agreed Sustainable Development Goals. Such objectives are not apolitical but command relatively broad global consensus and tend to be managed by IOs with substantive specialization and scope for autonomous initiative. Many of these objectives bear the characteristics of global public goods in the sense that once attained, many of their benefits are nonrival within and across nations. They often suffer from underprovision, however, due to limited political interest and resources for supplying governance with diffused benefits. In such contexts, public–private partnerships can help advance the implementation of

[22] Bradley and Kelley 2008; Hawkins *et al.* 2006.
[23] Tallberg *et al.* 2013.

consensual intergovernmental objectives. The literature on corporate social responsibility and on global public goods has argued that alignment of broadly agreed public purpose and private interest is likely to be a precondition for successful collaborative partnerships and social engagement by the private sector.[24] This implies, however, that certain public priorities are more likely to be tackled by global partnerships compared to others, depending on the degree of normative consensus and overlap of incentives.[25]

While agency autonomy is a fundamental precondition for IO influence in international life, existing applications of the principal–agent model have not sufficiently recognized the potential for more dynamic coalitions between agents and principals to stimulate endogenous institutional change. Accounts of change have been split, as we have already seen, between those that view preference alignment among powerful principals as drivers of reform[26] and those that explore how agency incentives and relative insulation can undermine the implementation of reforms or, alternatively, can actively shape institutional features.[27] The possibility of partial and tacit coalitions between IOs and a subset of principals has rarely been explored as a driver of endogenous institutional change.[28]

The more dynamic conceptualization of the relations between states, IOs, and their external environment (Figure 2.1) allows us to question the strict assumption about divergent incentives between principals and agents as a basis for agency activism. Entrepreneurial actors in IOs often have to define the scope of their initiative not only with respect to formal mandates of the organization but also by taking into account the level of political support they can muster. Moreover, states may differ in their interest to collaborate with nonstate actors and thus themselves may seek alliances with organizational entrepreneurs to export policy agendas. The following proposition therefore stipulates that moderate divergence among the preferences of state principals is likely to increase the scope for entrepreneurship of global partnerships.

---

[24] Kaul *et al.* 1999; Kaul 2005; Kaul and Conceicao 2005; Porter and Kramer 2006; Nelson 2002, 2004.

[25] Hale and Held 2012; Andonova 2010.

[26] Colgan, Keohane and de Graaf 2011; Hawkins *et al.* 2006; Nielson and Tierney 2003; Stone 2011.

[27] Hawkins and Jacoby 2006; Johnson 2014; Abbott *et al.* 2015.

[28] See, however, perspectives on the interplay between transnational networks and formal institutions: Slaughter 2004; Newman 2010; Andonova 2010; Andonova and Tuta 2014; Hale and Roger 2014; Farrell and Newman 2014.

Proposition 2: IOs are more likely to engage in the entrepreneurship of global partnerships when government policy preferences diverge moderately, providing incentives for principal–agent coalitions for institutional change.

Moderate preference divergence *among* principals implies that states are neither in broad agreement on specific governance objectives nor in a preference discord over policies and institutions. The latter condition would make cooperation difficult and agency engagement of external actors risky, as already discussed. Frequently, however, states' preferences lie between such extremes with respect to policies, instruments, or institutional arrangements for cooperation.[29] Global conservation issues alluded to earlier provide such an example. China and India are unlikely to object strongly to the conservation of tigers, although the intensity of their interest in conservation may be lower compared to that of industrial states and publics. Partnerships that link development to climate finance or conservation thus depend on political entrepreneurs, who can identify a political middle ground to bring together interested actors across the public and private spheres. The earlier example of peacekeeping illustrates this logic in relation to security. In the context of the Suez Canal crisis, the bipolarity of interests that characterized the Cold War cracked to give way to mixed incentives among larger and smaller powers to prevent the spiraling of the conflict. The initiative of the Secretary General spotted an opportunity to propose a new institutional intervention in the shape of a neutral force to preserve peace.

Moderate divergence of state preferences on global issues thus makes for a political environment ripe for agency activism and tacit agent-principal coalitions for change. This expectation is contrary to the prediction of models that focus on intergovernmental agreement as

---

[29] The emphasis on *moderate* preference divergence is important. Nelson and Tierney 2003 and Tallberg *et al.* 2013, for instance, hypothesize that any preference divergence among principals is likely to limit respectively the possibility of institutional reform or the granting of greater formal access to transnational actors. According to their analysis, in part because it focuses on formal institutional features, a substantial collective agreement among principals is necessary for institutional redesign. By contrast, Proposition 2 of the theory elaborated in this chapter, focuses precisely on the grey areas of moderate disagreement among principals, which can be exploited by agents, activist principals, and other actors to stimulate incremental and endogenous institutional change. See McCubbins, Noll and Weingast 1989; Milner 2006; Newman 2010; Urpelainen 2013.

a condition for institutional change, precisely because it allows for some fluidity in the political interpretation of the interests and motivation of states and international agencies. Activist governments may seek to influence agencies unilaterally or in small "like-minded" groups to advance informally a particular policy agenda.[30] Insider–outsider coalitions of multilateral actors with civil society or the private sector can increase the scope for experimentation with new institutions by leveraging additional resources, expertise, and possibly greater legitimacy with respect to specific global audiences or domestic constituencies of governments.[31] The dotted arrows in Figure 2.1 illustrate the possibility of multiple alliances around soft and nonbinding instruments of governance such as global partnership, which are nonetheless embedded within the intergovernmental structure of the system. Partnerships can be spearheaded or supported by a group of entrepreneurial states, IOs, and nonstate actors, which in isolation may have less influence over the institutional agenda.

Indeed, it becomes less surprising that with respect to complex problems such as HIV/AIDS, clean energy, or biodiversity, governance takes shape increasingly through numerous partnerships alongside formal norms and standards. Global partnerships carve separate political space for interested actors to pursue responses to such issues by focusing on a narrower subset of related problems, which may command greater consensus or only moderate divergence of views and objectives. Some initiatives may focus on the diffusion of medical or clean energy technologies, others emphasize financial instruments, while yet another set of partners may be more interested in local capacity to adapt and use technologies effectively.[32] Networks between agencies, select groups of principals, and transnational or local actors are key transmission belts in the dynamic organizational model elaborated in this book. The political logic of propositions 1 and 2 shows the limitations of functional accounts of partnerships as compensation for the governance gaps left by intergovernmental deadlock. While policy failures may motivate governance entrepreneurs to activate new public–private collaboration, the right sort of politics between states and international agencies must be in place.

---

[30] Pollack 1997; Newman 2010; Urpelainen 2013.
[31] Sikkink 2005; Fox and Brown 1998.
[32] Anadon *et al.* 2016.

Pressures for Change: Resources and Legitimacy

What pushes IOs to engage in the entrepreneurship of new governance? The makeup of IOs as bureaucracies controlled by states is intended to induce stability and continuity in the system rather than risk taking and experimentation. While principal–agent theories assume agency preferences and opportunistic behavior, sociological and public-choice theories have emphasized bureaucratic tendencies for inertia and mission creep to extend resources and toolkits. By contrast, engagement in partnerships to advance a set of global objectives is both a relatively recent phenomenon and a substantial departure from the traditional workings of the multilateral system, as elaborated in Chapter 1. It requires us to rethink how international bureaucracies can produce entrepreneurs willing to engage outside the comfort zone of their agencies. Organizational change may be triggered by some degree of turbulence in the external or internal environment of organizations, as sociological perspectives have indicated, associated with redistribution of resources, conflicting perspectives, and competition for legitimacy.[33] Proposition 3 anticipates the sources of organizational turbulence related to core concerns about resources and legitimacy and their impact on the incentives of international agencies to engage in global partnerships.

Proposition 3: IOs are more likely to engage in global partnerships when faced with heightened organizational turbulence in terms of budgetary threats and legitimacy pressures, all else being equal.

International agencies are particularly vulnerable to budgetary and legitimacy pressures. While they are visible public bureaucracies, closely associated with international policy outcomes (Figure 2.1), they have few *direct means* for implementing these mandates. This vulnerability of IOs in terms of resources and reputation has been overlooked by much of the principal–agent literature and sociological accounts. However, it has important implications for understanding agency incentives and strategy for innovation.

IOs, like all public bureaucracies, have strong preferences for stable and growing budgets to carry out their mandates and to advance

---

[33] Haas, E. 1990; March 1991; Powell and DiMaggio 1991; Abbott, Green and Keohane 2016.

their survival, political positions, and the careers of staff. Multiple manifestations of bureaucratic behavior such as turf battles, mission creep, and the projection of existing organizational solutions to new streams of policy problems are attributed in part to the imperative to secure resources.[34] From the perspective of political principals, however, budgets are first and foremost the strings attached to influence and discipline IOs.[35] The preference among IOs for stable and increasing budgets can thus clearly be at odds with that of states, which increasingly seek to minimize their relative contribution to the provision of cooperative benefits. Such contributions can be volatile as a result of domestic constraints, changing foreign policy priorities, or deliberate budget reductions and shifts to influence organizational work.[36]

An extreme example of a budgetary threat to organizational survival was the withdrawal in 2002 of U.S. financing from the UN World Population Fund, which overnight deprived the organization of 13% of its resources and related programming.[37] The chronic underfunding of organizations such as UNEP has historically resulted in growing reliance on project-based work funded by individual donors, while the dwindling resources of the WHO in the late 1980s and the shift of funding to the World Bank plunged the health agency into a veritable crisis.[38] Budgetary threats on IOs and the expanding resources of nonstate actors are, therefore, among the factors likely to prompt differential incentives between organizations to engage in the entrepreneurship of new mechanisms for additional financing.[39]

Resource limitations can, furthermore, undermine the performance and outcome-based legitimacy of organization. While standard principal–agent models do not necessarily anticipate disconnect between the behavior of principals and the legitimacy of IOs, the delegation of authority and consent by sovereign states is increasingly questioned as insufficient for the legitimacy of their agents. Political principals are often driven by considerations of political expediency, interests, and power, which may trump considerations of efficient,

---

[34] Barnett and Finnemore 2004; Cohen, March and Olsen, 1972; Mathiason 2007; Moe 1984; Murphy 2006; Vaubel 2006; Weber 1964.
[35] Hawkins *et al.* 2006; Nielson and Tierney 2003.
[36] Mathiason 2007; Weiss 2009.
[37] Left 2002.
[38] Conca 1995; Chorev 2012.
[39] Mathiason 2007; Murphy 2006; Tallberg *et al.* 2013.

equitable, or norm-conforming outcomes.[40] Yet as sociological theorists DiMaggio and Powel underscore, "Organizations compete not just for resources and customers, but for political power and institutional legitimacy, for social as well as economic fitness."[41] Sociological perspectives, furthermore, emphasize the legitimating role of IOs as an essential aspect of their authority alongside the intersubjective aspects of legitimacy that can be attributed or contested by the multiple audiences of multilateral outcomes.[42]

The dynamic model of IOs as public agencies that are embedded in a diversified public domain depicted in Figure 2.1 allows us to appreciate how the legitimacy of these agencies can be questioned by a wide variety of actors. IOs are most directly associated with international policy outcomes, as illustrated by Figure 2.1, which often makes them immediate objects of advocacy or public discontent (dotted arrows in Figure 2.1). The long delegation chain from domestic publics can thus put international agencies at a distinct disadvantage in terms of legitimacy and resource pressures. It is often difficult for external or domestic audiences to distinguish the extent to which international policy failures result from bureaucratic inefficiency and inept standard solutions, as opposed to lackluster cooperation and funding by states or limited implementation efforts and embezzlement at the domestic level. Are agencies or state principals to blame for the gaps and inequalities in international governance?

Even academic scholarship places differential emphases on the causes of international failures. While economist Jeffrey Sachs argues that the persistence of poverty despite decades of development cooperation reflects the insufficiency of resources committed by donor countries, William Easterly blames the development establishment itself and standard approaches by multilateral agencies.[43] In her acclaimed book on the Rwanda genocide, Samantha Power (2002) documented how limited political commitment by the United States and other permanent members of the Security Council resulted in a humanitarian tragedy. Another prominent account by Barnett and Finnemore (2004) analyzes the Rwanda tragedy as a manifestation of pathological behavior by the

---

[40] Buchanan and Keohane 2006; Keohane 2011; Moe 1990; Stiglitz 2002; Woods 2002; Gutner 2005; Gutner and Thompson 2010.

[41] DiMaggio and Powell 1983, p. 150.

[42] Barnett and Finnemore 2004; Finnemore and Sikkink 2001; Bernstein 2011, 2005; Hurd 1999.

[43] Sachs 2005; Easterly 2006.

UN and its conformity with the political party line at the expense of its normative mandate. The memoir *Shake Hands with the Devil: The Failure of Humanity in Rwanda* by General Roméo Dallaire, who led the last enclave of UN peacekeepers to save lives in Rwanda after the official withdrawal, blames both the indifference of powerful states and UN conformity.[44]

When faced with institutional failures, both principals and agents are likely to engage in buck passing. However, as impersonal international bureaucracies, IOs inadvertently become the epicenter of discontent or convenient symbols for domestic constituencies seeking to delegitimize or undermine multilateral cooperation.[45] Political disenchantment with international outcomes can, in turn, further diminish national commitments to the multilateral system and its capacity to support strong outcomes. The political logic of Proposition 3 therefore anticipates that IO entrepreneurship of new governance is likely to reflect core organizational imperatives such as existential threats related to diminishing budgets or legitimacy pressures, which visibly heightened in the globalization era.

The motivations for initiating more direct collaboration with non-state actors may be reactive (to appease advocacy pressure) as well as proactive (to benefit from the resources and opportunities of the new public domain). Partnerships can help deflect advocacy pressure by engaging critics selectively in problem solving and by increasing the flow of information and mutually enabled learning.[46] The involvement of business, in turn, increases the scope of governance dialogue and provides alternative mechanisms for the diffusion and implementation of organizational mandates, norms, and objectives.[47] The dotted arrows in the dynamic delegation model of IO (Figure 2.1) thus reflect the multiple directions of pressure for change in a globalized context, as well as possibilities for internal–external alliances that organizational entrepreneurs could exploit.

Partnerships may carry legitimacy risks, however, as discussed in Chapter 1. The involvement of powerful and publicly unaccountable corporate actors or large transnational NGOs with limited lines to

---

[44] Dallaire and Beardsley 2003.
[45] Tarrow 2001, 2005; Fox and Brown 1998; Mathiason 2007; Traub 2006.
[46] Börzel and Risse 2005; Fox and Brown 1998; Reinicke 1999; Ruggie 2002; Tallberg *et al.* 2013.
[47] Ruggie 2003a, 2003b.

domestic accountability could compromise procedural legitimacy of public–private arrangements.[48] Critics maintain that it could bring into question the normative power of international institutions should the inflow of private resources give rise to undue influence on policy agendas. Such considerations suggest that a theory of institutional change and global partnerships must reflect on the capacity of international institutions to exercise leadership in initiating change and also to manage the risks of external alliances and their conformity with institutional norms.

Knowledge and Capacity for Entrepreneurship

Knowledge is the primary source of internal capacity and power of international agencies, which they use to influence political outcomes. The extent and type of substantive specialization of IOs is likely, therefore, to shape in important ways both the motivations and capability of staff and leaders within these agencies to act as entrepreneurs of global partnerships. Proposition 4 captures the anticipated effects.

> *Proposition 4: IOs' facility for the entrepreneurship of global partnerships is likely to increase in line with their level of expertise. Furthermore, this expertise will also influence the nature of partners and governance instruments of collaborative initiatives.*

The logic of Proposition 4 rests on the premise of specialized knowledge as a source of identity, substantive interest, and influence of public bureaucracies.[49] The nature of their expertise shapes the ideas and practices that IOs project in international life to affect institutional practices and cooperative outcomes.[50] Sociological approaches also emphasize, however, that specialization can promote structural

---

[48] Dingwerth 2005; Börzel and Risse 2005; Grant and Keohane 2005; Ottaway 2001; Steets 2010; Andonova and Carbonnier 2014; Bäckstrand 2006; Bull and McNeill 2007; Beisheim *et al.* 2010; Beisheim *et al.* 2014. See Bexell and Mörth 2010 and Bexell, ed. 2014 (special issue of *Globalizations*, 11: 3)on democratic accountability and legitimation in global partnerships. .

[49] Allison 1969; Finnemore 1996; Kingdon 1984; Haas, E. 1990; March and Olsen 1983; Weber 1964.

[50] Barnett and Finnemore 2004; Finnemore 1996; Haas, E. 1990; Haas, P. 1989; Goldstein and Keohane 1993; Littoz-Monnet 2017; Weaver 2009; Chorev 2012.

stability and organization inertia as well as facilitate learning and change by fostering new epistemic census, ideas, and coalitions.[51] As March and Olsen observe,

> The development of competence...is primarily a stabilizing force. But it also creates foundations for new institutions and new objectives. Organizations not only become better and better at what they do, they also see new things to do. Having the capability of doing new things leads, in turn, to seeing their desirability. Capabilities stimulate recognition of the salience of problems to which they can provide solutions. By transforming capabilities, therefore, competence transforms agendas and goals.[52]

Specialized knowledge, therefore, is likely to shape in a number of ways the extent to which IOs influence the development of global partnerships. First, entrepreneurial actors within organizations are likely to draw on their expertise as the primary resource to formulate proposals for new governance solutions and to justify them in reference to the broader mandate of the organizations. From a sociological perspective, knowledge provides the capacity to navigate the often divergent normative agendas projected by member states and steer them in specific directions.[53] In this sense, large bureaucratic agencies with high degrees of specialization and epistemic capital do not necessarily behave as monolithic units. The knowledge that defines different departments and individual entrepreneurs within them shapes both the solutions proposed and the kinds of alliances and pathways they seek to promote them. Pressure for greening the World Bank, for example, came not only from NGOs and donor states but also from internal advocates, often experts with anthropology training, demanding greater accountability for compliance with the World Bank's own rules on social, environmental, and human rights impacts.[54] In the context of the WHO, Jonathan Mann, the founding head of the Global Programme on AIDS in the 1980s, was the first to raise concern about the social and human rights implications of the disease, despite internal administrative and political blockages at the time. However, the political recognition of the crisis came only in the late 1990s under new

---

[51] Haas, E. 1990; Finnemore 1996; Barnett and Finnemore 2004; March and Olsen 1983.
[52] March and Olsen 1988, p. 966.
[53] Chorev 2012.
[54] Fox and Brown 1998.

leadership of the WHO and growing advocacy movement, becoming a core motivation for the agency to develop global partnerships as new institutional solutions.

Second, the nature or organizational expertise affects the kinds of partners that are likely to become relevant in the formulation of global partnerships. Such alliances often depend on a common degree of understanding of the problem, or what Peter Haas terms an "epistemic consensus."[55] Studies of transgovernmental governance similarly high-light the role of networks in linking domestic and international agencies around common specialized portfolios on which they seek to deliver – be it environmental monitoring, food safety, health, or financial regulations. Epistemic capacity is likely to be even more important when agencies branch out of the public sphere to collaborate directly with private, advocacy, and charitable organizations, because such partnerships involve the negotiation of public and private purpose and the reconciliation of cross-sector collaboration with the intergovernmental nature of IOs.

Principal–agent models, in turn, associate organizational specialization with specific informational advantages vis-à-vis the principals that shape organizational interests and practice, as well as the capability to take initiative in political life. Studies in the public choice tradition have demonstrated a close correspondence between the nature of bureaucratic expertise and the type of policy options, tools, and institutional solutions that are promoted on the policy agenda by agencies.[56] Greater specialization in particular fields informs and facilitates in terms of agency autonomy a more activist position taken by international and domestic agencies alike, as demonstrated by studies of the U.S. Environmental Protection Agency, U.S. Congressional Committees, the European Commission, or the European Parliament.[57] Such agency position may diverge from the collective preference of political principals or be more closely aligned with the preferences of a subset of states, thus *creating* opportunities for dynamic coalition building with like-minded government bureaucracies and nonstate actors that share similar policy agendas.

---

[55] Haas, P. 1989, 1990.
[56] Allison 1969; Farrell and Héritier 2007; McCubbins, Noll and Weingast 1989; Pollack 1997; Vaubel 2006; Moe 1990.
[57] McCubbins, Noll and Weingast 1989, Pollack 1997, Schepsle and Weingast 1987, 1994; Farrell and Héritier 2007.

Sociological and rationalist perspectives thus converge in their observation that greater specialization in a particular field often motivates and facilitates, in terms of informational advantage and capacity for learning, a more activist role of IOs than traditionally assumed in international relations. Specialized agencies with large substantive portfolios are, therefore, more likely to take initiative in global partnerships compared to treaty secretariats, whose advantage is largely procedural. The technical and normative content of agency specialization informs, furthermore, both the extent and direction of agency initiatives. Trade institutions tend to place principles of free movements of goods before considerations of environmental or social externalities. Environmental and human rights agencies, by contrast, will seek to innovate in the direction of implementing stronger safeguards on environmental and social issues.

The facilitation of partnerships, as we shall see in the empirical chapters, frequently depends on the leadership of specialized units and even individuals to actively interpret mandates and to seek opportunities for dynamic coalition building. For this, they draw on the stock of knowledge and normative capital of their organizations. We can therefore anticipate significant variation across international institutions in the type of partners with whom IOs develop collaboration and the governance outcome they pursue.

The theory of dynamic institutional change thus directs us to take into account the agency of actors even within these massive edifices of bureaucracy. In other words, the exercise of autonomous influence assumed in principal–agent theories and substantiated in sociological accounts depends on entrepreneurs willing to interpret mandates and engage in collective action to pursue change. Such initiatives often go against standard procedures and established practices, and therefore endogenous change is important but also rare, because it contradicts the wiring of bureaucracies toward stability and standard solutions.

The Agency of Non-State Actors

The propensity for organizational change rather than stagnation is not just a matter of internal capacity but also stimuli and learning from their external environment. It is often the coupling of knowledge specialization and channels of interaction with external epistemic communities, which distinguishes the differential (and unusual) ability of

IOs to engage in learning and experimentation.[58] March and Olsen hypothesize, for example, that regular inflow of new expertise through a moderate degree of staff turnover is likely to be most conducive to institutional innovation, particularly in a context of organizational turbulence.[59] These theoretical observations direct our attention to the dramatic increase, since the late 1980s, in the density, agency, and resources of transnational nonstate actors that introduced new ideas, power, and resources. We observe a horizontal and vertical rescaling of international politics, as illustrated in Figure 2.1, with greater possibilities for domestic groups such as cities, NGOs, companies, communities, and even individuals to act transnationally and to construct private governance.[60] In the analysis of John Ruggie, this reconstruction of the "global public domain" has altered profoundly the streams of knowledge, ideas, and power for the management of global problems.[61] It has introduced new entrepreneurial actors and resources in closer proximity to the organizational milieus of IOs. Proposition 5 stipulates how this diversification of the organization environment of IOs has affected the incentives and capacity for institutional change in the multilateral system.

Proposition 5: IOs are more likely to engage in the entrepreneurship of global partnerships the greater the clustering of transnational nonstate actors and epistemic networks around their core mandates.

Proposition 5 highlights the qualitative differences in the organizational environment of international institutions brought about by globalization and by the rise of resources and governance claims of transnational actors (Figure 2.1). The spheres of transnational advocacy networks and IOs have never been completely separate. Advocacy networks have drawn strength from international platforms to diffuse

---

[58] See the seminal work of Ernst Haas (1990) on organizational adaptation and learning in international relations, as well as broader sociological perspectives on organizational learning Powell and DiMaggio 1991; Hannan and Freeman 1989; Haas, P. 1989; March and Olsen 1998.

[59] March and Olsen 1998.

[60] Andonova and Mitchell 2010; Andonova and Tuta 2014; Abbott, Green and Keohane 2016; Bruszt and McDermott 2014; Tallberg *et al.* 2013; Fox and Brown 1998; Boli and Thomas 1999; Tarrow 2001, 2005; Della Porta and Tarrow 2005; Scholte 2010; Abbott *et al.* 2015; Gereffi, Garcia-Johnson and Sasser 2001; Jönsson and Tallberg 2010; Prakash and Potoski 2006b.

[61] Ruggie 2004.

norms, which in turn have supported the implementation of the liberal agenda encoded in international law.[62] Increasingly, however, NGOs have demanded more direct access to international institutions as a means of achieving greater accountability, access to resources, and ultimately more influence.[63] Empirical work on IO reform such as the greening of development banks has demonstrated that once the institutional door is cracked open to some external accountability, insider–outsider coalitions of advocates and experts become stronger and instrumental in perpetuating change.[64]

The corporate social responsibility movement in the private sector similarly involves a range of incentives for business to get involved in voluntary regulation – ranging from consumer pressure and corporate leadership to interest to preempt stricter regulations. As part of such strategies, the direct engagement of business entities with international institutions is not necessarily obvious, as it increases the transactional costs of voluntarism and may potentially expose private-sector organizations to greater scrutiny by advocacy actors.[65] Research on business participants in global partnerships highlights the attractiveness of IOs as brokers of public–private interaction in complex political environments, conferring distinct reputational benefits.[66]

The increased density of transnational demand for participation in global governance has provided, in effect, a new menu of strategies for change-oriented entrepreneurs within IOs. As international agencies find themselves strapped for resources, they have become increasingly aware of private resources and the societal reach of NGOs. A growing number of foundations and campaigns – such as the Bill and Melinda Gates Foundation, the Clinton Foundation, the Carter Foundation, the UN Foundation supported by Ted Turner, or Rotary International – have "adopted" global issues ranging from new vaccines to clean energy and eradication of deadly pandemics. NGO campaigns have been instrumental in raising the salience of global issues and demanding direct action. Companies have been pressed to facilitate affordable

---

[62] Boli and Thomas 1999; Finnemore and Sikkink 2001; Keck and Sikkink 1998; Sikkink 2005; Weiss and Gordenker 1996.

[63] Betsill and Corell 2008; Fox and Brown 1998; Tallberg *et al.* 2013.

[64] Fox and Brown 1998; Gutner 2002; Keck and Sikkink 1998; Sikkink 2005.

[65] Nelson 2002, 2004; Witte and Reinicke 2005.

[66] Nelson 2002; Thomas and Fritz 2006; World Economic Forum 2005; Stadtler and Probst 2012; Bendell, Collins and Roper 2010.

access to technologies while retaining their preference for a strong intellectual property rights regime. In sum, the diversification of the global public domain has increased the pressures but also the incentives and opportunities for organizational entrepreneurs to engage in global partnerships.

However, such hybridization of private power and public mandates carries risks for international institutions as already discussed – in terms of accountability and possibility for undue influence. Again, the role of IOs becomes critical as mediators of change and interpreters of institutional rules to safeguard their normative integrity. Global partnerships are thus entrepreneurial initiatives in that they involve experimentation and management of risks in the political space. Partnerships, as we shall see, are not a single-shot exercise of institutional redesign; they are typically experimental governance initiated by entrepreneurial public–private coalitions that are only subsequently (and not always) fully institutionalized and legitimized as a feature of multi-lateral governance. The next section specifies three general stages in the life cycle of dynamic institutional change. While the five theoretical propositions elaborated in this section focus on the conditions for the variable emergence of global partnerships, the cycle stipulates their evolution and institutionalization.

Life-Cycle of Governance Entrepreneurship

The five propositions on the conditions for organizational entrepreneurship of global partnerships imply a certain gradation and dynamic in the process of institutional change. IOs that operate with greater autonomy are more likely to become agents of change in the first instance and to solicit the selective political support of a group of states (Propositions 1 and 2). The conditions in which IOs may initiate efforts to develop global partnerships reflect a range of plausible motives related to budgetary and legitimacy pressures (Proposition 3), as well as the ability to draw on internal epistemic capacity and networks of transnational actors and resources (Propositions 4 and 5). While each of these conditions may enable organizational entrepreneurship and experimentation, their interplay is likely to create reinforcing dynamics such as entrepreneurial coalitions between agencies, proactive states, and external entrepreneurs seeking windows of opportunity for advancing new, experimental mechanisms of governance. As legitimacy or budgetary pressures mount (Proposition 3), for instance, IOs may actively seek to enlarge their space for discretion and autonomous action through their capacity to interpret mandates (Proposition 4) or via informal coalitions with like-minded principals and external actors (Propositions 2 and 5). The process of change in this sense is dynamic and endogenous, since it is enabled from within the organizational structure of the system under a set of external and internal stimuli.

This perspective implies certain dynamism within multilateral institutions, which has been so far overlooked by the literature on IOs. The institutional engagement of the multilateral system with transnational actors has proceeded through an iterative cycle of organizational experimentation and incremental institutionalization rather than by intergovernmental design or capture by powerful transnational actors. It is possible to anticipate at least three stages in the life cycle of entrepreneurship of global partnerships: experimental adoption of partnership initiatives, their broader diffusion, and in some instances more permanent institutionalization.

At the stage of *experimental adoption*, a small group of organizational entrepreneurs identifies a set of problems and ideas for public–private governance solutions. At this stage, governance entrepreneurs play a particularly critical role – whether it is Gro Harlem Brudtland proposing as director general of the WHO to Roll Back Malaria in a broad public–private alliance or less visible groups of entrepreneurs who have succeeded in creating a community-based partnership program in the Global Environmental Facility to link global and local sustainability. Agency autonomy and leadership capability are critical to identify windows of opportunity and to circumvent potential opposition from principals or bureaucratic inertia for the experimental adoption of the initiative. Partnership entrepreneurs may have to develop frames for presenting collaborative initiatives as appropriate responses to global dilemmas and to place them within the scope of organizational mandate and autonomy. The adoption of partnerships is likely to be on an "experimental" and hence reversible basis to alleviate concerns by the principals about potential risks associated with agency activism and permeability to external actors. As we shall see in the empirical chapters, IOs have often engaged in partnership arrangements strategically but also opportunistically at times of crisis or in response to major international events. Private actors also approach partnerships with specific market-based, charitable, or ethical motivations in mind. Partnership experiments thus involve certain negotiations of purpose across the multilateral and transnational spheres, which IOs manage because of their visible role at that intersection. Similar to other entrepreneurs, governance entrepreneurs thus have to be "patient" and savvy,[67] responding to cross-fertilization of ideas, to signals from external actors, and to windows of opportunities within and outside the multilateral system.

The second stage of *diffusion of global partnerships* is essential for enlarging political support for public–private governance beyond the core coalition of governance entrepreneurs. At this stage, a specific partnership initiative is implemented and diffused by expanding participation beyond the core group of entrepreneurs and by replication across states, institutions, and contexts. The process of replication is important in all organizational fields as a means of creating familiarity, routines, and acceptance of experimental institutions as legitimate by the broader population of peer organizations and external audiences.[68] In the context of the multilateral system, the perception of successful implementation, diffusion, and experience of some partnerships, but not all, may foster their political and normative legitimation. Partnership initiatives can thus succeed or fail both at the agenda-setting stage, if experimental adoption is not secured, and even more so at the diffusion stage if the implementation, governance outcomes, or legitimacy of the initiative are substantially challenged.

The partnerships adopted at the World Summit on Sustainable Development in Johannesburg, South Africa are a case in point. The Summit recognized formally for the first time the relevance of cross-sector collaboration in environmental governance.[69] However, a large number of the 180 partnerships announced in Johannesburg remained ineffective or died off for lack of sufficient implementation effort and commitment.[70] At the same time, other Johannesburg partnerships such as the Coral Reef Initiative or the Amazon Regional Protected Areas succeeded in the process of implementation and diffusion of sustainability practice, leaving an important institutional imprint.[71] When partnerships create benefits for participants and for addressing global issues, they are more likely to be mimicked by other units within

[67] Mintrom 1997.
[68] DiMaggio and Powell 1983; Jordan and Huitema 2014.
[69] Andonova and Levy 2003; Hale and Mauzerall 2004.
[70] Pattberg *et al.* 2012.
[71] Andonova 2014.

the organization and other organizations in their field.[72] We hear more readily about global success stories of large partnerships that save lives, reduce the cost of treatment, empower women and children through education or microfinance, or achieve visible gains in sustainability, food security, and conservation compared to those that did not make the full cycle of governance entrepreneurship. Through instances of successful implementation, deliberation, and diffusion across jurisdiction and organizations, partnerships can contribute over time to the acceptance of a de facto norm in the multilateral sphere for greater collaboration with nonstate actors.[73] The practice of partnership governance can in effect create new organizational and political constituencies supportive of cooperation with nonstate actors as well as facilitate across the multilateral system a network of partnership entrepreneurs and culture of greater cross-organizational collaboration.

The third stage in the entrepreneurship of global partnerships involves a process of *reverse institutionalization* as a more permanent structure within a governance regime. The process of institutionalization is reverse, because the collective principal agrees on the constitutional fit of partnerships as a form of governance within the multilateral system only *after* their experimental adoption and implementation. Such reverse institutionalization can be triggered by several mechanisms. The champions of partnerships can move toward more permanent institutionalization via the modification of the governance status quo – once a set of partnerships is established, they can create new constituencies, as discussed earlier, and focal points for collaboration, making the undoing of collaborative governance more difficult.[74] As Hawkins and Jacoby anticipate in their discussion on IOs as active agents, "agents can ask principals to formalize a practice that agents have developed informally.... As always, principals can end the contract, but agent access to large amounts of data and expertise enables them to pursue and defend independent reinterpretations with vigour."[75]

Reverse institutionalization can be also prompted by principals, who may be concerned that the experimental institutional feature is becoming a *de facto* fixture and who will seek to adopt mechanisms of more

---

[72] DiMaggio and Powell 1983.
[73] Bexell and Mörth 2010.
[74] McCubbins, Noll and Weingast 1987; Pollack 1997.
[75] Hawkins and Jacoby 2006, p. 207.

direct control over partnerships. Governance entrepreneurs can furthermore advance a broader normative framework that legitimizes collaborative governance beyond individual cases. Many of the large partnership institutions that we know nowadays such as the Global Fund, the World Bank Climate Finance Funds, or the Global Reporting Initiative have gone through the entire cycle of dynamic institutional change from uncertain experiments to salient institutional features of international governance.

In sum, similar to entrepreneurship and innovation in other political spheres, global partnership initiatives are likely to be opportunistic, not be always successful, and to entail a cycle of dynamic institutional change. The change is initiated and facilitated from within the organizational structure of the multilateral system, even if it may be prompted by external turbulence and opportunities to align with nonstate agents of governance. This theoretical perspective provides us with an analytic tool to understand not only the opening of multilateralism to collaborative arrangements with nonstate actors but also the variations in the patterns of partnership governance, their institutionalization, and outcomes across international institutions.

Theory Implications and Methods

The observable implications of the dynamic theory of institutional change, which will guide the empirical study of global partnerships, depart quite significantly from the more traditional state-centric views of multilateral institutions. Realist theorists tend to belittle the significance of new modes of governance such as partnerships either as a development of little consequence or as an artifact of powerful states' interests to create and exploit multiple forums of cooperation to their advantage.[76] Such multiplication of governance forms is deemed to undermine multilateral cooperation and to shift global governance increasingly toward the priorities of powerful states and the corporate actors that influence them. Even some applications of the principal–agent perspective – which, contrary to realist theory, take into account the agency of IOs – attribute institutional form and change primarily to state preferences, functional imperatives, and collective action.[77]

---

[76] Drezner 2004; Krasner 2003; Waltz 1999.
[77] Abbott and Snidal 1998; Hawkins *et al.* 2006; Nielson and Tierney 2003.

Writing in the institutionalist tradition on the role of informal governance in international organizations, Randall Stone argues that "The
existence of power politics, the frequency of informal manipulation
and the possibility of forum shopping by powerful states put important
limits on the autonomy of international organizations. Far from mar-
ginalizing international organizations, however, these practices high-
light their significance as instruments of power."[78]

Compared to state-driven explanations of institutional form, the
theory of organizational entrepreneurship of global partnerships
implies a very different sequence of institutional change. Rather than
by principal design, institutional innovation happens within existing
institutions through informal coalitions that involve agents, principals,
and external actors. The mediation and frequent leadership by IOs
imply that partnerships are likely to be structured to reflect and
reinforce agency mandates, norms, and toolkits rather than to undermine multilateral institutions. This account joins an emergent literature
on the influence of IOs on institutional life. However, it anticipates a
much more dynamic and politicized interaction among principals and
agencies with respect to external actors compared to works that place
the spotlight largely on the bureaucracies. State interest and power do
play a role in the creation of global partnerships, often tacitly to the
extent that powerful actors and intergovernmental bodies have no
interest in blocking experimental adoption (Proposition 1) or more
actively by lending selective political and financial support for entrepreneurial coalitions (Proposition 2). The cycle of institutional change
may thus provide opportunities for proactive states to craft niches for
policy experimentation within larger issue areas that stagnate due to
limited interest on the part of large players.

Evidence that partnerships emerge through a process of IO–enabled
entrepreneurial coalitions despite limited interest on the part of powerful states will be particularly supportive of the organizational theory of
institutional change. The implementation of experimental approaches
could in turn contribute to learning and greater commitment by formerly disengaged powers, as reflected in the subsequent endorsement
by large industrialized and emerging countries of informal and formal
initiatives on business and human rights, climate change, or transboundary chemical pollution.

[78] Stone 2011, p. 2.

The theory also has important implications for understanding the agency behind global partnerships and their uneven clustering around some global challenges but not others. The perspective on dynamic institutional change can account for the substantial intertemporal increase in the development of partnerships, as related to the rise of transnational actors and the legitimacy and resource pressures associated with globalization and stagnating intergovernmental commitments (Propositions 5 and 3). Partnerships create opportunities of innovative governance for specific global problems while bypassing other governance failures that are either tightly controlled by states or fall outside the interests of entrepreneurial coalitions. Such uneven clustering of partnerships challenges functional accounts that conceptualize global partnerships largely as new institutional means to address the gaps in global governance and to support the supply of global public goods. We cannot overlook the differential incentives and capacity of political agents to act as governance entrepreneurs in the face of global challenges.

For critical political economy theorists, the clustering of global partnerships around some global problems but not others is symptomatic of the capture of the multilateral agenda and its steering toward neoliberal ideology and market-based practices.[79] The theoretical framework developed here suggests, however, a process of negotiation between the public objectives of international agencies and the interests, resources, and ideology of nonstate actors. In this interplay, IOs and their normative and epistemic capital are anticipated to take center stage in influencing both the nature of external partners and the governance outcomes of partnerships in terms of issues tackled and instruments deployed (Proposition 4). For partnerships to succeed through the cycle of governance entrepreneurship, they have to reconcile private participation with the normative frameworks of IOs and expectations of some degree of internal and external accountability. Some organizations have normative mandates that are particularly sensitive to associations with corporate power, for example the WHO because of concerns about conflict of interest in interacting with entities that are regulated by international health norms or UNICEF and humanitarian organizations wary that undetected practices that

---

[79] Levy and Newell 2005; Utting and Zammit 2006, 2009; Bull and McNeill 2007; Newell 2012.

harm the most vulnerable carry enormous legitimacy risk.[80] In such organizational environments, we anticipate a more contested process of change involving both internal and external scrutiny and that depends critically on the implementation of institutional safeguards to integrity.

The cycle of incremental institutional change thus implies an imprint of IO norms, culture, and knowledge on the nature of their external partners and governance instruments championed by collaborative initiatives rather than the marketization of the multilateral system, even in issues such as health, where private actors have been significant in terms of both financial resources and access to technologies.

In sum, the logic of agency entrepreneurship of public–private partnerships has a number of observable implications that can be examined systematically against plausible alternative explanations. It leads us to expect a specific sequence of institutional change from within existing organizations, strengthening rather than undermining mandates, tacitly backed by a small number of principals, and gradually achieving reversed authorization by their broad membership. Such initiatives are likely to follow peaks in budgetary shortages, advocacy campaigns, private philanthropy, or other windows of opportunity for governance entrepreneurs. Moreover, the outcomes of global partnerships are likely to vary across organizations to reflect the scope for autonomous initiative and their knowledge specialization and capacity to facilitate change. The theory of entrepreneurship of global partnerships thus lends itself to broadly generalizable and extensive empirical cross-examination.

The empirical chapters of the book shed light on these alternative expectations and debates by examining the politics of partnership emergence, institutionalization, and outcomes across multiple policy issues and five IOs: the UN Secretariat, UNEP, the World Bank, UNICEF, and the WHO. One of the important contributions of the book is the new empirical evidence on partnership governance across policy arenas in the multilateral system. The selection of these institutions is motivated by the opportunity to analyze comparatively organizational domains characterized with different sources and degrees of agency autonomy and, importantly, different types of expertise and stimuli in their organizational environment associated

---

[80] Andonova and Carbonnier 2014.

with globalization. The propositions of the theoretical framework lead us to expect that such variation is likely to have a visible imprint on the process and outcomes of partnership governance. The analysis is structured to examine the intertemporal rise of global partnerships as well as their variable outcomes across organizations. The evidence is collected through a mixed-methods approach, which best allows us to assess the validity of the theory of dynamic institutional change and its observable implications.

The original Global Partnerships Database, constructed for this book and elaborated in the Annex, provides the basis for evaluating assumptions and arguments on the political drivers and outcomes of partnership governance. The methodology of populating the Global Partnerships Database includes a comprehensive survey of partnership initiatives in which the World Bank, UNEP, UNICEF, and the WHO participate. Such information was obtained either directly from the partnership units of individual IOs or by surveying their websites and secondary material; it was subsequently complemented on the basis of interviews where needed. The documents and websites of each partnership were hand-coded for key characteristics of partnerships related to the observable implications of the argument and alternative perspectives.[81] Additional data was provided from the Global Compact and the United Nations Fund for International Partnerships.[82] This data allows us to evaluate in broad and generalizable strokes the agency of IOs, states, and a variety of nonstate actors in spearheading coalitions for change. It sheds new light on so-far-unresolved debates on the nature of private and public authority implicated in global partnerships. The quantitative data also provides a basis for analyzing comparatively for the first time the variation in the outcomes of partnership governance in terms of governance instruments, issue focus, and financial partners, as anticipated by the theory.

The qualitative analysis follows the stages of the cycle of institutional change across the five organizations of the multilateral system, which have been selected to capture differences in key explanatory variables of the theoretical framework such as institutional structure, the nature of organizational turbulence in their internal and external environments, and the type of epistemic capacity on which IOs draw

---

[81] See Annex for further detail on the Global Partnerships Database.
[82] See Chapter 3 for more detail.

to facilitate entrepreneurial coalitions. The strategies of governance entrepreneurs and the political coalitions involved in the development of global partnerships are documented through extensive archival research of UN materials, interviewing, and text analysis of primary documents. The interviewing relied on a snowballing technique of referencing within and outside the five organizations under study. The research draws similarly on perspectives from external experts and on primary and secondary documents. These qualitative methods and the comparative approach across issue domains are essential for assessing the consistency and generalizability behind the entrepreneurial life cycle of institutional change.

The empirical chapters that follow embark on the journey to examine the politics and variable geometry of change in the multilateral sphere that have produced new hybrid governance. This study reveals the significant variation in approaches exposed by the relevant partnership portfolios across institutions, even in similar issue areas or with respect to shared partners. This speaks of the anticipated imprint of IO mandates and norms on the nature, purpose, and tools of public–private alliances. It challenges preconceived assumptions of collaborative governance and, for the first time, documents what kinds of instruments, resources, and priorities such initiatives bring to the multilateral system.

3 | The UN Secretariat
Crafting Normative Space for Partnerships

Introduction

When UN Secretary-General Kofi Annan proposed the Global Compact at the 1999 World Economic Forum in Davos, Switzerland, he did so without an intergovernmental blueprint. His office took the initiative and risk of engaging business and other nonstate actors in the core affairs of the UN, including human rights, social justice, and the environment. Supported by an informal coalition of like-minded member states, UN agencies, and nonstate entrepreneurs, the Office of the Secretary-General actively created institutional space and policy justification for global partnerships with the private sector.

The initiative of the Secretary-General was not without its challenges. This chapter explores the tensions between the political constraints associated with the delegated nature of the authority of the UN Secretary-General and the pivotal role of the Office in enabling new governance. Drawing on legal and historical literature, as well as on primary documents and interviews, the analysis examines the nature of the authority, agency autonomy, and leadership that facilitated organizational change in the post–Cold War era. Case studies of the United Nations Fund for International Partnerships (UNFIP) and the UN Global Compact (UNGC), the two most prominent UN platforms for global partnerships with the private sector, provide empirical evidence for the hypothesized effect of organizational turbulence associated with budgetary and legitimacy pressures, IO entrepreneurship, and tacit political coalitions in the cycle of experimentation, diffusion, and institutionalization of global partnerships.

The Secretary-General: Unlikely Entrepreneur?

For the UN Secretary-General to play an activist role by creating new collaborative governance with nonstate actors is unexpected, to say the least, when examined from the traditional state-centric view of the UN.

According to the UN Charter, the Secretary-General is the "chief administrative officer" of the organization, serving its main intergovernmental organs and performing functions "entrusted" by them.[1] The very appointment of the Secretary-General is a highly politicized process dominated by the five permanent members of the Security Council and the U.S. in particular. What then are the sources of autonomous influence of the Office of the Secretary-General and its ability to facilitate agent–principal coalitions which the theoretical framework identifies as important conditions for endogenous institutional change? How can we account for the active role of the UN Secretariat in creating platforms for partnership collaboration?

In an insightful volume on the history and evolving role of the Office, Simon Chesterman captures the tension between the broad public purpose and the political constraints of the post: "At once civil servant and the world's diplomat, lackey of the UN Security Council and commander-in-chief of up to 100,000 peacekeepers, he or she depends on states for both the legitimacy and resources that enable the United Nations to function."[2]

I would argue, however, that it is precisely the broad public mandate and degree of ambiguity surrounding the formal responsibilities of the Secretary-General that imply scope for agency discretion and initiative. Agency autonomy is only partially defined with constitutional clarity; its extent can be rather established through interpretation, informal practices, and specific formal decisions and precedents. As anticipated in the theoretical discussion on dynamic institutional change, both the political conditions and personal initiative of entrepreneurs to interpret mandates matter for the scope of agency entrepreneurship. The second UN Secretary-General, Dag Hammarskjold, famously referred to "Chapter Six and a half" as the legal basis for the creation of the first UN peacekeeping force during the 1956 Suez crisis.[3] The proposal by the Secretary-General and approval by the General Assembly for UN Peacekeeping entailed willful interpretation of the UN Charter provisions for resolving disputes peacefully (outlined in Chapter VI) and for more forceful action with respect to threats to peace (Chapter VII).[4] Similarly, the "good offices" function

---

[1] UN Charter, Articles 97 and 98.
[2] Chesterman 2007, p. 1.
[3] See UN 2008.
[4] See Chesterman 2007; Tharoor 2007; Morgenthau 1966.

of the Secretary-General has been established through informal practice and entails active exercise of agency through quiet diplomatic engagement in disputes to prevent conflict escalation.[5] According to Chesterman, the function has "intentionally vague formulation," and its influence in preventing conflict among countries "is routinely underestimated . . . in part because successes draw so little attention."[6]

The moral authority of the Office of the Secretary-General furthermore allows its leadership to interpret the normative ends of the organization and to act as entrepreneur with agency autonomy to advance such ends.[7] Johnstone qualifies cases such as the sending of a UN observer mission to the civil conflict in Yemen (1963) by Secretary-General U Thant, the adoption of the Agenda for Democratization (1996) under Secretary-General Boutros Boutros-Ghali, and the legal formulation of the Responsibility to Protect principle for humanitarian intervention by Kofi Annan as specific instances of norm entrepreneurship, which are sometimes at odds with the preferences and ideologies of the members of the Security Council.[8]

Historically, however, the variable ability of the Secretary-General to define an autonomous space for his office to stimulate change has depended critically both on personal leadership and on an ability to manage relations with member states and in particular with Security Council principals. In an early reflection on the UN, Hans Morgenthau pointed to the incremental expansion of the role of the Secretary-General beyond what is constitutionally envisaged by the Charter:

By virtue of delegations of power, generally vague, by the Security Council or the General Assembly, his office took over political functions which the Security Council or the General Assembly themselves should have performed but were unable to. This transformation of the office owes much to the initiative and skill of Dag Hammarskjold . . .. This enlargement of the Secretary General's office into something approaching supranational political agency was bound not only to evoke the opposition of particular nations to particular measures taken by the Secretary-General but also to pose in acute form the inner contradiction between . . . national sovereignty and the effectiveness of international organizations.[9]

[5] Chesterman 2007; Whitfield 2007; Traub 2006.
[6] Chesterman 2007, p. 3.
[7] Annan 2013.
[8] Johnstone 2007.
[9] Morgenthau 1966, p. 472.

This account of the organizational workings of the UN supports the theoretical premise of this book that a *dynamic* organizational model of interactions between IOs as bureaucratic and normative agents, states as principals, and their external environment is necessary to grasp the conditions for institutional innovations produced by the UN system. To advance or facilitate change, international agencies and their leadership have to navigate a fine line between defining the scope for initiative and securing sufficient support from principals, often through "informal and issue-specific small coalitions of states known as 'groups of friends.'"[10] As we shall see, the creation of the Global Compact and UNFIP as organizational responses to the challenges of globalization has depended on the leadership and capacity of the Office of the Secretary-General to navigate the constitutional framework of the organization and to elicit political support for collaborative governance.

Organizational Turbulence and Capacity for Entrepreneurship

Scholars of the UN and biographers speak of Kofi Annan as an activist Secretary General.[11] According to close associates, Annan viewed collaboration with the private sector as an important and not-sufficiently-explored mechanism to advance the objectives of the UN; such partnership was to be one of his legacies as Secretary-General.[12] Although Annan was appointed Secretary-General in 1997 from within the UN bureaucracy, his ability to appreciate the relevance of business and other global actors to the UN's mission has often been attributed to his background as the son of an enterprising family in Ghana and his broad international education, including at the Institut Universitaire des Hautes Etudes Internationales in Geneva and at the Sloan School of Management of the Massachusetts Institute of Technology.[13] His leadership, however, while important, was only one of several factors that paved the way for the entrepreneurship of public–private partnerships. As posited by the theoretical framework on dynamic institutional change, turbulence in the political environment

---

[10] Whitfield 2007, p. 86.

[11] See Chesterman 2007; Johnstone 2007; Adebajo 2007; Traub 2006, 2007.

[12] Interviews with John Ruggie, former Assistant Secretary-General for Strategic Planning, February 2008, Cambridge, MA; discussion with Kemal Dervis, former Administrator of UNDP, March, 2010, Geneva.

[13] Traub 2006.

of the UN associated with globalization and decline of resources, as well as internal organizational capacity to facilitate coalitions with supportive states and external actors, were essential ingredients in the development of global partnership platforms.

The signs of organizational pressures on the UN, associated with resources and legitimacy, were unmistakable by the second half of the 1990s. The early post–Cold War cooperation honeymoon had given way to increased civil conflicts, failures of humanitarian intervention, and transnational contestation of economic globalization. At the same time, donor countries, and in particular the U.S., were reducing their financial support to the UN system. State principals demanded greater efficiency and reorganization, often without sufficient political backing for such changes. The organization increasingly appeared in the public perception as overly bureaucratic and slow to react to new social and security issues. Questions about UN (in)efficiency and donor states using the power of the purse to demand reforms in the bureaucracy became increasingly prominent, particularly in the domestic political context of the U.S.[14] Figure 3.1 analyzes the frequency with which the terms "UN reforms" and "UN budget" have appeared in the *New York Times* and the *Washington Post* (two major U.S. newspapers) to illustrate the rise in public awareness of UN budgetary issues and pressure for reforms.

Meanwhile, there was also a growing imbalance between public and private international finance. Flows of official development assistance (ODA), which support many UN causes and programs, stagnated after 1990. Arrears in unpaid UN membership dues also increased substantially in the 1990s, while the U.S. gradually reduced the share of its contribution to the UN budget from approximately 30% down to 22% by 2000.[15] The trend of stagnating and uncertain public finance stood in sharp contrast to the exponential expansion of foreign direct investment (FDI), which outstripped ODA by a factor of forty by the year 2000 (Figure 3.2).

UN entrepreneurs of collaborative governance were sensitive not only to the pressures on the organization to redefine its role but also to the opportunities associated with the expanding resources and global reach of the private sector. The number and density of international

---

[14] On the UN in the post–Cold War context, see Kennedy 2007; Weiss 2009; Murphy 2006; Kuyama and Fowler 2009; Traub 2006; Bull and McNeill 2007; Brühl and Rittberger 2001.

[15] Bond 2012.

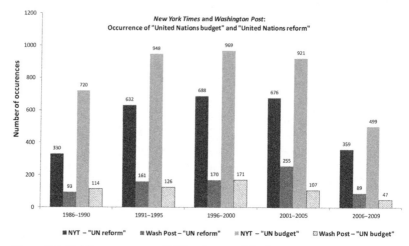

Figure 3.1 Public awareness of UN reform and budget concerns
Sources: New York Times 2012, archive, http://query.nytimes.com/search/sitesearch, *Washington Post* 2012, Archive, http://www.washingtonpost.com/wp-adv/archives/advanced.htm.

NGOs expanded, as did their presence in governance, for example through UN ECOSOC observer status or the creation of civic global regulation such as the SA8000 or Forest Stewardship Council certification (Figure 3.3). By the mid-1990s, global companies had started to adopt corporate social responsibility (CSR) strategies and voluntary certification, a trend that continued into the new millennium (Figure 3.4). The creation and diffusion of voluntary standards for environmental management (such as the ISO14000 certification series) and social accountability (for example, the SA8000 certification, which establishes a set of voluntary standards on working conditions and safety) signaled new interest and capacity among corporate actors to engage in governance.

The financial and political pressures on the UN system along with the opportunities associated with the rise of private finance and governance provided important stimuli for institutional change. External turbulence alone, however, was not sufficient to bring about change. Change also necessitated organizational capacity for entrepreneurship, as specified in the theoretical framework in Chapter 2. Three components of such organizational capacity were reinforced under the leadership of Kofi Annan and subsequently under that of his successor, Ban Ki-moon.

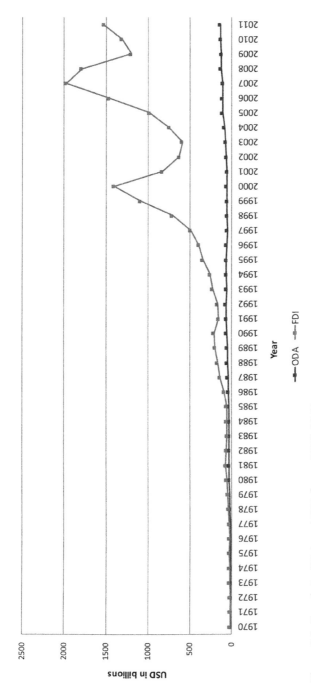

Figure 3.2 Trends in ODA and FDI flows, 1970–2000

Sources: UNCTAD 2013; OECD 2013.

73

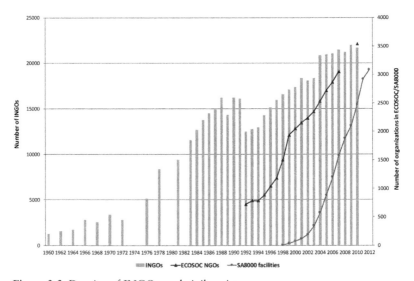

Figure 3.3 Density of INGOs and civil society governance
Sources: Union of International Associations, 2011; UN 2012; Social Accountability Accreditation Service, 2012.

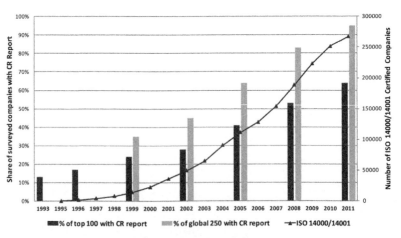

Figure 3.4 Rise of business self-regulation and Corporate Responsibility (CR) reporting
Sources: KPMG 2005; KPMG 2011; ISO 2011.

First, shortly after his appointment, Annan created a new organizational structure, the Office of the Assistant Secretary-General for Strategic Planning, and appointed as its head John Ruggie, then the Dean of the School of International and Public Affairs at Columbia University. One of the main tasks of that office was to develop strategies and assist the Secretary-General in launching special programs or projects for greater collaboration with the private sector and for better coordination across agencies as part of the UN reform agenda. The Office's small team exchanged ideas and generated political support for experimentation with new governance through informal networks both within UN organizations and with governments and external entrepreneurs. The willingness of the UN leadership to deliberately reach out to external experts and policy networks enhanced the capacity for organizational learning and entrepreneurial change.[16] That same capacity remained essential for strengthening the institutionalization of collaborative governance with private actors within the intergovernmental structure of the UN under Secretary-General Ban Ki-moon.

Second, the Office of the Secretary-General suggested a new framing for cooperation with the private sector as a means to increase the relevance of the UN in an era of globalization and to find new ways to advance UN objectives. While previous reform efforts under Secretary-General Boutros Boutros-Ghali had focused primarily on the intergovernmental agenda of the UN, Secretary-General Annan famously talked about the mismatch between "problems without passports" and institutions that were organized around state borders. He thus emphasized the need to devise institutional solutions that included actors who are truly global in character.[17] According to former Assistant Secretary-General for Strategic Planning John Ruggie,

Annan believed that cooperation with the private sector in particular was an important and hitherto not sufficiently explored path to reinvigorate the UN and to strengthen the social pillars of economic globalization. Cooperation with global actors was an opportunity to overcome a range of constraints, including resource constraints and institutional constraints, and to pursue the objectives and norms of the organization via new means. It was a means

---

[16] Interview with Peter Maurer, Secretary of State of Switzerland, June 2011, Bern; and with George Kell, Global Compact, UN Office of Secretary-General, July 2010, New York. See also theoretical work on this point by Haas, E. 1990 and March and Olsen 1998.

[17] Annan 2009.

to increase the relevance and reputation of the UN in the era of globalization and to generate new and potentially powerful support for UN causes.[18]

Such ideas were not confined to the UN Secretariat. As we shall see in the case studies and later chapters of this book, units within UN agencies had already begun exploring engagement with nonstate actors in their operational work. Several governments entertained new ideologies in the 1990s on collaborative ways to tame the social risks of globalization.

In sum, the entrepreneurship of new global partnerships with non-state actors required organizational capacity and willingness to interpret the constitutional statutes of the UN in order to situate such collaboration within the scope of agency authority. Cooperation with nonstate actors had to be crafted in such a way as to safeguard the public purpose and reputation of the organization while securing sufficient principal support for experimental implementation, diffusion, and broader institutionalization. Drawing on its position of organizational leadership, moral authority, and public purpose, the Office of the Secretary-General had an important role to play in creating such institutional space. The case studies of UNFIP and the Global Compact present further empirical evidence on the political conditions for endogenous institutional change elaborated in Chapter 2 by examining the sources of organizational pressures, agency capacity, and political support in the entrepreneurship of partnership governance. The parallel structuring of the cases around the three stages of the life cycle of dynamic institutional change – from experimental adoption of new governance to its diffusion and subsequently to institutionalization – reflects on the hypothesized process of change and its contextualization in the specific circumstances that opened opportunities for political entrepreneurship.

The United Nations Fund and the UN Office for Partnerships

Window of Opportunity: The Turner Gift

In 1997, the U.S. Congress failed to allocate the U.S. contribution to the UN, then equivalent to roughly 30% of the organization's budget.

---

[18] Interview with John Ruggie, February 2008, Cambridge, MA.

Along with unpaid arrears by member states, this served to create the deepest budgetary deficit in the history of the UN. In a gesture that surprised many, U.S. philanthropist Ted Turner announced a donation of US$1 billion to "compensate" for the gap in dues from the U.S. and to support UN causes. This was the largest private donation in the history of the UN. The confluence of budgetary threats, interest of an external entrepreneur, and initiative by the Secretary-General triggered the cycle of institutional change toward public–private collaboration.

The Turner gift coupled with acute budgetary crisis opened a unique window of opportunity for the Secretary-General to establish, on an experimental ten-year basis, the UNFIP. This was the first institutional platform within the UN Secretariat to facilitate partnerships between the UN and nonstate actors. The United Nations Foundation was created to manage the Turner donation. The Foundation is a body with public charity status outside the UN system whose mission has been to leverage additional private resources and advocate for UN causes, including within the U.S. political context. The Secretary-General acted within the digression of his agency autonomy to facilitate the experimental creation of UNFIP in 1998 as the interface between the United Nations Foundation and UN agencies by following accepted institutional procedures. He relied on advice from the Advisory Committee on Administrative and Budgetary Questions of the General Assembly.[19] A paper by UNFIP Board Members on the history of UNFIP describes the relevance of agency initiative and epistemic capacity:

...[T]he Secretary General mobilized a team to work with the Foundation and establish the internal mechanisms within the UN for coordination and the arrangements that would be required for programming the planned gift. This important initial series of negotiations produced what came to be known as a "concept paper" on Mr. Turner's gift that the Secretary-General made available to the Chairman of the Advisory Committee on Administrative and Budgetary Questions in a letter dated 30 January 1998. In that letter, the Secretary General outlined his reasons for planning to establish a trust fund – the United Nations Fund for International Partnerships (UNFIP) – to coordinate, channel and monitor contributions from the United Nations Foundation. UNFIP would report directly to the Secretary General.[20]

---

[19] See UNGA 1998.
[20] Chen *et al.* 2006.

The General Assembly subsequently adopted Decision 52/466, in which it "took note" of UNFIP and mandated the Secretary-General to provide regular reporting on the activities,[21] a step indicative of entrepreneurship by the agency rather than the member states.[22] As an experimental initiative, UNFIP had a ten-year sunset clause. However, it provided a substantially new organizational platform for logistical and financial support to partnerships between UN agencies and private actors.

For the first time in UN history, the formal agreement between the UN and the United Nations Foundation on the structure and functions of UNFIP included the objective of "mutual collaboration" between the UN and nonstate actors "to work together to achieve the goals and objectives of the Charter of the United Nations through implementation of innovative, forward-looking and pro-active projects and activities that make contributions to the collective future and well-being of the planet."[23] The Executive Director of UNFIP reported directly to the Secretary-General. The Advisory Board of UNFIP, chaired by the Deputy Secretary-General and including representatives of UN agencies, academia, business, and societal organizations, provided policy guidance and contributed to identifying and reviewing the eligibility of partnership proposals for support from the partnership platform.

Despite the substantial exercise of agency discretion and private initiative in the creation of UNFIP, there was surprisingly little substantive opposition by UN member states in the General Assembly[24] beyond concern voiced by some states that partnerships "might alter and potentially exert outside influence on United Nations priorities."[25] This is due to the fact that most member states and UN agencies initially viewed UNFIP primarily as another limited mechanism for fundraising rather than as a new model for a truly collaborative approach to governance.[26] From the perspective of principals, the

---

[21] UNGA 1998.

[22] The language of "taking note" implies adopting a proposal or ex-post approval without necessarily a ringing endorsement by the intergovernmental body.

[23] UNGA 1998, p. 8. The full text of the agreement is reprinted in the Report of the Secretary-General to the General Assembly on the UNFIP; see UNGA 1998.

[24] UNGA, 1998–2011, Secretary-General Reports United Nations Fund for International Partnerships.

[25] Chen *et al.* 2006, p. 5

[26] Interviews with John Ruggie, February 2008, Harvard University, Cambridge, MA; and with Gawaner Atif, Chief of Office/Secretary to the Advisory Board, UNFIP, July 2007, New York. See also UNGA 1998; 1999.

initiative was a low-risk opportunity for experimentation with partnerships in a period of budgetary crisis.

The establishment of the United Nations Foundation, which provided an extrabudgetary funding mechanism, and the UNFIP as a partnership platform, expanded both the means and autonomous space for the UN Secretariat to stimulate greater collaboration with non-state actors.[27] This was seemingly incremental institutional change in political terms but much more significant for advancing collaborative governance between the UN and the private sector compared to merely incorporating the Turner gift toward UN programming. The United Nations Foundation, purposely structured as a public charity, was further intended as an autonomous mechanism to *advocate* for the UN both in the private sector and in the U.S. political context.[28] It is telling that former U.S. Senator Timothy Wirth became the first president of the United Nations Foundation. Two major public campaigns launched by the Foundation during its first ten years of existence include Better World – to "strengthen the relationship between the United States and the United Nations through outreach, communications, and advocacy" and The People Speak.org – "to educate and engage young people on global issues... of poverty reduction, global health, climate change and more."[29] As Andrea Gay, Executive Director of Children's Health at the United Nations Foundation, explained in an interview, "Telling the UN story is to this day an important aspect of the work of the Foundation."[30] The United Nations Foundation has advocated in the U.S. political context through public–private campaigns to support specific UN causes and by showcasing the role of the UN in tackling global problems related to health, human security, youth, women, and the environment and by advocating for U.S. Congress to deliver its dues.[31]

In effect, the governance entrepreneurs of the United Nations Foundation and UNFIP purposely steered these partnerships to address

---

[27] Chen *et al.* 2006; Dossal 2004a, 2004b.

[28] Interview with Shamir B. Shahi, Head of Executive Office, United Nations Foundation, July 2014.

[29] United Nations Foundation 2008.

[30] Interview with Andrea Gay, United Nations Foundation, Washington, DC, January 2008.

[31] Interview with Shamir B. Shahi, United Nations Foundation, Washington, DC, July 2014; UNOG Executive Briefing with Kathy Calvin, President and Chief Executive Officer of the United Nations Foundation, May 2014, Geneva.

legitimacy and resource pressures facing the UN, including with respect to public opinion and domestic politics of key state principals such as the U.S., and by supporting the capacity of the agency to advance global objectives. If we look back to Figure 2.1 on dynamic interaction and institutional change in Chapter 2, we would detect that both the UN and its private partners through the United Nations Foundation and UNFIP reached back to domestic constituencies, as well as to global actors, in order to advance via other means the resources, political legitimacy, and programming of the organization.

Diffusion of Partnerships in the UN

The funding and programmatic activities of the two partnership platforms, UNFIP and the United Nations Foundation, supported in turn the initiatives of organizational entrepreneurs within UN agencies and facilitated access by nonstate actors. By the 1990s, some UN agencies had already experimented with collaborative governance in their operational activities. The UNEP and the United Nations Development Program (UNDP), for example, had supported discrete instances of collaboration with civil society or business from the bottom up, often quietly aided by the relatively decentralized structure of the organizations and motivated by operational objectives on the ground.[32] UNICEF had used various forms of operational cooperation with NGOs and had experience with private fundraising.[33]

UNFIP supported the diffusion of partnership governance by providing resources to scale up successful partnership models such as the International Coral Reef Action Network or the African Rural Energy Enterprise Development facilitated by UNEP. In other instances, UNFIP and the United Nations Fund sowed the seeds of major new partnerships, for example, the program on Mother-to-Child Transmission for HIV/AIDS Prevention and Increased Rate of Survival, a joint

---

[32] Interviews with Garrette Clark UNEP DTIE, October 2011, Paris; with Delphin Ganapin, February 2008, UNDP, New York; and with Craig Murphy, Professor of Political Science, UN Historian, September 2008, Wellesley, MA. See also Chapter 4 for more detail on the history of UNEP partnership governance; and Murphy 2006 on UNDP.

[33] See Steets and Thomsen 2009 and Chapter 5.

effort among UNICEF, WHO, a coalition of eight foundations, and the Columbia University Public Health School. In the run-up to the 2002 Johannesburg Summit on Sustainable Development, the office worked closely with the Under-Secretary-General for Economic and Social Affairs, Nitin Desai, to support the adoption of partnerships as an official outcome of the intergovernmental summit.[34]

The UNFIP office further promoted recognition of partnerships by UN staff and intergovernmental bodies as a substantively *collaborative* mode of governance. Even though leveraging funding has been a key aspect of UNFIP's mission, senior staff have on multiple occasions explained that one of the main objectives and challenges for the UN has been to move away from the traditional view of the private sector as a source of charitable giving toward one of more integrative collaboration and strategic partnering.[35]

The UNFIP served as a point of entry by private-sector and civil-society actors to the UN and a broker of partnerships at a very high level in the UN administration. As argued in the theoretical framework of the book, this partnership platform effectively increased the opportunities for internal–external coalitions. Increasing awareness among business and NGOs about opportunities for collaboration on UN causes was critical, because for private actors, such partnerships were neither obvious nor without transaction costs. Programmatic collaboration with the United Nations Foundation was particularly important for mobilizing additional private-sector interest and contributions. For example, this kind of leveraging of political and private interest was critical for the work of UNEP's Energy Branch. Created in 1997, when clean energy was still a difficult topic for political discussion in the UN, the Energy Branch found tremendous support in terms of funding, programming, and access to a large network of actors interested in

---

[34] The Johannesburg partnerships have attracted considerable political and scholarly attention because of the visible high-level recognition of partnerships as a form of governance. Paradoxically, their management and implementation have been rather uneven in some cases as a result of limited commitment of resources and loosely defined objectives. See Andonova and Levy 2003; Bäckstrand and Kylsäter 2014; Biermann *et al.* 2007; Pattberg *et al.* 2012.

[35] Interview with Gawaher Atif, Chief of Office/Secretary to the Advisory Board, UNFIP, July 2007, New York; with Camilla Schippa, UNFIP, July 2007, New York; and with William Kennedy, UNFIP, February 2008, New York. See also Dossal 2004a; Chen *et al.* 2006.

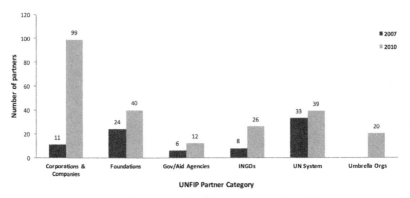

Figure 3.5 Expansion of non-state funding partners of UNFIP

Sources: Report of the Secretary-General: Programme budget for the biennium 2010–2011; UNGA 2010, (A/65/347), Annex 1; UNFIP report on file for 2007 data.

clean energy, on the basis of which it developed a substantial clean energy portfolio, including through partnerships.[36]

During the initial ten-year period of UNFIP's work, the UN Foundation supported its partnerships with more than US$1.1 billion, of which US$465 million were from the original Ted Turner gift and an additional US$665 million were provided by corporate actors, foundations, governments, and NGOs.[37] Data on the major categories of UNFIP funding partners (Figure 3.5) illustrates the growth in private engagement and suggests that the diffusion of partnerships relied substantially on support from external entrepreneurs – most prominently private-sector foundations, international business and NGOs – and financial support from government agencies of several donor countries, as well as the facilitation of UN agencies. The uptake and implementation of partnerships, in turn, has depended on active collaboration with government agencies of developing countries. Such patterns of actor support for the partnership model of governance would suggest more limited ex-ante intergovernmental steering than the traditional model of IOs would assume. They reflect active coalition building between interested governments, UN agencies, and nonstate actors, emphasized by the theoretical model of dynamic institutional change.

[36] Phone interview with Mark Radka, July 2015, UNEP DTIE Energy, Paris.
[37] United Nations Foundation 2008.

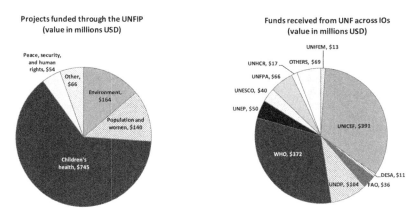

Figure 3.6 UNFIP projects and financing across issue areas and UN agencies
Sources: UNGA 2011a (A/66/188).

The data in the biannual report of the Secretary-General to the General Assembly on UNFIP and interviews furthermore reveal the central role of UN agencies in the diffusion of the partnership model of governance. In practice, private-actor participation in specific partnerships supported by UNFIP has often been agreed at the agency level, while backing by UNFIP and the United Nations Foundation has smoothed the wheels of such collaboration politically and financially.[38]

The facilitation of partnerships has been highly uneven, however, across UN organizations and issues. Figure 3.6 shows that the WHO, UNICEF, and UNDP are the three organizations with the largest share of partnership funding from UNFIP; they are followed by UNEP, UNESCO, UNFPA, and FAO. These organizations have very different mandates and organizational structures. However, they have in common a high reliance on technical expertise, extensive epistemic networks, and policy focus characterized by lower sovereignty cost concerns as compared to security, trade, or human rights organizations.[39]

---

[38] Interviews with William Kennedy, UNFIP; February 2008, New York; Camilla Schippa, UNFIP, July 2007, New York; and with Garrette Clark, UNEP DTIE, October, 2011, Paris.

[39] Haas, P. 1989; Haas E. 1990; Finnemore 1996; Murphy 2006. The relative autonomy of UNESCO and UNFPA in promoting specific programs has been

The patterns of IO leadership and partnership clustering across issues lend credence to the theoretical hypotheses on the role of relative agency autonomy and capacity, along with a degree of consensus or moderate preference divergence among principals as conditions likely to create space for the development of global partnerships (Chapter 2). The programmatic frameworks, which UNFIP and the United Nations Foundation presented to the General Assembly, proposed four main areas for partnership collaboration: children's health, biodiversity and sustainable use of natural sites designated by the 1972 World Heritage Conventions, sustainable energy and climate change, and the rights and well-being of adolescent girls and women.[40] Some of these issues, for example children's health and rights, had achieved relatively high intergovernmental consensus on the need for new governance. Others such as clean energy, biodiversity conservation at World Heritage Sites, or issues related to adolescent girls and women allowed the partnership platforms to carve out areas of moderate divergence of state preferences and opportunities to advance causes incrementally with the support of proactive states and nonstate actors. The issue focus of UNFIP partnerships furthermore reflected the leading role and expertise of highly specialized UN agencies (Figure 3.6). In comparison, there are very few UNFIP partnerships related to core areas of UN competence such as peace, security, and human rights, which are associated with relatively high sovereignty concerns among principals and more limited autonomy of UN organizations.

As anticipated by the theoretical positions in Chapter 2, UNFIP partnerships responded also to the density of interests by nonstate entrepreneurs in global issues such as biodiversity, clean energy, or better access to health. Private-sector participation tended to emphasize specific measurable outcomes toward UN goals and to avoid

---

contested by different U.S. administrations, which withdrew support for the respective agencies. These examples illustrate that agency autonomy can be at times perceived as politically costly but is difficult to reverse altogether even by the most powerful principal, in this case the U.S. Partnerships can be important in expanding agency resources and implementation capacity.

[40] See UNGA 1999 (A/54/664), 2000a (A/54/664/Add.1), 2000b (A/54/664/Add.2), 2000c (A/54/664/Add.3). See also UNF and UNFIP 1999, 2001; UNFIP 2013a, 2013b, 2013c.

policy problems that are perceived as politically sensitive or fraught with deadlock on the part of states. According to Andrea Gay of the United Nations Foundation:

The priorities emphasized in the programmatic documents reflect an interest of United Nations Foundation leadership in areas of strong consensus likely to attract donor interest and provide space for implementing results-oriented interventions. This approach intersected with the Secretary General's ambition to engage the private sector in addressing global issues in ways that also create cross-cutting linkages and cooperation among UN agencies.[41]

Institutionalization: UN Office for Partnerships

It was the practice of UNFIP partnerships and their diffusion and implementation by a large majority of developing countries that established the political basis for their more permanent institutionalization. UN agencies and nonstate entrepreneurs played a central role in the formulation and facilitation of the partnership model in the early experimental stages of the life cycle of dynamic institutional change. However, broader political acceptance, particularly by developing countries, remained important for the more permanent institutionalization of hybrid governance.

Between 1998 and 2010, the UNFIP platform facilitated some 507 partnership projects across 124 countries.[42] The formulation and implementation of these partnerships depended critically on governmental and nongovernmental entrepreneurs *within* states. The Galapagos Sustainable Electricity Partnership, for example, started as an initiative of the mayor of the island of San Cristóbal, facilitated by UNDP and a partnership with E8, an association of some of the world's largest energy companies. The African Rural Energy Enterprise Development partnership involves collaboration between local nonprofit and financial organizations in Ghana, Mali, Senegal, and Zambia, facilitated by UNEP Energy and with financial support from UNFIP and the Swedish Agency for International Cooperation. Global

---

[41] Interview with Andrea Gay, United Nations Foundation, January 2009, Washington, DC.
[42] UNGA 2011a (A/66/188).

initiatives such as those for polio eradication or measles vaccination have depended on international political support as well as close collaboration with national public health services and local communities and health providers.[43] It is such experiences, coupled with regular and detailed reporting to the General Assembly on the portfolio and financing of UNFIP across countries and issue areas, that contributed to firmer political endorsement of partnerships as an institutional feature of UN governance.[44] The diffusion, reporting, and debate on partnerships contributed to strong legitimation of this form of governance through social processes identified in the theoretical framework, such as familiarity, mimicry, and replication of successful practices across UN organizations and member states.

This demonstrates the dynamic of "reverse" institutionalization whereby institutional acceptance follows experimental adoption and perception of successful diffusion and normalization of experimental practices. A statement by Karen Lock of South Africa on behalf of the G77 plus China illustrates how expanding political support has been based on experience with partnership diffusion and implementation:

The Group of 77 and China commend the Fund, which through its collaboration with the United Nations Foundation has supported US$809.5 million in programming in the areas of children's health, population and women, environment, and peace, security and human rights. Since 1998, funding has been allocated to 376 projects in 121 countries involving 39 United Nations organizations ... The work of UNFIP illustrates the positive contribution that public–private partnerships could make towards the work of the United Nations, as envisaged by the Secretary-General when he urged business leaders in 1998 to increase their investment in developing countries and work in partnership with the United Nations system ... The Group remains appreciative of the positive contribution made by the UNFIP to projects in developing and least developed countries.[45]

---

[43] Interviews with former Ambassador John Lange, United Nations Foundation, July 2014, Washington, DC, and with William Kennedy, UNFIP, February 2008, New York.

[44] For the repetition, consistency, and detail of annual reporting on UNFIP to member states, see UNGA 1998 (A/53/700), 1999a (A/54/664), 2001c (A/55/763), 2002b (A/57/133), 2003b (A/58/173), 2004b (A/59/170), 2005b (A/60/327), 2007b (A/61/189), 2010b (A/65/347).

[45] Lock 2006.

The creation of a larger political constituency for global partnerships through practice and implementation provided space for the UN Secretary-General to advance their institutionalization within the inter-governmental framework of the UN. Indicatively, an earlier attempt by Kofi Annan to create an Office for Partnerships in 2002 had failed. This was a result of the relatively short experience with partnerships and the persistent high-level skepticism within the UN bureaucracy about its misfit with the intergovernmental nature of the organization. In addition, there was disagreement as to whether the Global Compact should be included within an integrated partnership platform. Kofi Annan eventually succeeded in creating the UN Office for Partnerships in 2006, pursuant to General Assembly resolution 60/1 on the 2005 World Summit Outcomes, which reaffirmed the role of partnerships in advancing development objectives and finance. The UN Office for Partnerships included UNFIP, the United Nations Democracy Fund created in 2005, and a new Partnership Advisory and Outreach Service.[46] In 2008, the UN and the United Nations Foundation renewed their agreement on UNFIP for ten additional years, subject to raising an additional US$1 billion in support of UN causes.

Continued leadership by Secretary-General Ban Ki-moon, coupled with the political support that he elicited on the basis of wider diffu-sion of partnership practices, was ultimately essential for the greater institutionalization of global partnerships as a mechanism of UN governance. In 2009, the UN Office of Internal Oversight Services conducted the first audit of UNFIP. It noted that "by leveraging activities…UNFIP secured recognition in the system, as attested by successive General Assembly resolutions and related reports."[47] At the same time, the audit report recommended clearer specification of the mandate of the Office for Partnerships, remarking that "…there is no formal United Nations mandate assigned to UNOP."[48] Following the recommendations of the report, a special Secretary-General Bul-letin on the Organization of the United Nations Office for Partnerships in December 2009 formalized its structure and role within UN insti-tutions. Over the course of a decade, global partnerships had become a

---

[46] United Nations Secretariat 2009 (ST/SGB/2009/14).
[47] UN Office of Internal Oversight Services 2009, p. 7.
[48] UN Office of Internal Oversight Services 2009, pp. 7–8.

more widely recognized and legitimized sphere of UN governance, in which public and private actors cooperate on specific objectives that fall within the mission of the organization. In 2015, the Sustainable Development Goals reaffirmed global partnerships as important institutional means to advance the implementation of these broadly endorsed objectives.

The United Nations Global Compact

The United Nations Global Compact is currently the world's largest corporate social responsibility (CSR) initiative. The Office of the Secretary-General positioned the Global Compact not as an operational partnership but as a strategic initiative to rearticulate the UN relationship with the private sector and to establish its role for advancing broadly adopted norms and stability in an era of global change.[49] As such, it was a more risky undertaking for organizational entrepreneurs than UNFIP. By engaging transnational corporations directly to advance human rights, labor rights, environmental protection and transparency through voluntary commitments, the UN norms continue to gain greater resonance globally. Such engagement also brings legitimacy risks, however, by association with potential corporate malpractice. The initiative furthermore had to overcome the traditional mistrust between the UN and the business community. Many staff members viewed corporations as largely irrelevant to the UN work or worse, as footloose entities whose prioritization of global markets has often eluded or worked contrary to international norms. In the formulation of this initiative, the Office of the Secretary-General had to actively safeguard against the ethical risks and contradictions that such a partnership may entail. The cycle of governance entrepreneurship, from agency-driven experimentation to broader political acceptance and institutionalization, is reflected in the name of the initiative. Originally created as *The* Global Compact without formal intergovernmental recognition, it has now become acknowledged as the *UN* Global Compact by General Assembly resolutions.[50]

---

[49] Interviews with Peter Maurer, June 2010, Bern; John Ruggie, February 2008, Cambridge, MA. See also Brugger and Maurer 2010.
[50] UNGA 2007c (A/RES/62/211), 2010a (A/64/223).

Experimental Adoption

Kofi Annan articulated the idea for the Global Compact not in the UN General Assembly but in a speech to the 1999 World Economic Forum in Davos, Switzerland. Text analysis of the speech suggests a careful crafting of a normative framework to justify collaboration between the private sector and the UN and to situate it within the agency authority of the organization. The speech advanced several core ideas. First, Annan made the case for the *relevance of the UN* in an era of globalization. Globalization brought prosperity but also fragility: it implied greater need for global cooperation and stability for world commerce to flourish. The UN had cultivated a body of normative frameworks on a set of broadly agreed principles, and it was thus offering a lot of institutional capital that could be used to stabilize the system.[51]

In addition, the speech advanced explicitly the idea that business and the UN have common interests in promoting peace and stability by advancing core UN values. According to Georg Kell, who worked closely with John Ruggie and Kofi Annan on the formulation of the initiative and later became its first executive head, this aspect of the speech presented "a radical step forward for the United Nations and the business community and an important paradigm shift from the more traditional patterns of UN regulation through weak or failed codes of conduct and business resistance."[52] The speech called on business "to embrace, support and enact a set of core values" embedded in "the Universal Declaration, the International Labor Organization's Declaration on fundamental principles and rights at work, and the Rio Declaration of the United Nations Conference on Environment and Development in 1992."[53] A strategy note prepared for the Davos speech justifies the focus on the provisions of these three UN documents: "These components were chosen because they are backed by international law or declarations and relevant to business operation. Issues related to business ethics that are not covered by the UN are not included. Doing so would create the undesirable impression of yet another business ethics code."[54]

---

[51] Annan, 1999.
[52] Interview with George Kell, July 2010, New York.; UN Office of the Secretary-General 2008.
[53] Annan 1999, p. 2.
[54] United Nations Office of the Secretary-General 1998, p. 3.

The Secretary-General's proposal for a compact between the UN and the business community thus involved deliberate agency initiative and communicative action to actively establish the normative space, justification, and scope for new governance. Its organizational entrepreneurs took care to ensure that the idea fit with the mandate for implementation of the UN Secretariat and that it did not create a new regulatory threat for business or for developing countries. They also engaged in mobilization of relevant organizations within the UN, among member states, and in the transnational NGO and business community to create supporting political coalitions, as anticipated by the dynamic theory of institutional change.

The Global Compact was nonetheless not without risk for its entrepreneurs. Some officials within the UN bureaucracy, including at very high levels, viewed it as a dangerous departure from standard frameworks and the intergovernmental nature of the institution[55] or, even worse, as a potential capture of the UN by corporate interests.[56] To secure sufficient organizational and political support for the experimental implementation of a radically new venue for collaboration with business, the Office of the Secretary-General relied on extensive consultation with relevant UN agencies and with governments that shared the desire for closer partnership with private actors. Discussion with the International Labor Organization, UNEP, and the Office of the High Commissioner for Human Rights (OHCHR) led to the formulation of the Global Compact principles on labor, the environment, and human rights.

The OHCHR was perhaps most sensitive to the ethical risks entailed in closer collaboration with corporate actors because of the moral basis of its statute and the possibility that companies may become associated directly or indirectly with human rights abuses.[57] Moreover, human rights laws impose limits and obligations pertaining to the sovereign machinery of states. Their translation to the business sector thus entails higher risk, on one hand of raising sovereign concerns and objections, and on the other hand the possibility of diluting responsibility away from the state as the primary addressee of the law. The

---

[55] Interviews with Georg Kell, July 2010, New York; John Ruggie, February 2008, Cambridge, MA.
[56] Utting 2002; Utting and Zammit 2006.
[57] Clapham 2006; Robinson 1999; Weissbrodt 2008.

Office of the High Commissioner undertook a series of legal analyses to evaluate such ethical considerations and the normative bases for engaging corporate entities directly in the protection of human rights. These studies provided a legal understanding on which Commissioner Mary Robinson based her support for the Global Compact.[58]

In sum, as the theoretical model on governance entrepreneurship suggests, the authority of the Secretary-General to initiate the Global Compact was actively examined and established by its entrepreneurs within the constitutional framework of the organization, rather than given by its formal structure or political oversight. The proposal for the adoption of a new partnership platform with business was situated carefully within the scope of agency autonomy. It targeted broadly institutionalized norms, as anticipated by Proposition 1 of the theoretical framework.

In this process, political support by a group of states was another essential element of the creation of the Global Compact and the agent–principal coalitions behind dynamic institutional change. The governments of the UK, Germany, Norway, Switzerland, and France tacitly endorsed the initiative in its conception. These were states either with domestic traditions that favored dialogue with the business community or that were experimenting domestically with new ways of reconciling economic globalization and social purpose.[59] For instance, the UK Labour government of Tony Blair had embraced the "third way" ideology of reconciling in a more collaborative and less interventionist manner global capitalism and social risks. The UK Overseas Development Agency actively supported partnerships as instruments for advancing human security and sustainability. Switzerland embraced ideas of human security and rights as central to the development paradigm, in which the business community would have a role to play. For the Swiss government, which was preparing for a second popular vote on UN membership (following the failure of the 1986 vote), reframing the relationship between the UN and the business community was important for domestic audiences to view the organization as relevant in a

---

[58] Interview with Andrew Clapham, Professor of Law, Graduate Institute of International and Development Studies, Geneva, June 2010. See also Robinson 1999.

[59] Interview with John Ruggie, February 2008, Harvard University, Cambridge, MA.

new era of globalization.[60] While the Clinton administration in the U.S. did not directly endorse the initiative, it nonetheless shared an interest in experimenting with soft regulatory mechanisms for advancing social concerns. Informal discussions also took place with NGOs such as the World Wildlife Fund for Nature (WWF) and the International Union for Conservation of Nature (IUCN) and with business organizations including the International Chamber of Commerce, the United States Council for International Business, and the World Business Council for Sustainable Development (WBCSD) to establish the extent of private actor interest and support for the initiative.[61]

The launch of the Global Compact presents compelling illustration of the conditions and political dynamics of organizational entrepreneurship for new governance and its initial experimental adoption. The turbulence of globalization, agency leadership, and confluence of ideas across supportive agent–principal coalitions and external networks made such action possible, as anticipated by the theory of dynamic institutional change. In line with this theoretical perspective, the internal capacity of the Office for Strategic Planning for normative interpretation of the mandate of the Secretary-General and its ability to advance epistemic deliberation and coalitions within the UN and with external actors was another key dynamic in the entrepreneurship of the Global Compact. The strategy note for Kofi Annan's Davos speech, furthermore, identifies the venue and the moment in history as a window of opportunity for such partnership:

As international business and global economic rule making are increasingly under pressure to respond to the vague but growing uneasiness of the public with the globalization process, a new window of opportunity has emerged. Projecting UN values and principles as defining a framework of universal standards against which corporate behavior can be judged promises to create new awareness about UN goals and significantly advance their implementation.[62]

Following positive reception of the speech by the business community, the Office of the Secretary-General established the Global Compact in July 2000 with forty signatories. The signatories undertake to

---

[60] Interview with Peter Maurer, Federal Department of Foreign Affairs of Switzerland, June 2011, Bern.
[61] Interview with Georg Kell, July 2010, New York.
[62] United Nations Office of the Secretary-General 1998, p. 1.

publicly advocate the nine principles of the Global Compact on human rights, social justice, and the environment through mission statements, annual reports, and partnerships for UN development objectives, as well as to publicly communicate progress in their implementation. The Global Compact added a tenth principle on Anti-Corruption in 2004.[63]

The Global Compact was created on the basis of a call for action by the Secretary-General within the authority of his Office without formal General Assembly recognition or funding. A paper by Markus Eggenberger of the Swiss Department for Foreign Affairs eloquently summarizes the leading role of agency initiative in the experimental adoption of the Global Compact: "Despite their defining role as members of the UN General Assembly, one has to recognize that governments per se did not play an essential role within the original Global Compact governance structure."[64] Norway, Sweden, Switzerland, Germany, and France created a trust fund with voluntary contributions for the operation of the Global Compact and, under a Swiss initiative, constituted a Friends of the Global Compact group.[65] This political support is illustrative of the selective agent–principal coalitions that typically back the experimental adoption of new governance. The support of states for the Global Compact initiative was deliberately "light footed" in order to enhance the autonomy of the Office of the Secretary-General to experiment with new institutional approaches that involve risks and may not be readily accepted by its intergovernmental bodies.[66]

Diffusion of UN–Business Collaboration

The politics of the Global Compact took on fresh vigor in the aftermath of its creation. The legitimacy of the initiative was contested on several fronts. NGOs challenged the voluntary, open-ended nature of Global Compact commitments; as one NGO put it, "a paper tiger could not possibly be more toothless."[67] Advocacy critics charged that the Global Compact amounted to blue-washing of corporate practices

---

[63] For the full formulation of the ten Global Compact Principles, see UNGC 2016.
[64] Eggenberger 2011, p. 58.
[65] Eggenberger 2011; Kell 2012; UNGC 2011.
[66] Thérien and Pouliot 2006; Eggenberger 2011.
[67] Bern Declaration 2007, p. 8.

and "a venue for opportunistic companies to make grandiose statements of corporate citizenship without worrying about being called to account for their actions."[68] In other words, skeptics feared that the voluntary pledges to advance principles on human rights, labor rights, and sustainability might amount to window dressing and undue influence on the part of business. The Alliance for a Corporate-Free UN and CorpWatch mobilized a campaign to expose "the flawed human rights and environmental records of companies forming partnerships with the UN," calling for restrictions of corporate influence in the UN system.[69] Critics cautioned that corporate agendas could be fundamentally at odds with UN principles of fairness, equity, and accountability. In effect, the Global Compact was seen as a vehicle to legitimize the corporate power that drives economic globalization.[70] As Thérien and Pouliot observe: "The denunciation of the Global Compact is all the more pronounced because of the widespread perception that it epitomizes a regrettable ideological shift on the part of the UN."[71]

Another fundamental line of initial political opposition had to do with the lack of intergovernmental mandate or approval of the Global Compact and hence its uncomfortable fit with a strict view of the UN as an intergovernmental organization. Critics deplored "that UN member states themselves were pushed to the side lines of the project and were consulted only several months after Kofi Annan's speech at Davos."[72] The G77 plus China issued a Ministerial Statement in September 2000 calling for intergovernmental oversight and guidelines on UN engagement with the private sector.[73] Reportedly, a group of G77 ministers asked Kofi Annan who authorized him to establish the Global Compact, to which the Secretary-General replied that he did not realize that he needed a mandate to help implement the Universal Declaration of Human Rights.[74] The Secretary-General explicitly positioned the initiative within the delegated authority of his office.

---

[68] Williams 2004, p. 762.
[69] CorpWatch 2001. See also CorpWatch 2000; Transnational Resource & Action Center 2000; Paine 2000; Bendell 2004; Bull and McNeill 2007.
[70] Utting 2002; Utting and Zammit 2006, 2009.
[71] Thérien and Pouliot 2006, pp. 66–67.
[72] Thérien and Pouliot 2006, p. 68. See also Boisson de Chazournes and Mazuyer 2011.
[73] UNGA 2000e (A/55/459), p. 5. See also King 2001.
[74] Interview with John Ruggie, February 2008, Harvard University, Cambridge, MA.

Nonetheless, the architects of the Global Compact were keenly aware that enlarging support by principals, particularly among developing and emerging economies, was a necessary condition for its more permanent institutionalization and legitimization.

The Office for Strategic Planning responded to external and internal contestation with extensive communication, justification, and ethical risk management. The dominant frame of this discourse was the juxtaposition of the Global Compact as a learning network for advancing UN norms with traditional (and failed) attempts to adopt corporate codes of conduct. An open letter by then-Assistant Secretary-General John Ruggie emphasized that "...the Global Compact is not a code of conduct... Instead, ours is a learning model, utilizing the powerful tool of transparency...you will be able to see and judge the same actions because all of the information will be in the public domain."[75] In 2000, the Secretary-General issued *Guidelines on Cooperation between the United Nations and the Business Sector*, which established conditions on the use of the UN emblem and selection of business partners. These include specific limitations on the noneligibility of "business entities that are complicit in human rights abuses, tolerate forced or compulsory labor or the use of child labor, or are involved in the sale or manufacture of anti-personnel mines or other components..."[76]

The creation of domestic business networks of the Global Compact has perhaps been the most important mechanism for gaining wider diffusion and political support. Several local networks were launched as early as 2000–2001 and expanded rapidly over time and across regions (Figure 3.7), establishing a presence in all major emerging economies including Argentina, Brazil, China, India, South Africa, South Korea, Mexico, and Russia. Focusing on national networks in emerging markets was no accident; it was directly related to the initial G77's ambivalence. Support from business leaders and CEOs in the national networks of India and China, for example, eventually translated into political support of the countries' leadership for the initiative. The establishment of local networks was often supported by UNDP local offices and involved collaboration at the subnational level among business associations, companies, UN entities, and public

---

[75] Ruggie 2000. See also Ruggie 2002; Kell, Slaughter and Hale 2007; Williams 2004; McIntosh, Waddock and Kell 2004.

[76] United Nations Office of the Secretary-General 2000, p. 2.

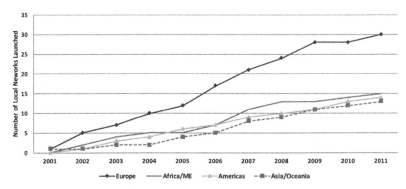

Figure 3.7 Expansion of local networks of the Global Compact
Source: UNGC, 2013a.

institutions.[77] The main function of these initiatives has been to promote the norms of the global CSR initiative among companies in developing countries and emerging economies. Their role has been to raise awareness among the business community, to diversify the Global Compact membership across geographic regions, and to help reach small and medium enterprises. In Asia and Africa, for instance, approximately 70% of Global Compact companies are also engaged in a local network, which speaks to their significance for broadening business participation.[78] Local networks have furthermore facilitated opportunities to engage both business and governmental actors in informal discussions on human rights, labor, the environment, and global operations. There was thus a political agenda to create domestic constituencies and consolidate greater political support for the partnerships platform from developing countries.[79]

The rapid diffusion of Global Compact initiatives during its first decade across regions and states brought the number of members to approximately 10,700 by 2012, of which about 7,090 are business signatories and 1,666 NGOs, making them the two largest constituencies

[77] Kell and Levin 2003; Rasche and Kell 2010; Bremer 2008; UNGC 2010a, 2010b. The faster initial expansion of Global Compact local networks in Central and Eastern Europe, for instance, is attributed in part to early engagement by UNDP regional offices (Whelan 2010).

[78] Whelan 2010; Gilbert 2010; Fuertes and Liarte-Vejrup 2010; UNGC 2010a, 2010b; Mwangi *et al.* 2013; UNGC 2009, 2010a, p. 22. See Perkins and Neumayer 2010 on diffusion patterns of Global Compact membership.

[79] UNGA 2015.

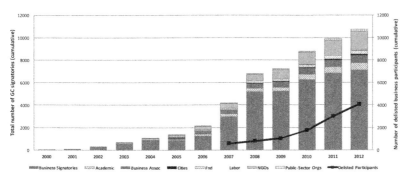

Figure 3.8 Expansion of Global Compact Membership
Source: UNGC 2007 and 2013b.

of the partnership (Figure 3.8). As Bremer observes, "The Global Compact has adopted an explicit strategy of growing rapidly to scale. Its definition of scale encompasses not only the number of companies participating, but the achievement of a membership base that is large, diverse and truly global."[80]

NGO membership has been also of importance for gaining political support, given the significant role of societal organizations as vocal critics of the program, particularly with respect to limited monitoring of signatories' performance.[81] However, watchdog NGO alliances have remained outside the Global Compact and maintain their critiques.[82] Over time, the governments of countries such as China, Brazil, and the other large emerging economies, many of which were initially suspicious or hostile to the initiative, saw value in the Global Compact as a universal platform for CSR, including for companies from the South, and as a soft mechanism for stabilizing discourse about CSR and commercial relations. It is telling that by 2010, the governmental "circle of friends" financially supporting the Global Compact had expanded to thirteen governments, still predominantly from Europe but also including Korea, Colombia, China, and Brazil.[83] The diffusion of Global Compact membership and its activities across

---

[80] Bremer 2008, p. 232.
[81] Berliner and Prakash 2012; Amnesty International *et al.* 2004.
[82] See, for example, Global Policy Forum, accessed via https://www.global policy.org/, November 2016.
[83] UNGC 2010a.

the Global South has been in many ways the litmus test and necessary condition for its political survival as a feature within the intergovernmental structure of the UN.

Institutionalization: The UN Global Compact

The case of the Global Compact is an even clearer example of the reverse nature of the institutionalization in the cycle of dynamic, entrepreneurial change of institutions. While the General Assembly "took note" of and thus acknowledged the UNFIP at its very creation, intergovernmental bodies only recognized the Global Compact in a piecemeal manner during the first decade of its existence. This process depended on the enlargement of political support by principals, and by developing countries in particular, through the diffusion of membership but also via the gradual formalization of such support through discursive and procedural actions.

The discursive and procedural path toward institutionalization of the Global Compact and partnership collaboration in general proceeded in tandem. The language of partnerships with global actors and references to the Global Compact became increasingly prevalent in high-level UN reports endorsed by member governments. The Secretary-General's report *We the Peoples: The Role of the United Nations in the 21st Century*, prepared for the 2000 Millennium Summit, was the first document that explicitly justified global partnerships as a UN mode of governance to a high-level diplomatic audience. It famously underlines that "even though the United Nations is an organization of states, the Charter is written in the name of 'we the peoples.' Ultimately, then, the United Nations exists for, and must serve, the needs and hopes of people everywhere."[84] The document makes the case for collaborative governance as another means of advancing human well-being in the context of globalization:

Better governance means greater participation, coupled with accountability. Therefore, the international public domain – including the United Nations – must be opened up further to the participation of the many actors whose contributions are essential to managing the path of globalization. Depending on the issues at hand, this may include civil society organizations, the private

---

[84] Annan 2000, p. 6.

sector, parliamentarians, local authorities, scientific associations, educational institutions and many others.[85]

The 2000 *Millennium Declaration* adopted by heads of state affirms that "partnerships with the private sector and with civil society" are tools for advancing the UN development agenda.[86] The Millennium Development Goals launched at the Summit included *Goal 8 on Developing a Global Partnership for Development*. Over time and across subsequent intergovernmental documents such as the *2002 Monterrey Consensus of the International Conference on Financing for Development*[87] and the General Assembly Resolution on *The 2005 World Summit Outcomes*,[88] partnerships included the mention of the Global Compact, which became normalized in sociological parlance as part of UN discourse on governance and development.

Formal procedures for the institutionalization of the Global Compact were advanced cautiously by its political supporters within the UN and couched in the broader theme of partnerships as a new mode of UN governance. In 2001, Germany and other European states introduced in the General Assembly the first Resolution A/55/215 *Towards Global Partnership*, which affirms in its first and second paragraphs the central role of the intergovernmental body in the promotion of partnerships while "underlining the intergovernmental nature of the United Nations."[89] The resolution further requires "the Secretary General to submit a comprehensive report on the matter, containing a compilation of views of Member States..." thereby bringing the partnership model more closely within the purview of its principals.[90] The Office of the Secretary-General then proceeded to submit biannual reports to the General Assembly titled

---

[85] Ibid., p. 13. The fact that the Assistant Secretary-General for Strategic Planning and his office were centrally involved in the drafting of the report *We the Peoples* and in the formulation of the *Millennium Declaration* is furthermore indicative of the interconnection between several initiatives for incremental but important institutional change by Secretary-General Kofi Annan. This further illustrates the role of this office and its epistemic capital in facilitating the entrepreneurship of such change, as anticipated by the theoretical framework.

[86] UNGA 2000d (A/RES/55/2).

[87] UN 2002 (A/Conf.198/11, Sales No. E.02.II.A.7); UNGA 2002a.

[88] UNGA 2005c (A/RES/60/1).

[89] UNGA 2001a, (A/55/215).

[90] Ibid.

Cooperation between the United Nations and All Relevant Partners, in Particular the Private Sector.[91]

The first of these documents reiterates the justification for closer engagement of nonstate actors as part of the UN reform effort.[92] It relates the views of member states and UN agencies elicited through a consultation process. In line with the theoretical propositions on the conditions for sufficient agency autonomy for the entrepreneurship of new collaborative governance, unattributed quotes by member states show mild divergence among principals with respect to partnership engagement. Some quotes clearly support the discourse of the Secretary-General: "We must ensure that globalization is a force that will benefit all of us. The private sector must be encouraged to promote the public good."[93] Others project concerns that "Such cooperation should not challenge the intergovernmental nature of the UN, in particular its intergovernmental decision-making," but there is no direct governmental challenge expressed to the ideas of partnerships or specific initiatives featured in the Secretary-General's report.[94] The subsequent biannual reports to the General Assembly tended to emphasize the functional advantages of global partnerships and best practices, thus projecting a largely uncritical discussion of partnership initiatives. On the basis of the Secretary-General's biannual reports, the General Assembly endorsed a series of resolutions *Towards Global Partnerships* that broadly support practices of collaborative governance, including the Global Compact.[95]

As with UNFIP, the formal mechanisms for the institutionalization of the Global Compact were subsequently activated by Secretary-General Ban Ki-moon, whose support for partnerships as a means of UN governance was essential for the continued active role of the Secretary-General's Office. In 2007, the General Assembly adopted Resolution A/RES/62/211 *Towards Global Partnership*, which for the first time in its paragraph 9 formally recognized the Global Compact

---

[91] UNGA 2001b (A/56/323), 2003a (A/58/227), 2005a (A/60/214), 2007a (A/62/341), 2009a (A/64/337).
[92] UNGA 2001b (A/56/323), p. 8.
[93] Ibid., p. 9.
[94] Ibid., p. 9.
[95] UNGA 2001a (A/RES/55/215), UNGA 2002a, 2004a, 2006 (A/RES/60/215), 2007c (A/RES/62/211), 2010a (A/64/223), 2012 (A/RES/66/223), UNGA 2015 (A/RES/70/224), UNGC 2015.

as the *United Nations* Global Compact, in effect attributing the initiative a place within the intergovernmental structure of the UN.[96] The reverse institutionalization of the Global Compact, which is the last stage in the cycle of governance entrepreneurships, thus proceeded incrementally through a social process of repetition and vetting (tacit or explicit) to master sufficient political support by the broad intergovernmental constituency. Brugger and Maurer eloquently summarize the gradual process of the Global Compact's reverse institutionalization as follows: "Over the years, the Global Compact has found its recognized place in the UN system. With strong institutional independence and a 'license to operate' endorsed by Heads of Government at the 2005 Summit, by G8 and African Union statements, national and regional governmental meetings and in General Assembly resolutions, the Compact managed to become an entity '*sui generis*' in the UN System."[97]

The cycle of governance entrepreneurship of the Global Compact has introduced substantial change within the UN, providing a formal platform for regular interface between the UN, companies, and non-profit organizations. It opened avenues across the UN system for joint programmatic work and advocacy on global issues, among which are climate change (Caring for Climate), water (Water Action Hub), responsible investment (Principles for Responsible Investment with UNEP), and children's rights (Children's Rights and Business Principles with UNICEF and Save the Children). Compared to the case of UNFIP, the entrepreneurs of the Global Compact engaged with several layers of politics to mobilize support in the process of change. At the stage of experimental adoption, they navigated internal organizational politics to alleviate warranted skepticism within the bureaucracy about transnational corporations and their normative intent to take into account the positions of relevant UN agencies and to secure the backing of liberal states interested in experimentation with new hybrid governance. Leadership coalitions within the institutional structure of the UN were in many ways the motor behind the cycle of change. The capacity of the Office of the Secretary-General to tap into external expertise and networks was similarly an important factor for the

---

[96] Interview with Georg Kell, UN Global Compact Office, July 2010; UNGA 2007c (A/RES/62/211).
[97] Brugger and Maurer 2010, p. 388; see also UNGC 2008.

entrepreneurship of new governance. The diffusion of Global Compact participation across North and South tackled another set of politics, namely the buy-in of the broader body of state principals, particularly by developing countries and large emerging economies. This was a necessary condition for the subsequent process of more permanent institutionalization of the partnership platform within the structure of the UN.

The process of institutionalization reintroduced a third political front: the pressure for greater accountability of the Global Compact and its signatories. With expanding membership and institutional acceptance, it was increasingly clear that limited information on companies' implementation efforts and norm-conforming behavior was the weakest link in the legitimacy of the program as an instrument of UN governance.[98]

In 2009, Secretary-General Ban Ki-moon issued updated *Guidelines on Cooperation between the UN and the Business Sector* in response to General Assembly recommendations for greater emphasis on assessment of impact and transparency of UN partnerships, including the Global Compact. The new *Guidelines* extend the limitations on signatories to exclude companies that violate UN Security Council sanctions and entities that "systematically fail to demonstrate commitment to meeting the principles of the UN Global Compact."[99] Under internal and external scrutiny, The Global Compact Board also adopted a set of "integrity measures." These included a procedure for handling of external complaints on "systemic and egregious abuses" by Global Compact member companies, as well as, since 2007, the delisting of members who fail to post progress reports and are thus "noncommunicating" for two consecutive years. By 2012, 4,078 participants had been delisted (Figure 3.8), introducing some degree of peer accountability and efforts at transparency.[100] A 2010 audit report by the UN Joint Inspection Unit made further recommendations for the institutionalization of the Global Compact, of which almost half related to improved

---

[98] See Clapham 2006; Boisson de Chazournes 2009; Boisson de Chazournes et Mazuyer 2011; Berliner and Prakash 2012; Thérien and Pouliot 2006; Brugger and Maurer 2010.

[99] United Nations Office of the Secretary-General 2009, p. 3.

[100] Grant and Keohane 2005; Mwangi *et al.* 2013; UNGC 2008; Fall and Zahran 2010.

transparency, outcome-based accountability, more transparent implementation of the integrity measures, and oversight by member states.[101]

Despite the adoption of procedures for greater accountability, important tensions persist between the structuring of the Global Compact as a voluntary learning platform and the expectations by external audiences for more systematic action by signatories to implement Global Compact principles.[102] A Global Compact survey conducted in 2010 revealed that about three-quarters of the surveyed members assess their implementation of the ten principles to be "at the beginner or intermediate level." Moreover, companies tend to follow environmental and labor commitments with which they have longer experience more readily, compared to principles related to human rights and transparency.[103]

Recent academic research provides evidence of the normative effect of the Global Compact on the corporate social responsibility practices of participating companies. This is precisely the effect intended by the political entrepreneurs of the program, who designed it as a learning network. A quantitative analysis by Bernhagen and Mitchell, for example, concludes that "the program increases the likelihood of firms developing human rights–related company policies and receiving positive external assessments of their performance."[104] Berliner and Prakash also find that companies with stronger internal policies on human rights and the environment are more likely to join the Global Compact, which improves further their normative commitment and reputation, after controlling for the selection effect. The study reveals, however, that signatories also remain associated with higher levels of environmental externalities and human rights failures, which questions the on-the-ground effectiveness of the initiative and its limited institutional provisions for measurable changes in behavior and monitoring.[105] The corporate accountability movement and advocacy watchdogs, similarly, maintain the pressure for less talk and more walk on the norms of the Global Compact.[106]

[101] Fall and Zahran 2010.
[102] Fall and Zahran 2010; Berliner and Prakash 2012, 2014.
[103] UNGC 2010c.
[104] Bernhagen and Mitchell 2010, p. 1.
[105] Berliner and Prakash 2015. See also Berliner and Prakash 2014; Sethi and Schepers 2014.
[106] Paine 2000; Bendell 2004; Utting and Zammit 2009.

In sum, while the normative impact of the Global Compact platform has extended across a range of global issues with which the UN is grappling, the political battle for a greater and different kind of accountability is likely to remain salient. The UN has become more relevant to global actors as a consequence. Transnational actors lent support to Secretary-General Ban Ki-moon to keep up the political heat for action on climate, women, energy and other issues when they stagnated at the intergovernmental front. At the same time, peer pressure, advocacy fire alarms, and epistemic scrutiny remain critical for the integrity of hybrid initiatives such as the Global Compact. Contestation and learning to establish the legitimacy of new governance are part of the politics of dynamic institutional change, as we shall also see in subsequent chapters.

Broader Institutional Implications

In parallel to the greater institutionalization of the UN Global Compact, the UN Human Rights Council unanimously approved in 2008 the report *Protect, Respect and Remedy: A Framework for Business and Human Rights* presented by John Ruggie in his capacity as UN Special Representative on Business and Human Rights. The framework elaborated an intergovernmentally endorsed normative basis for corporate responsibility to protect human rights.[107] It placed the issue in the purview of the Human Rights Council after the failure in 2004 of the Commission on Human Rights to adopt the draft Norms on Business and Human Rights, which were intended to be legally binding but did not gather sufficient governmental support.[108] In 2011, the Human Rights Council further endorsed *The UN Guiding Principles on Business and Human Rights,* in effect advancing a soft-law instrument with greater authoritativeness granted by the intergovernmental body.

The two documents of the Human Rights Council moved the concern about business practices and their impact on the protection of fundamental human rights beyond the learning structure of the Global Compact. They explicitly clarify a set of normative obligations for both companies and states and recommend mechanisms

---

[107] Ruggie 2013.
[108] Weissbrodt 2008.

for their domestic implementation through practices, standards, and regulations. Nonetheless, the six-year process that led to the adoption first of the Framework and then of the UN Guiding Principles benefited from the Global Compact experience insofar as the partnership platform had already raised the visibility of questions of business and human rights. As discussed, the Global Compact provided an important mechanism for deliberation among UN agencies, business entities, large advocacy organizations, and member governments both at the UN level and from the bottom up through its local membership networks in emerging and developing countries. The partnership had thus created a certain trust of the business community and other actors that facilitated the consultations that fed into the formulation of the two documents of the Human Rights Council.

These developments illustrate the possibility of interplay between global partnerships as entrepreneurial initiatives and larger institutional changes that affect intergovernmental decisions. It would have been hardly possible to imagine the political acceptance of a normative framework on business and human rights, even in its soft-law form, without the experimentation, ongoing contestations, and learning stimulated by global partnership platforms. In 2013, another initiative of UN Secretary-General Ban Ki-moon, Human Rights Up Front, was launched to strengthen the role of UN agencies in prevention of "serious and large-scale violations of international human rights and humanitarian law."[109] The initiative targets UN culture to assure greater responsibility "to act with moral courage" and "accountability" and recommends operational changes for better early warning and response and more "proactive engagement with member states" to prevent large-scale human rights atrocities. It aims to address precisely the kind of complacency within the UN and its member states that has been implicated by prominent analyses in the Rwanda genocide and other humanitarian failures.

Conclusion

At the dawn of the twenty-first century, the UN profoundly transformed its level and means of collaboration with the private sector

---

[109] Ki-moon 2013, p. 1, 2016; Human Rights Up Front 2016.

and other nonstate actors. Traditionally viewed as a forum for state negotiations of industry codes of conduct or for granting observation rights to civil society, the organization took a more entrepreneurial role in constructing opportunities for partnering on a host of UN causes. This chapter has documented the quintessential role of the Office of the Secretary-General together with UN agencies with a relatively high degree of knowledge specialization and organizational autonomy as agents of change. Contrary to the assumptions of classic theories of international relations, the agency and authority of the Office of the Secretary-General to initiate governance experimentation was not predetermined by a fixed principal–agent relation with member states. The organization and its leadership took risks to actively establish an institutional space and supportive coalitions with principals and external actors, which enabled the cycle of experimentation, diffusion, and institutionalization of new governance.

The stories of UNFIP and the Global Compact also challenge conventional wisdom about the UN system and global partnerships. First, it is difficult to view these initiatives as a corporate takeover of the UN given the active steering of partnerships by the UN organizations and their intergovernmental mandates and the necessary vetting (albeit in reverse order) of such initiatives by the majority of states, particularly developing countries, for their more permanent institutionalization. The relevance of UN steering, mandate, and expertise cannot be more evident in the UNFIP portfolios of partnerships. To be sure, governance foci on collaborative initiatives are actively negotiated between units of international organizations and the corporate and social concerns of transnational actors. Inadvertently, they advance via other means a set of liberal goals that are often related to the operation and indeed social failures of global markets and the norms embedded in UN institutions.

Second, the analysis of the entrepreneurial life cycles of UNFIP and the Global Compact provides limited evidence of the realist hypotheses (and early concern by developing countries) about new forms of governance as platforms for exporting the influence of the North via other means. In the case of the Global Compact, a handful of likeminded donor states, including two members of the Security Council, France and the UK, played a crucial role in supporting politically and with seed funding the UN to undertake a new governance initiative. While such backing came from donor countries, it did not involve the traditionally most powerful principals of the organization. Rather, it projected a set of ideas for institutional experimentation to reconcile global capitalism and social objectives in direct deliberation and cooperation with the private sector. The evidence shows, furthermore, that the political "friends of the Global Compact" deliberately adopted a hands-off approach in shaping the actual structure of the initiative. UNFIP and the Global Compact also followed an explicit strategy for engaging the interest and participation of a broad swath of developing countries and emerging economies. Such a strategy was essential for the implementation and broader diffusion of partnerships to establish their worth and political relevance as a new mode of UN governance.

Finally, the evolution of the two initiatives has demonstrated that creating channels of accountability to multiple audiences including UN intergovernmental bodies, external advocates, and affected communities is one of the most important challenges for the sustainability of this new model of governance. These conclusions have important implications for further studies on the conditions for effectiveness of global partnerships and for policy evaluation of their practical contributions to problem solving.

4 UNEP and the World Bank
Extending Sustainability via Partnerships

Introduction

Global environmental problems are characterized by unenviable complexity. Addressing them requires coordination across multiple jurisdictions and scales to manage the interplay between natural and social systems. As a consequence, collective action for environmental sustainability is often hindered by classic dilemmas associated with the coordination of a large number of actors, distributive and normative concerns, short-term horizons, or the difficulty of assuring credible commitments. Some success stories of international environmental agreements have been paralleled by increasing stagnation or diversion of intergovernmental cooperation.[1] At the same time, global partnerships have become a prominent feature of sustainability governance since the 1990s.[2] In such a context, it is not surprising that many scholars have qualified the proliferation of partnerships as endemic to a broader tendency of neoliberalization of sustainability governance and its fragmentation, implicitly to the detriment of multilateral institutions and binding agreements.[3]

This chapter takes a closer look at the politics of partnerships for sustainability in the multilateral sphere. In particular, it seeks to understand the rise and outcomes of global partnerships across the institutional domains of UNEP and the World Bank. The analysis reveals a more dynamic picture of the interplay between traditional and new forms of governance than previously recognized and in line with the theoretical framework on endogenously enabled institutional change.

---

[1] Conca 2015; Hale, Held and Young 2013; Young 2010.
[2] Andonova and Levy 2003; Andonova 2009, 2010, 2014; Andonova and Assayag 2015; Bäckstrand 2006; Glasbergen, Biermann and Mol 2007; Pattberg *et al.* 2012; Vollmer 2009; Dingwerth 2005; Beisheim and Liese 2014.
[3] Bexell and Mörth 2010; Biermann *et al.* 2009; Mathews 1997; Utting and Zammit 2006; Zelli and van Asselt 2013.

It argues and shows empirically that IOs have facilitated entrepreneurial coalitions of public and private actors to *extend* the institutional means for sustainability governance within multilateral mandates, particularly when their missions have been unsettled by intergovernmental stalemates, inadequate resources, or advocacy pressures. Rather than displacing or undermining multilateral institutions, global partnerships for sustainability appear closely embedded around the mandates of IOs and the types of expertise and toolkits they manage. Indeed, public–private partnerships rarely prove to have regulatory or universal roles that are characteristic of international treaties. But they have not resulted in the marketization of the multilateral system either. The partnerships of UNEP and the World Bank have focused primarily on advancing new informational tools for governance, policy consensus, or implementation capacity around specific environmental issues of overlapping interest for IOs, nonstate actors, and state agencies. As such, partnerships have been instrumental in advancing a range of global objectives such as clean energy, biodiversity, financing action on climate change, or reducing chemical and industrial risk, often in advance of and as a vehicle toward fully fledged intergovernmental endorsement.

The comparative analysis of the life cycle of the emergence and institutionalization of sustainability partnerships and their governance outcomes illuminates the politics of dynamic institutional change in the contexts of UNEP and the World Bank respectively. The organizational case studies examine in parallel fashion the sources of agency autonomy and the nature of organizational turbulence and epistemic capacity, which, according to the theoretical framework (Chapter 2), shape the motivations and processes of entrepreneurship of new governance, its diffusion, and reverse institutionalization. The analysis also includes a focused discussion of the microdynamics of specific partnerships. The empirical evidence draws on interviews, primary documents, the Global Partnerships Database, and cases within each organization to consider what kinds of coalitions between public and private actors have spearheaded the iterative cycle of institutional change.[4] The chapter sheds new empirical light on the outcomes of

---

[4] The *Global Partnerships Database* is the source of data for all figures in the chapter. The Annex explains in detail the methodology of data collection and coding. The database represents a snapshot of the partnership work of these international organizations at the time when the data was collected.

partnerships for environmental sustainability across the two organizational domains and in terms of their governance instruments, issue focus, and financial partners. The comparative research design and new data allow us to assess if and how the differential organizational structures, circumstances, and expertise of UNEP and the World Bank have shaped the patterns of their partnership engagement and ultimately the outcomes for sustainability.

UNEP: Leveraging Resources and Mandate through Partnerships

Agency Autonomy but Mission Impossible?

UNEP was established following the first high-level international Conference on the Human Environment, in Stockholm, 1972. The UN General Assembly resolution 2997 (XXVII) defined its status as a UN Programme with a "small secretariat" to "serve as a focal point for environmental action and coordination within the United Nations system in such a way as to ensure a high degree of effective management."[5] UNEP's mandate includes strong specialization in policy-relevant knowledge to support the facilitation of international agreements and the coordination of environmental action within the UN. The UNEP Governing Council, composed of 58 member states elected by the General Assembly, oversaw the organization until 2013, when the Council was replaced by the United Nations Environment Assembly (UNEA) as a governing body with universal membership. The organization's budget consists of allocations from the regular UN budget (3–5%), voluntary governmental contributions to the UNEP Environmental Fund, and an increasing share of earmarked contributions and trust funds (approximately 45% in the period 2014–15).[6] In addition to its Secretariat in Nairobi, Kenya, UNEP has six regional offices and a Division of Technology, Industry and Economics (UNEP DTIE) in Paris, France.

From the perspective of both principal–agent and sociological standpoints on organizations, UNEP has a high margin of agency autonomy and potential for agency influence thanks to its extensive specialization

[5] UN General Assembly 1972, Section II, 1.
[6] http://www.unep.org/about/funding, accessed October 2016.

in policy-relevant knowledge, its formal agenda-setting mandate, and an active epistemic network.[7] In the 1970s and 1980s, UNEP indeed developed a reputation as an activist secretariat under the leadership of Maurice Strong and subsequently of Mustafa Tolba. This secretariat is credited with the successful facilitation of an epistemic consensus to advance multilateral environmental agreements for the management of regional seas, ozone depletion, biodiversity, and hazardous chemicals.[8] UNEP played an instrumental role in sponsoring ideas and providing institutional space for governance innovations such as the Multilateral Fund and the Technology Assessment Panels under the Montreal Protocol, the first set of targeted funding and technology diffusion mechanisms in global environmental governance with involvement of the private sector.[9]

From the perspective of a public bureaucracy, however, UNEP's position as "small, chronically underfunded and marginal within the UN constellation" has undermined its core coordination mission and its effective capacity for agency activism in intergovernmental politics.[10] UNEP's position as anchor for the environment became increasingly compromised by bureaucratic politics and turf battles as other UN agencies started to compete for limited environmental funding in the 1980s.[11] UNEP serves as the umbrella for a set of international agreements, which has produced tensions with Convention Secretariats that emphasized their responsibility to member states and saw limited value in coordination and additional layers of UN bureaucracy.[12] The organization expanded its project-based activities at national and subnational levels as a means to increase earmarked financing from donor governments, but its lack of operational mandate and stable resources resulted in overstretch. The woes of the organization came to a head in the second half of the 1990s, when accusations of mismanagement and failed reforms by then Executive Director Elizabeth Dowdeswell prompted major donors such as the U.S. and Japan to reduce or freeze their contributions to the Environmental Fund.[13]

---

[7] Andresen 2007; Haas, E. 1990; Haas, P. 1989.

[8] Haas 1989; Najam 2003; Mee 2005; Andresen 2007; Parson 2003.

[9] I am grateful to Calestous Juma for directing my attention toward some of these examples of early governance innovations, enabled by UNEP.

[10] Conca 1995, p. 450.

[11] Ivanova 2007.

[12] Andresen 2007; Juma 2000; Conca 2015.

[13] Heimer 1998.

As anticipated by the theoretical framework, mounting turbulence in the organizational environment of UNEP, associated with endemic resource scarcity and concerns about political support and legitimacy, prompted a search for reinvention of its practices and financing. Under subsequent Executive Directors Klaus Toepfer and Achim Steiner, UNEP established a Global Ministerial Environment Forum for closer coordination with member states. The Forum launched a dialogue on an institutional framework for sustainable development, which became one of the major themes of the Rio+20 UN Conference on Sustainable Development in 2012. While the UNEP leadership emphasized high-level diplomacy to bring states into the fold, units within the organization leveraged their knowledge-based agency to increasingly work with nonstate actors in project-based or programmatic collaboration.[14] Such alliances became the precursor of the rise of many public–private partnerships for environmental sustainability.

Experimentation with Partnerships: From the Bottom Up

UNEP's partnership engagement with nonstate actors was not part of an organization-wide strategy, unlike that of the World Bank or the UN Secretariat discussed in Chapter 3. It was most often expert groups within UNEP departments that worked out partnership arrangements with the private sector or with societal and expert organizations around programs or projects they were putting in place. Garrette Clark, a Business and Industry Outreach Officer with UNEP DTIE, summarized in an interview such processes as gradual and bottom-up experimentation: "[Y]ou have to look at UNEP partnerships organically, as part of the broader experience of the organization with the private sector and other actors."[15] UNEP has enjoyed good relations with NGOs and an extensive network of collaboration with scientific and research institutions.[16] As anticipated by the theoretical framework on dynamic institutional change and emphasized in multiple interviews, the professional networks that UNEP staff had developed with experts, nongovernmental organizations, and specialized units of

---

[14] Haas, E. 1990.
[15] Interview with Garrette Clark, October 2011, UNEP DTIE, Paris.
[16] Conca 1995; Haas, P. 1989, 1990; UNEP 2004.

government influenced profoundly the opportunities for public–private partnerships and their substantive nature.[17]

The 1992 Summit on Sustainable Development in Rio was the first high-level platform that opened its doors to nonstate representation and where ideas for closer collaboration between UNEP and private actors resurfaced. The staff of UNEP DTIE, a division established in the 1970s to engage industry on environmental matters, assumed leadership as entrepreneur of partnering activities, often referring directly to the concepts of environmental management, waste minimization, and corporate responsibility endorsed at the Rio Summit. Such an activist role was enabled by the relative agency autonomy of the division and supported by its informal networks with the private sector and expert communities around issues such as sustainable production, energy, and economics. Jacqueline Aloisi de Larderel, as Deputy Director and then Director of UNEP DTIE, is credited with spearheading and formalizing organizational engagement in public–private collaboration. Aloisi de Larderel emphasized in an early article the direct impact of business activity on environmental problems and the necessity of involving the private sector in advancing the business case for acting in an environmentally responsible manner.[18] Such framing provided broad rationales for public–private collaboration, similar to those advanced by governance entrepreneurs in other contexts, such as the UN Secretariat (discussed in Chapter 3), while at the same time attaching them to the immediate mandate and priorities of the agency.

The UNEP Finance Initiative was the first formal partnership with the private sector, announced at the Rio Summit in 1992 (Figure 4.1). The proposal came from Swiss banks, while UNEP DTIE sponsored a space for financial institutions to engage on issues related to finance

[17] Interviews with Guido Sonneman, UNEP/SETAC Life Cycle Initiative; Maria-Milagros Morales and Eric Usher, African Rural Energy Enterprise Development Programme (AREED); Tomas Marques, UNEP Responsible Production Programme; Helena Rey, Global Partnership for Sustainable Tourism, October 2011, UNEP DTIE, Paris. Discussion with Curt Garrigan, UNEP Sustainable Building and Climate Initiative, UNEP DTIE, October 2013, Paris.

[18] Aloisi de Larderel 1995. See also Van Der Lugt and Dingwerth 2015 on the role of UNEP DTIE.

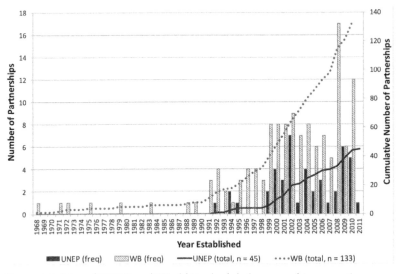

Figure 4.1 Rise of UNEP and World Bank global partnerships over time

and environmental responsibility.[19] The initiative uses a range of specific informational tools and advocacy "to steer financial institutions into voluntarily identifying, promoting, and realizing sustainable practices in all levels of operation..."[20] Its work became an important basis for formulating a set of Principles on Responsible Investment advanced jointly by the Global Compact and UNEP in 2005.[21] Over time, partnerships became mechanisms for entrepreneurial units within UNEP to engage in new governance activities for the environment and to generate new private as well as public streams of financing for specific programs. Thus, these units extended the means for pursuing issues that fell within their purview. Such a strategy was a response to the volatility of state contributions to the UNEP budget and the need to generate soft financing to support the core mandates of the organization. Indicative of such organizational incentives is the fact that by 2012, approximately 50% of UNEP staff was funded on a project basis.[22]

[19] Interviews with Yuki Yasui, November 2011, UNEPFI, Geneva, and with Garrette Clark, October 2011, UNEP DTIE, Paris. See also Yasui 2011.
[20] Yasui 2011, p. 21.
[21] Van Der Lugt and Dingwerth 2015; Yasui 2011.
[22] Interview with Garrette Clark, UNEP DTIE, October 2012, Paris.

According to the 2011 evaluation of UNEP's partnership portfolio, between 2008 and June 2010, UNEP engaged with "over 750 partners (private sector, NGOs, governments) contributing to the project budgets over 65 million USD, according to data compiled by each of its divisions."[23] In comparison, the governmental contributions to the UNEP Environmental Fund for the 2007–2008 biennium amounted to US$174 million, while earmarked contributions and trust funds contributed an additional US$233.3 million to the budget of the organization.[24]

In sum, as anticipated by the theory of incremental and quasi-endogenous change, a confluence of budgetary and performance pressures, coupled with relative agency autonomy and expert capability, spurred the early steps in the cycle of entrepreneurship of global partnerships and new mechanisms for governance within UNEP. As in other cases discussed in this book, governance entrepreneurs used windows of opportunity such as the Rio Conference on the Environment and Sustainable Development and later the Johannesburg Summit on Sustainable Development to advance partnerships on an experimental basis and to situate them within the mandate of the organization.

Diffusion of Partnership Governance

UNEP's early partnerships built either on preexisting epistemic networks of cooperation (the Coral Reef Initiative; the Interactive Map Service; Resource Efficiency and Cleaner Production Programme) or specific opportunities presented by external actors (UNEP Finance Initiative; the Global Reporting Initiative). The trend for partnership collaboration, recorded in the Global Partnership Database, accelerated quite substantially around the turn of the millennium, similar to trends in other organizational fields such as that of the World Bank (Figure 4.1).[25]

The creation of several partnership platforms at the level of the UN Secretariat as detailed in Chapter 3, namely the UN Fund for International Partnerships (UNFIP) and the Global Compact, contributed

---

[23] UN Office of Internal Oversight Services 2012, p. 2.
[24] UNEP 2011.
[25] The *Global Partnership Database* is the source of data for all figures in this chapter. See Annex 1 on the methodology of the database.

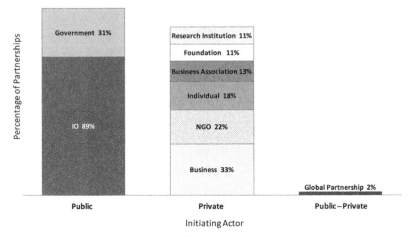

Figure 4.2 Initiating actors of UNEP partnerships by type of authority

to the replication of the partnership model by supporting entrepreneurial actors with resources, legitimating strategies, and common institutional space. The 2002 World Summit on Sustainable Development in Johannesburg, South Africa, endorsed partnerships as an official type II outcome of the intergovernmental summit. These partnership platforms were important for UNEP's organizational entrepreneurs to justify partnership activities that had been initiated from the bottom up rather than from UNEP headquarters.[26] The Global Partnerships Database shows that about one-third of the partnerships recorded in the database were launched or extended at the Johannesburg Summit. Initiatives such as the African Rural Energy Enterprise Development or the Principles of Responsible Investment were in turn developed in close coordination with UNFIP and the Global Compact, respectively.[27]

As anticipated by the theoretical framework and Proposition 2 in particular, entrepreneurial coalitions between organizational units within UNEP, proactive states, and nonstate actors constituted the political impetus behind the proliferation of partnership practice. Figure 4.2 illustrates that along with UNEP as a core governance entrepreneur and facilitator of such coalitions, units of governments played a role in the adoption of at least one-third of the UNEP

---

[26] Interview with Garrette Clark, October 2011, UNEP, Paris.

[27] Interviews with Will Kenneday, UNFIP, July 2010, New York; witg Georg Kell, Global Compact Office, July 2010, New York; and with Yuki Yasui, UNEPFI, November 2011, Geneva.

partnerships, keeping in perspective that each partnership is typically initiated by a coalition of multiple public and private actors. Importantly, nonstate actors also lead a large share of such initiatives (Figure 4.2).

Government agencies initiated some 31% of the partnerships in the UNEP portfolio (Figure 4.2). As anticipated by the theoretical framework, partnerships have provided opportunities for proactive governments to advance unilateral or mini-lateral influence on specific policy agendas around which there is mild or moderate divergence of state preference. Such policy agendas are often part of more complex environmental issues on which fully fledged environmental agreement has proved difficult to reach.

The database on Global Partnerships reveals that European countries (for example Germany, France, Norway, Sweden, Switzerland, Italy, the UK) and the U.S. engaged with greatest frequency and resources in the initiation of collaborative partnerships with UNEP and nonstate actors. However, countries from other regions, including Africa, Asia, and Central and South America, have also taken initiatives to advance partnerships that pertain to specific, domestically salient environmental problems such as access to energy in rural areas or the management of chemicals and industrial risk.[28]

Moreover, the process of diffusion of partnership governance has involved not only the multiplication of such initiatives but also expanding participation and recognition on the part of governments and nonstate actors. The Renewable Energy Network (REN21) is a case in point. It was established through a Memorandum of Understanding between UNEP, the German Ministry of the Environment, and the German Ministry and Federal Ministry for Economic Cooperation, with the participation of the European Renewable Energy Council, a business association. In an interview, the Executive Director of REN21, Christine Lins, underlined the importance of UNEP for governments and business alike as a convener and source of credible expertise on global partnerships such as REN21: "We do a lot of work with the Energy Branch of UNEP DTIE. The hosting status of UNEP gives us access to UN networks; REN21 publications are taken up by all UN organizations because they come from UNEP. Our convening

---

[28] Interviews with Maria-Milagros Morales, African Rural Energy Enterprise Development; Helena Rey, Global Partnership for Sustainable Tourism; Tomas Marques, October 2011, UNEP DTIE, Paris; and with William Kennedy, UNFIP, July 2010, New York.

power in countries and across sectors increases through these UNEP networks."[29] By 2016, REN21 had indeed grown from what Lins described initially as a "coalition of the willing" to a network extending across the globe and involving a multitude of state and nonstate core partners and participants.[30] The informational tools developed by REN21 have been subsequently referenced in UN documents as one of the main authoritative sources on technology and policies related to renewable energy.[31] Over time, UNEP has facilitated a number of partnerships related to clean energy (amounting to 30% of its partnership portfolio as recorded in our database), with broad participation across the jurisdictions of developed and developing countries.

UNEP's expert capacity as a hub of environmental expertise has also been instrumental in enabling coalitions with nonstate actors. As we see in Figure 4.2, a substantial variety of nonstate actors have partaken in the diffusion of the partnership model of governance. These include traditional UNEP constituencies such as NGOs and research organizations as well as a substantial number of business actors. A more detailed case analysis of the UNEP Programmes on Safer Production and Industrial Risk Reduction illuminates the micro-level dynamics of entrepreneurship and incremental institutional change from experimental adoption of initiatives, diffusion of partnership practices, and their reverse institutionalization.

The Life Cycle of Partnerships for Safer Production

It was a disaster of global significance, a chemical leak from a Union Carbide plant in Bhopal, India, causing thousands of deaths and injuries, that prompted the creation of the first UNEP program for safer production and industrial risk management. The program Awareness and Preparedness for Emergencies at Local Level (APELL) intended to facilitate more direct cooperation with local communities for the management of industrial risk. A document summarizing the history of APELL captures the importance of organizational turbulence, agency initiative, expertise, and convening power in the

---

[29] Interview with Christine Lins, October 2011, REN21, Paris.
[30] See http://www.ren21.net/about-ren21/about-us/, accessed October 2016.
[31] UNGA 2011b.

entrepreneurship of new governance approaches, as well as its subsequent endorsement by principals (emphasis mine):

In late 1986, after the major industrial accidents in Seveso, Bhopal, Mexico City and Schweizerhalle resulted in serious adverse impacts on the local communities and environment, *UNEP proposed a series of measures* to minimize the occurrence and harmful effects from industrial accidents. One of these measures involved establishing a programme to enable governments, in co-operation with industry, to work with local leaders to identify the potential hazards in their communities and to prepare measures to respond to and control emergencies that might threaten public health, safety and the environment. *In 1987, UNEP's Governing Council requested that the Secretariat continue these efforts with governments, industry, and other United Nations bodies, taking into account existing international initiatives.* As a result, UNEP prepared a draft APELL Handbook, building on the "Community Awareness and Emergency Response" (CAER) programme developed by the U.S. Chemical Manufacturers Association ... UNEP then convened a group of international experts to review the draft, including officials from developed and developing countries, industry leaders, and representatives of other international organizations with related activities.[32]

The initiative of UNEP DTIE's industry and chemicals branch responded to the realization following the Bhopal disaster that "local preparedness was a simple concept but very difficult to implement, as information, capacity and systems for reacting to industrial incidents were lacking at that level."[33] Over 20 years, the project-based approach of APELL has been diffused transnationally across 80 communities in more than 30 countries, leveraging information systems and capacity for preparedness as primary governance technology.[34] Building on the APELL model, in 2007, UNEP DTIE initiated the Flexible Framework Initiative for Chemical Accident Prevention and Preparedness.[35] The initiative supports the development of governmental frameworks for improved chemical accident prevention and preparedness. The governance approach involves the convening of a national task force with diverse representation to build expertise, to secure political buy-in, and to provide tools for policy

[32] UNEP 2011, p. 4.
[33] Interview with Tomas Marques, UNEP DTIE, October 2011, Paris.
[34] UNEP 2011.
[35] Marques 2011.

development. The emphasis on a *Flexible* framework allows policy to be tailored around country-specific issues and priorities in industrial accident prevention. The primary influence of UNEP is described as that of a convener of an internal–external coalition of actors: "…[E]verybody comes when we [UNEP] organize a demonstration project or an expert meeting. We bring Ministries of Health, Environment, Industry, Industry Associations, huge multinational companies, civil protection, chemical industry association, and other stakeholders to the table."[36]

In 2010, UNEP expanded its governance activities related to safer production and chemical risk with the Responsible Production partnerships, initiated together with the International Council of Chemical Associations, the NGO Accountability, and the International Council on Mining and Metals. The objective of the new program was to "build capacity for chemical safety management in Small and Medium Size Enterprises…"[37] Within that partnership, the project PROMOTING SAFER OPERATIONS AND EMERGENCY PREPAREDNESS IN THE VALUE CHAIN OF THE CHEMICAL SECTOR IN CHINA combines information systems, enterprise training, local community preparedness, and work with national authorities and university experts to increase domestic capacity for industrial accident prevention and risk management, including at the enterprise and industrial park levels. It also aims to support a new policy framework for chemical safety and risk management at the governmental level.

The partnership initiatives under UNEP's Safer Production and Industrial Risk Programmes have enabled the organization to develop in coordination with external actors new governance tools in one of its core areas of specialization related to environmental risk management and chemicals. Over time and through overall successful experimentation and diffusion, they have leveraged multiple governance instruments, starting with information systems tailored around specific industrial sites and including in the course of time capacity building, finance, and policy support. It is precisely such processes of institutional experimentation and their subsequent uptake by an increasing number of actors that have contributed to the more permanent institutionalization of global partnerships as mechanisms of governance within the institutional structure of UNEP.

---

[36] Ibid.
[37] Ibid.

Institutionalization of UNEP Partnerships

The institutionalization of global partnerships at UNEP has proceeded relatively slowly compared to other organizations such as
the World Bank, for example. This is in part a reflection of the
fact that it was primarily specialized divisions and departments
that experimented in a decentralized manner with partnerships.
The UNEP Secretariat, contrary to the secretariats of the UN, the
World Bank, or the WHO, remained largely disinterested in collaborative initiatives until a critical mass of such governance had clearly
taken place. Indeed, some early initiatives such as the UNEP Finance
Initiative and the Global Reporting Initiative were viewed as separate
from UNEP and had limited direct interaction with the core organizational bureaucracy, although they followed UNEP administrative
procedures. A degree of de facto institutionalization was brought
about through the renewal of partner commitment and diffusion of
partnership practices, as illustrated by the expansion of the Safer
Production initiatives, REN 21, the UNEP Finance Initiative, and
other partnerships.

The broader processes of legitimization of collaborative governance in the UN system started to take off in the year 2000, as documented in Chapter 3. Following the adoption of updated *Guidelines on
Cooperation between the United Nations and the Business Sector* by
Secretary-General Ban Ki-moon in 2009, UNEP's senior management
adopted its first policy document on collaborative initiatives, titled
UNEP Policy on Partnerships and Guidelines for Implementation.[38]
The policy provided a common definition of partnerships and an
overview of practices. It also articulated for the first time a set of
guiding principles for UNEP's entry into partnerships, as well as a
requirement for legalized contracts between UNEP and its partners,
along with regular evaluation and an integrated database of such
initiatives. Shortly afterward, the UN Office of Internal Oversight
Services released an Audit Report titled UNEP PROJECT DELIVERY
ARRANGEMENTS VIA PARTNERSHIPS.[39] Text analysis of the
Audit Report speaks of the reverse nature of the institutionalization of global partnerships within UNEP's structures in a number of
ways. The document notes that "UNEP is engaged in a significant

[38] UNEP 2009.
[39] UN Office of Internal Oversight Services 2012.

number of successful partnerships... However, during the period under review, partnership arrangements were managed in a decentralized manner with inadequate controls..."[40] Among the report's seventeen recommendations, two emphasize that the UNEP administration should formally "authorize Divisional and Regional Directors to sign Project Cooperation Agreements within the established limit"[41] and that the "delegation of [such] authority to Divisional and Regional Directors" should be clarified.[42] The audit report further recommends more institutionalized oversight and "regulatory framework for management of partnerships, centralization of partner selection, and financial monitoring..."[43]

UNEP's partnerships have thus allowed the organization to push the envelope of its agency autonomy, to pursue via new means multiple areas of environmental governance under its mandate, and to expand its activities at subnational and transnational scales. Through the cycle of governance entrepreneurship and dynamic institutional change, partnerships have become a recognized approach for addressing environmental issues and an integral part of UNEP's broader international cooperation programs. It is indicative that the Green Growth Initiative, endorsed by the organization's intergovernmental body in 2012 as the new direction for UNEP's programmatic work, incorporates public–private partnerships as a core governance approach together with more traditional approaches such as policy advising and facilitation of international accords.[44]

The World Bank: Partnerships for Global Public Goods

The Unbearable Lightness of World Bank Greening

At its creation in 1945, the World Bank had no environmental mandate. It supported the postwar reconstruction of Europe and later shifted attention to poverty alleviation and development.[45] As the global political and normative context changed, the organization faced increasing pressure to incorporate sustainability considerations into its

[40] Ibid., p. 6.
[41] Ibid., p. 5.
[42] Ibid., p. 6.
[43] Ibid., p. 1.
[44] Steiner 2013.
[45] Finnemore 1996; Weaver 2009.

policies and projects. Studies on the greening of the World Bank capture the sources of turbulence in its organizational field, which have stimulated, at least in part, the search for new institutional solutions such as global partnerships.

First, the rise of transnational civil society movements since the 1980s against the negative environmental and social effects of Bank-supported projects has pressured the Bank for more direct accountability and greater consideration of societal and environmental conditions in its portfolio.[46] The initial response to transnational pressures was partial and halfhearted reform, according to different assessments, with formal environmental safeguards adopted but persistence of organizational culture and incentives to prioritize traditional large projects.[47] Second, principal–agent accounts of the stopgap greening of the organization argue, in turn, that only after a change in the environmental preferences of donors could the collectivity of these core principals demand more earnest reforms.[48] A third strand of the literature projects a more complex interpretation of the often elusive objective of closing the gaps between institutional policy and performance. These gaps have lasted in part as a result of the persistence of traditional bureaucratic culture[49] but also reflect the dual role of recipient countries of development finance as both principals and clients of the Bank, with limited interest in borrowing for sustainability.[50]

The rich literature on the contestation of the World Bank greening thus reveals the position of the organization as a visible international bureaucracy with substantial agency autonomy in managing development issues but limited *direct* influence on the implementation of more sustainable approaches. The confluence of rising organizational turbulence associated with accountability and legitimacy pressures throughout the 1990s, coupled with the relative agency autonomy and epistemic capacity of the World Bank, makes this case, as we shall see in the next sections, an almost textbook illustration of the core conditions stipulated in the theoretical chapter for agency entrepreneurship of global partnerships.

---

[46] Keck and Sikkink 1998; Fox and Brown 1998.
[47] Rich 1994; Wade 1997.
[48] Nielson and Tierney 2003.
[49] Park 2007, 2010; Weaver 2009.
[50] Gutner 2002, 2005.

Experimental Adoption: Public Goods Framing

The World Bank engagement with global partnerships was a deliberate strategy of its leadership. This was a strategy intended to manage the pressures of globalization and growing public expectations, which were often difficult to deliver via traditional lending mechanisms. Shortly after his appointment in 1995, World Bank President James D. Wolfensohn persuaded the Executive Board to increase the administrative budget of the organization by 10% for three consecutive years to support his Strategic Compact initiative for reorganizing and retooling the organization. Within this 10% increase, there was significant money allotted to promoting collaboration on global issues, including through partnerships with nonstate actors. The Development Grant Facility was established in 1997 as a new instrument for grant financing of global partnerships and programs.[51]

The World Bank thus acted on its agency autonomy to propose new mechanisms of governance. The additional resources in effect expanded the scope of agency autonomy to experiment with a new governance agenda related to global issues such as the environment or health. The World Bank leadership justified this strategy to the Executive Board using the dilemma of growing expectations on the part of global civil society and the belief of some principals that the World Bank should contribute to addressing global problems such as the environment or health pandemics, which do not always benefit from strong ownership among recipient countries or availability of appropriate financing. The country-based nature of its core lending operations tended to steer Bank activities away from global issues and toward the priorities of its client states.[52]

The organizational entrepreneurs within the World Bank, including Wolfensohn, argued for the establishment of new mechanisms of financing and governance for the provision of "global public goods," a concept it advanced collaboratively with research units of the UN

---

[51] Interview with Christopher Gerrard, Independent Evaluation Group, World Bank, November 2010, Washington, DC. See also World Bank Operations Evaluation Department 2001.

[52] Interview with Christopher Gerrard, Independent Evaluation Group, World Bank, November 2010, Washington DC. See also World Bank Operations Evaluation Department 2001.

Development Program (UNDP) and external experts.[53] As in the case of the Global Compact (Chapter 3), the interpretive and discursive strategy of the governance entrepreneurs around the mandates of their organizations had the effect of expanding incrementally the political space and justification for agency initiative. The World Bank adopted the following definition of global public goods:

Global public goods are distinguished from national and local public goods by their reach. Their nonrivalry and nonexcludability spill across national boundaries. People in more than one country can benefit from the provision of a global public good, whether or not they contributed to the cost of supplying the good.[54]

It is notable that the public goods framing is derived from economic theories of public finance and thus resonates with the core economic expertise of the World Bank staff and national finance officials as immediate principals of the World Bank.[55] Such framing helped place on the agenda the question of funding new institutional mechanisms for global issues that may be underprovided by traditional intergovernmental and national policies. It allowed engaging principal constituencies to support institutional experimentation. An address by Jan Piercy, the U.S. Executive Director to the World Bank Board of Directors for the Clinton administration, speaks of agency initiative but also, as anticipated by the theoretical framework, of the role of dynamic agent–principal coalitions behind institutional change:

In the last three years there has been a remarkable evolution in the Bank's thinking about how to finance global public goods. Various shareholders have been wrestling with the question to what extent is it appropriate for the World Bank, which is primarily a lender, to move into financing on a grant basis? Three years ago, the Bank created a Development Grant Facility to bring together efforts in various parts of the Bank to provide grant financing… I must be candid, however: the Development Grant Facility is not yet well established, and within the Bank we continue to have quite a debate about the appropriateness and the criteria for Bank grant financing… Both Bank President Wolfensohn and U.S. Treasury Secretary Summers are keenly focused on the question of how to finance global public goods that we are convinced absolutely require global action – including the growing

---

[53] Kaul *et al.* 1999; World Bank Operations Evaluation Department 2001.
[54] World Bank Operations Evaluation Department 2004, p. 5.
[55] Kaul *et al.* 1999; Héritier 2002.

HIV/AIDS crisis. Clearly we must increase – even double – the size of the Development Grant Facility, and for global public goods we must learn how to do things on a grant basis.[56]

This statement reflects the political process of dynamic and quasi-endogenous institutional change examined in this book. The World Bank initially acted in response to external turbulence associated with accountability and performance pressures, in ways intended to advance the legitimacy, resources, and mission of the organization by proposing new governance. Subsequently, the dynamic is one of generating sufficient principal support for experimentation, diffusion, and institutionalization. It involves the justification of agency initiative and its situation in the mandate of the institutions, along with deliberation of new ideas and coalition building within and outside the organization (see Figure 2.1 in the theoretical Chapter 2 for an illustration of these dynamics). The World Bank approach was leadership driven and more strategic compared to the bottom-up entrepreneurship of partnerships within UNEP. This reflects important differences in organizational structures and imperatives but also the role of ideas and leadership. World Bank Presidents James Wolfensohn and later Robert Zoellick, like the UN's Kofi Annan and later Ban Ki-moon, invested substantial personal initiative in formulating ideas and using the scope of their agency discretion to advance new initiatives in collaboration with nonstate actors. UNEP, by contrast, operates as a more decentralized organization. Hence, the experimental adoption of the partnership model proceeded often from the bottom up through its specialized departments while being subsequently sanctioned and supported by the leadership of Executive Director Achim Steiner.

Diffusion of Partnership Programs

After the approval of the Development Grant Facility, the World Bank rapidly expanded its partnership activities (see Figure 4.1). This expansion of the partnership model reflected the broader development mandate of the organization and its interdependence with a host of global issues. Prior to the 1990s, the organization had some unique collaborative programs such as the Consultative Group on International

---

[56] Piercy 2001, p. 5.

Agricultural Research (CGIAR), an initiative of the Rockefeller Foundation, the World Bank, the Food and Agriculture Organization (FAO), and UNDP. Indeed, World Bank advocates of partnerships for global public goods referred to the success of CGIAR in diffusing knowledge and new seed technologies for global poverty reduction and food security.

In contrast with UNEP, where partnership started small and from within the work of a particular unit, a number of the World Bank's partnerships involve large-scale programmatic coordination with other IOs, nonstate actors, and governments. This is the case, for example, in the creation of a series of partnerships for global health, including the Global Forum for Health Research, Roll Back Malaria, the Medicines for Malaria Venture, the Global Fund to Fight AIDS, Tuberculosis, and Malaria, the Global Alliance for Vaccines and Immunization, and the Stop Tuberculosis Partnership. The creation of the Development Grant Facility provided internal organizational space and resources for the entrepreneurships and replication of the partnership model, particularly in areas such as health and the environment, where Bank performance was lagging behind and facing persistent public scrutiny from advocacy actors. Not surprisingly, a large share of the World Bank partnerships convened by 2011 focus on global issues such as environmental sustainability (36%) and health (15%).[57]

The replication and diffusion of World Bank partnerships proceeded even faster compared to those of UNEP, in part thanks to the institutional space and resources generated by the organization's leadership and its broader engagement with development issues. As in the case of UNEP, however, the uptake of the partnership model relied on an expanding set of entrepreneurial coalitions involving state principals and nonstate actors. Figure 4.3 summarizes information on the type of actors that initiated global partnerships within the institutional context of the World Bank and thus the nature of the political coalition behind the diffusion of this governance model.[58]

Figure 4.3 shows the substantial organizational entrepreneurship on the part of the World Bank, which along with other IOs has been one

[57] Global Partnerships Database.
[58] Since multiple types of partners can play entrepreneurial roles in any given partnership, the percentages in Figure 4.3, as in Figure 4.2, are not intended to add up to 100%. They reflect the relative share in leadership of such initiatives by different types of actors.

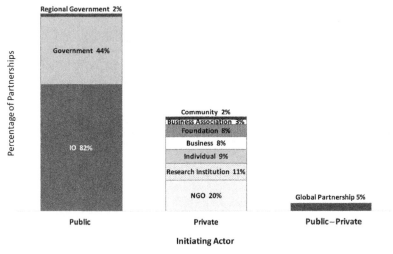

Figure 4.3 Initiating actors of World Bank partnerships

of the lead entrepreneurs of more than 80% of global partnerships. Governments (and particularly donor countries) have also played significant roles as initiating actors in about 44% of World Bank partnerships. The role of units of states as part of the entrepreneurial coalitions behind the rise of partnerships governance is more strongly pronounced compared to UNEP because of the paramount importance of soft public finance as an instrument of governance in the majority of World Bank partnerships. By contrast, UNEP partnerships have intended in part to address the relative dearth and unpredictability of public funding flowing to the organization.

The divergence of state preferences with respect to global issues that have characteristics of public goods, as anticipated by Proposition 2 of the theoretical framework, has motivated proactive agent–principal coalitions in the World Bank context of financial expertise for new mechanisms of funding and incremental influence over the broader institutional agenda.

Somewhat surprisingly, given the market-based orientation of the World Bank, the private sector has not been strongly involved as a lead actor in global partnerships. While in the case of UNEP, business actors took initiatives in some 33% of collaborative initiatives and business associations in 13% (Figure 4.2), in the case of the World Bank, the private sector assumed a direct lead in approximately 8% of the partnerships and business associations in 3% (Figure 4.3). Such trends reflect the fact that the World Bank has other institutional means of working with the private sector, including the International Finance Corporation (IFC) and the Multilateral Investment Guarantee Agency (MIGA).[59] At the same time, the greater role of NGOs and foundations, compared to market-based actors, reflects the fact that in its partnership entrepreneurship, the World Bank was responding to specific types of organizational turbulence and legitimacy pressures associated with scrutiny by advocacy networks.[60] In relation to the environment, for instance, large and visible partnerships such as the Global Water Partnership, the Inter-American Biodiversity Information Network, the Meso-American Biological Corridor, the Global Tiger Initiative, or the Critical Ecosystem Partnership exemplify engagement with visible environmental issues and major advocacy organizations globally. The following analysis of the life cycle of the World Bank partnerships for climate finance provides greater detail on the entrepreneurial coalitions behind the adoption, diffusion, and institutionalization of collaborative governance around the issue of climate change.

The Life Cycle of Partnerships for Climate Finance

The World Bank had a limited explicit climate change mandate in the 1990s, beyond its role as one of the three implementing agencies of the Global Environmental Facility. The Prototype Carbon Fund (PCF), established in 1999, was the first experimental initiative in what later became a large portfolio of trust funds for climate change.[61] The signing of the Kyoto Protocol in 1997 and its provision for three market mechanisms – emissions trading, Joint Implementation (JI), and Clean Development Mechanism (CDM) – provided both the impetus and a window of opportunity for the Bank's engagement in climate-related governance as part of a larger imperative to green its operations and contribute to the provision of global public goods. The initiative came out of the World Bank Environment Department, whose size and expertise had expanded substantially in the 1990s.[62] Drawing heavily on environmental economics and financial expertise, this technical unit has promoted the implementation of a variety of policy instruments linking markets

[59] Park 2010.
[60] Fox and Brown 1998; Keck and Sikkink 1998; Park 2010.
[61] World Bank 2010b.
[62] Kelly and Jordan 2004.

and the environment, such as tradable permits, green accounting, valuation, and waste minimization.[63]

As anticipated by the cycle of dynamic institutional change, the Environment Department proposed the creation of the PCF as an experimental institution for learning by doing to support the implementation of project-based reductions of greenhouse gas emissions envisaged by the Kyoto Protocol.[64] The JI and CDM were intended to benefit developing and transition countries. However, interest in climate change action among these countries was limited in the 1990s. Furthermore, the implementation of market instruments for project-based mitigation required considerable capacity and institution building in the areas of project preparation, assessment of baseline scenarios, carbon accounting, granting of emission reduction credits, and transaction transparency. The World Bank viewed the PCF proposal as an opportunity to engage core principal constituencies, for example, developing and transition countries, in experimentation and institutional building for new mechanisms of governance. It would also allow the organization to extend its environmental portfolio in a direction that corresponded closely to the economic expertise of its lead organizational unit dealing with sustainability.

The entrepreneurial coalition that supported the agency initiative and experimental adoption of the PCF included those industrialized countries that were interested in promoting the flexible mechanisms within the Kyoto framework (Canada, Finland, Japan, the Netherlands, Norway, and Sweden) and 17 private companies, mostly from the energy and financial sectors. They jointly committed a total of US$180 million for the operational period 2000–2012.[65] With the support of World Bank President Wolfensohn, the World Bank Executive Board approved the creation of the PCF in 2000, *before* an intergovernmental consensus on the implementation of the Kyoto Protocol flexible mechanisms was achieved at the Conference of Parties in Marrakesh (2001) and well before the entry into force of the treaty in 2005 with a sufficient number of state ratifications. The PCF was proposed as a prototype fund, which would serve an intermediary function of creating sufficient capacity and knowledge to enable the takeoff of carbon markets. The design of the PCF as a pilot facility

---

[63] Gutner 2002.
[64] Newcombe 2001, p. 73.
[65] Freestone 2003.

reduced the perceived risk of agency activism to the broader body of principals by making the new institutional mechanism, at least in theory, easily reversible. David Freestone, then chief legal counsel of the World Bank, described the PCF as, "[...] unique in that it is the first trust fund established by the World Bank which permits contributions from both the public and the private sectors and which also provides something in return."[66] Ken Newcombe, the chief architect of the PCF, rationalized the agency initiative in a 2001 paper, saying,

[...] the regulatory framework for the Kyoto Protocol still doesn't yet exist. We have in some sense been granted the legitimacy of testing the application of the protocol through rules that are still being negotiated. Often in the process of developing a product, we were accused of getting ahead of the convention.[67]

The justification for agency activism was thus deduced by World Bank environmental staff on the basis of advancing valuable knowledge, capacity, and institutional infrastructure to support the treaty and the participation of developing countries. As Proposition 3 of the theoretical framework anticipates, the PCF closely reflected the expertise and epistemic networks of the agency. Newcombe emphasized in a published interview shortly after the approval of the fund that "[t]he key asset of the PCF is knowledge, to inform negotiators about the rules about previous PCF experiences on efficient and inefficient markets."[68]

Early facilitation by the PCF of carbon-offset projects and institutional development in developing and transition countries expanded support, both within the Bank and among state principals, for the replication and diffusion of carbon finance partnerships. Between 2000 and 2007, ten new carbon funds were created within the institutional context of the World Bank: the Community Development Carbon Fund (2003), the Bio Carbon Fund (2004; tranche 2, 2007), the Netherlands Clean Development Mechanism and Facility (2002), the Netherlands European Carbon Facility (2004), the Italian Carbon Fund (2004), the Danish Carbon Fund (2005), the Spanish Carbon Fund (2006), the Umbrella Carbon Facility (2006), the Carbon Fund for Europe (2007), and the Forest Carbon Partnership Facility.[69] The names of these facilities are telling of the relatively specific political backing and governance agendas they promoted. Such facilities

---

[66] Freestone 2003, p. 1–2.
[67] Newcombe 2001, p. 74.
[68] Newcombe 2001.
[69] World Bank 2009.

reduced some of the political and transaction costs of bilateral engagement in CDM and JI activities and provided a vehicle for entrepreneurial coalitions to export more activist climate agendas. The early success of the PCF and other facilities in large emerging countries such as Brazil and China and transition economies enlarged political support across the principal constituency of the organization.

Trust funds leveraged new resources, including both from traditional government agencies and from private and nonprofit actors, for a specific global purpose. In turn, this stream of new soft financing in effect increased the autonomy of World Bank staff to act in such ways as to enlarge political support among states constituencies and initiate new partnerships via coalitions with states and nonstate actors, fueling the cycle of diffusion of the fund-based partnerships for climate action.

The World Bank carbon finance portfolio did not go uncontested, however. Early carbon finance facilities aimed to demonstrate the feasibility and cost efficiency of project-based mitigation, investing a large share in "brown" offsets such as the destruction of hydrochlorofluorocarbons (HCFCs) or methane capture from coal mines.[70] Critics rightly argued that such projects prioritize investor interests and target primarily opportunities for large-scale offset projects in emerging markets, doing little for least-developed countries as a core constituency of the organization.[71] There was further concern that the operations of many of the early climate funds largely bypassed least-developed countries, which did not have large polluting industries to attract mega-offset projects. Such patterns of carbon fund projects put into question the extent to which such activities contribute to the broader objective of environmental and socially inclusive sustainable development.[72] Advocacy critics charged that in parallel to carbon fund activities, the Bank had not sufficiently integrated climate change considerations in its energy lending portfolios or country strategies.[73] The World Bank had to address concerns about the legitimacy of its climate finance activities not just with respect to immediate principals but with larger audiences and advocacy scrutiny.

---

[70] Andonova 2010; World Bank 2009.
[71] Arce and Marston 2009.
[72] Michaelowa and Michaelowa 2011; Nakhooda 2011.
[73] Nakhooda 2008; Nakhooda and Ballesteros 2009.

Over time, the climate finance initiatives of the World Bank diversified to include creation of a capacity-building program and new facilities focused on community- and forestry-based offsets to support greater participation by least-developed countries. The third wave of climate finance expansion included the Climate Partnership Facility, the Forest Carbon Partnership Facility, and Climate Investment Funds. The Climate Investment Funds (CIFs) included, for the first time, contributions from all major donors of the organization, including large initial contributions from the United States (31%), the UK (22%), Japan (18%), Germany (13%), and France (5%).[74] Interviews with Smitha Nakhooda, a climate finance expert formerly with the World Resources Institute (WRI), and with a former employee of the UK's Department for International Development (DFID), characterize the CIFs as an effort to follow up on the commitments made at the Glenn Eagles Summit and to "help the development banks to do more on climate change as it relates to development."[75] The CIFs include the Climate Technology Fund and the Strategic Climate Fund, the latter supporting programmatic activities in developing countries that relate to adaptation and resilience to climate change, forestry programs, and renewable energy programs. Under pressure by NGOs and developing countries for more equitable governance, the CIF board has equal representation of developed and developing countries (eight each) along with more direct collaboration with regional development banks and active observers from the private sector (two) and civil society (four).

By 2010, the World Bank had become the most important multilateral source of financial assistance for climate change by generating, through a series of experimental institutional mechanisms, approximately US$16 billion in climate finance during the period 2000–2011.[76] The carbon finance activities of the World Bank were widely regarded as successes both within the organization and by the majority of its shareholders. These new institutional mechanisms served as a platform for a new stream of donor contributions for

---

[74] Interview with Richard Zechter, Carbon Finance Unit, World Bank, Nov. 2010. For data, see Carbon Partnership Facility 2016.

[75] Interviews with Smitha Nakhooda, Overseas Development Institute, February 2013, London; Philip Lewis, Climate and Development Knowledge Network, February 2013, London.

[76] World Bank 2010c, 2010d, 2010e.

climate-related activities at a time when intergovernmental resources and commitments were stagnating.[77] The view of successful organizational experimentation, which generated new resources and engaged a growing number of developing countries and substate actors, became the basis for the more permanent institutionalization of climate finance and subsequently policy within the World Bank.[78]

In 2010, the World Bank published its first policy document on climate change titled *Development and Climate Change: A Strategic Framework for the World Bank Group*. In 2014, the World Bank appointed Rachel Kyte as vice president and special envoy for climate change, overseeing the growing portfolio of work on climate change, including adaptation, mitigation, climate finance, and disaster risk and resilience across the institutions of the World Bank Group. By way of a counterfactual, it is hardly possible to imagine that the intergovernmental principals of the organization could have agreed on institutional change that mandates the World Bank to engage in financing climate projects in 1999 and in a portfolio of climate policy 2010, respectively, while intergovernmental politics have remained deadlocked. The role of the organization in climate governance will remain controversial, as critics see it as a potential diversion from the authority of the UNFCCC. However, from the point of view of understanding the evolving structure and roles of international institutions, the life cycle of climate finance at the World Bank captures the relevance of governance entrepreneurship and global partnerships as mechanisms for substantial institutional change.

Institutionalization of Global Partnerships

The broader institutionalization of global partnerships as a new means of World Bank governance proceeded relatively swiftly following their rapid rise in the 1990s. This was a result of early engagement between the agency and its key financial principals on the role of the Bank in the provision of global public goods via partnerships. Moreover, the oversight culture and procedures introduced in the organization since the

---

[77] Interviews with Kristalina Georgieva, Corporate Secretary and Vice President of the World Bank, June 2008; Chris Warner, World Bank Carbon Finance Unit, February 2008; Ari Huhtala, Overseas Development Institute, February 2013, London; Prof. Gilbert E. Metcalf, Tufts University, August 2014, Medford, MA.
[78] World Bank 2006.

1980s, along with concerns about potential legitimacy challenges of the hybrid approach, prompted provisions for greater transparency and faster institutionalization compared to other organizations such as UNEP or the UN Secretariat.

The Executive Board of the World Bank requested in 2001 a review of World Bank engagement in global partnerships, which produced specific recommendations for their institutionalization and periodic oversight.[79] The World Bank Operations Evaluation Department, which reports directly to the World Bank Board of Directors, as well as staff in the organization's legal department, produced a series of documents on the institutional governance of global partnerships.[80] A report of the Independent Evaluation Groups speaks of a relatively early effort of greater institutionalization and oversight of World Bank global partnerships at the level of organizational management, including the adoption in 2005 of *A Strategic Framework for the World Bank's Global Programs and Partnerships*:

The Bank has taken steps to strengthen its oversight of GPPs [Global Programs and Partnerships]. The Global Programs and Partnership Council was established in response to a recommendation made in the Phase 1 evaluation. The Bank issued a strategic framework paper in 2005, which took steps to strengthen the accountability of the VPUs [Vice Presidential Units] for overseeing GPPs, including more effectively linking GPPs to the Bank's country and regional strategies and revising the choice of issues for engagement.[81]

By 2008, it became clear that trust funds, many of which support partnership programs, had surpassed in volume for the fiscal years 2003–2008 the traditional intergovernmental instrument of concessional finance, the International Development Association under the World Bank (IDA).[82] In response, the organization created a new department on Global Partnership and Trust Fund Operations under the Vice Presidency for Concessional Finance and Global

---

[79] World Bank Operations Evaluation Department 2001, 2004.
[80] Interviews with Sophia Drewnowski, Global Partnerships and Trust Fund Operations; Charles Di Leva, Legal Counsel, World Bank, Washington, November 2010. See also World Bank Development Committee 2007; World Bank Operations Evaluation Department 2005.
[81] Independent Evaluation Group 2006, p. 46. See also World Bank 2005; World Bank Operations Evaluation Department 2005.
[82] Independent Evaluation Group 2011, p. 10.

Partnerships,[83] thus institutionalizing collaborative activities and providing for more direct principal oversight.[84] Global partnerships have become part of the institutional repertoire of the World Bank, particularly for extending its governance on global issues such as environmental sustainability.

The analysis of the opening up of UNEP and the World Bank to direct collaboration with nonstate actors for sustainability sheds new light on the ways in which organizational entrepreneurs and supportive policy coalitions have steered partnership governance. These two agencies reacted to very different circumstances in the late 1990s. Yet as anticipated by the theory of dynamic institutional change, in both instances, the organizational entrepreneurship of new governance related to concerns about legitimacy, resources, and sufficient autonomy and epistemic capacity to facilitate selective alliances with states and external actors. At the same time, and in line with the observable implications of the theoretical framework, the nature of partnership engagement and the type of collaborative alliances have differed substantially across the two institutional domains, reflecting their organizational structure, expertise, and approaches to governance.

Partnership Outcomes across Institutions

The theory of dynamic and partially endogenous institutional change implies that the portfolio of partnerships and their outcomes should reflect important differences in the expertise, mandates, and fields of the two agencies. As we saw in the preceding analysis, different types of organizational circumstances motivated the search for new public–private alliances. The Database on Global Partnerships allows us to assess the observable implications of the theoretical framework by examining comparatively the patterns of the outcomes of partnerships for sustainability across the two organizational fields. In the case of the World Bank, the comparison considers the subset of global partnerships with explicit environmental focus (forty-eight partnerships, or 36% of the total number of World Bank global partnerships in the database) to assure compatible samples and units of analysis. The analysis can thus proceed to assess substantively the extent to which

---

[83] Later transformed to Development Finance Vice Presidency.
[84] Kirby-Zaki 2009; Wu and Rey 2009.

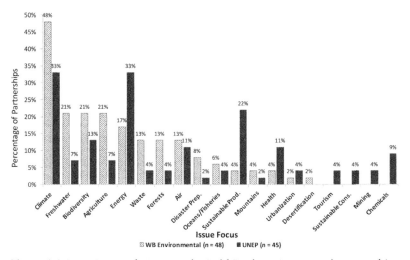

Figure 4.4 Issue Focus of UNEP and World Bank environmental partnerships

different organizational circumstances have impacted the nature and outcomes of partnerships for sustainability.

Three leading questions structure the comparative analysis of partnership outcomes: What kind of environmental issues do global partnerships address predominantly? What type of instruments do they introduce for addressing such issues? Who are the main financial partners, and what kind of resources are leveraged toward environmental issues via partnerships?

Figure 4.4 presents a comparison of the issues on which the environmental partnerships of UNEP and the World Bank focus predominantly.[85] It reveals some telling differences across the portfolios of the two organizations. To begin with, the partnerships in which UNEP participates are spread across a somewhat broader range of environmental problems, which reflects its extensive environmental policy mandate and expertise. A substantial number of partnerships have furthermore developed around the expert authority of UNEP DTIE branch, the main entrepreneurs of public–private collaboration, including clean energy, sustainable production and consumption, air pollution, chemicals, and related health and environmental issues. By

---

[85] The issue focus of partnerships is coded based on the language of their mission statements or comparable documents. A single partnership can identify one or several related issues as primary foci.

contrast, World Bank partnerships are more highly concentrated around global issues such as climate change and biodiversity or traditional areas of World Bank lending such as agriculture, water, and waste infrastructure.

Figure 4.4 furthermore indicates that three global issues – climate change, clean energy, and biodiversity – have attracted substantial attention from public and private partnership entrepreneurs. Such patterns correspond to the observable implications of the theoretical framework on dynamic institutional change. These policy arenas are among the most densely populated with transnational advocacy and private actors and initiative.[86] As anticipated by Proposition 4 of the theoretical framework and recognized by documents of the two organizations, such arenas present greater external pressure and opportunities for organizational collaboration via partnerships.[87]

At the same time, differential preferences by governments exhibited with respect to climate and clean energy policy can account for the willingness of proactive state actors to support partnership coalitions, as illustrated by both the cases of clean energy partnerships of UNEP and the climate finance partnerships of the World Bank. In both instances, partnerships steered toward more narrowly defined parts of these complex problems, where preference divergence became moderated and some common ground across industrialized and developing countries was beginning to emerge. According to Mark Radka, the founding Director of the UNEP's Energy Branch created in 1997, UNEP made "a strategic decision to occupy an organizational niche that was opening up as several policy streams converged."[88] With the adoption of the Kyoto Protocol, clean energy was gaining some political resonance compared to the disinterest and avoidance within the UN in earlier time periods. UNEP reacted to growing interest among industry and policy circles in renewable energy, which was viewed as likely to become increasingly compatible with conventional technologies cost-wise. Partnership platforms such as UNFIP allowed experimentation in small coalitions for clean energy governance that cut across local and global concerns and constituencies of the organization.

---

[86] Andonova 2014; Bulkeley *et al.* 2014; Newell 2012.
[87] World Bank Development Committee 2007; UNEP 2009.
[88] Phone interview with Mark Radka, July 2015, UNEP DTIE Energy, Paris.

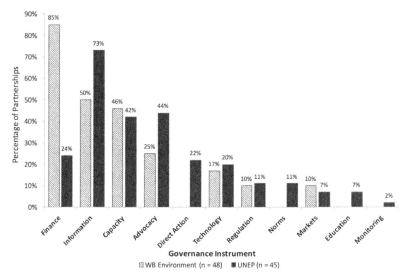

Figure 4.5 Governance instruments of UNEP and World Bank environmental partnerships

Figure 4.4 also illustrates how, in two related arenas, the World Bank framed partnerships predominantly in terms of climate change as a type of global public good, while UNEP's partnerships placed greater premium on the diffusion of a set of clean energy technologies (solar cook stoves, efficient buildings, efficient lighting, sustainable biofuels, rural access to clean energy, etc.), which reflects the entrepreneurial role of the Energy Unit of UNEP DTIE. Hale and Roger furthermore find that the World Bank has orchestrated a range of transnational initiatives for climate governance, reflecting a similar tendency to coalesce with transnational and substate actors on global issues.[89] These patterns of issue clustering in global environmental partnerships are thus indicative of their nature as niches for experimental governance, which allow the partition of complex problems into narrower subsets of issues, characterized by moderate divergence of principal interests, epistemic capability of IOs, and the possibility for cross-sector alliances.

The governance instruments of global partnerships for sustainability (Figure 4.5) similarly exhibit the imprint of the organizational fields within which they are embedded, along with some cross-cutting commonalities. Information and capacity building are important

---

[89] Hale and Roger 2014.

instruments of partnership governance for both UNEP and the World Bank, and indeed for transnational governance more broadly.[90] Given the high degree of knowledge specialization of the two organizations, these are the types of instruments they can develop best and for whose implementation they are likely to find more agency autonomy.[91] As we saw earlier in the chapter, UNEP has fostered a range of partnerships in which the supply of reliable environmental knowledge, timely information, and capacity to react to such information are fundamental steps in reducing environmental risks and managing environmental problems such as industrial accidents, chemical safety, energy efficiency, or access to renewable technologies. UNEP joined the private entrepreneurs of the Global Reporting Initiative for corporate sustainability to promote more rigorous information standards, reflecting the belief of one of the lead organizational entrepreneurs within UNEP that "...what you don't measure you don't manage."[92] The entrepreneurs of World Bank climate finance partnerships similarly justified the establishment of new experimental carbon funds by referring to the need to build credible knowledge, accounting, and capacity for implementing carbon offset projects envisaged by the Kyoto Protocol. The space for IO–facilitated agency entrepreneurship of global partnerships indeed appears to be greatest with respect to knowledge-based and capacity-building instruments.

The comparative information presented in Figure 4.5 is notable also for the surprisingly low share of partnerships that use markets as governance instruments even in the case of the market-oriented World Bank. This distinguishes global partnerships quite considerably from private transnational governance, which relies to a large degree on market-based instruments.[93] The data also shows that very few of the UNEP and World Bank environmental partnerships engage in any type of regulatory activity, and none have explicit monitoring provisions. This is not surprising given that regulatory agreements within the multilateral sphere tend to be strictly in the domain of the intergovernmental

[90] Bulkeley *et al.* 2014.
[91] Tallberg *et al.* 2013.
[92] Aloisi de Larderel 2002, p. 4. See Brown, de Jong and Levy 2009 and Brown, de Jong and Lissidrenska 2009 on information as governance strategy promoted by the GRI and its achievements and limitations.
[93] Clapp 2005; Prakash and Potoski 2006b; Pattberg 2007; Büthe and Mattli 2011; Vogel 2005, 2008.

bodies and thus, as anticipated by Proposition 1, will tend to leave limited space for agency facilitation of new governance.

The variation in the partnership instruments across the two organizational spheres is also telling. The partnership portfolio of UNEP uses a somewhat wider variety of tools, including greater promotion of issue advocacy, norms, and direct action with subnational communities (Figure 4.5). Meanwhile, in the World Bank, financial instruments appear to be the means most frequently leveraged by its environmental partnerships, along with information and capacity. These patterns reflect the nature of the Bank's expertise and its approach to the environment as an issue ripe for new financial instruments for the supply of global public goods that are underprovided for by traditional lending mechanisms.[94] Not surprisingly, norm diffusion, education, and direct action on environmental problems are largely absent from the instruments of the World Bank partnership portfolio (Figure 4.5).

Finally, the database on Global Partnerships also allows us to shed new light on the type of financial partners that have supported the entrepreneurship of hybrid governance in the multilateral sphere. Figure 4.6 reveals that the World Bank, an IO characterized by relatively high financial autonomy, has relied to a large extent on its own resources (67% of all environmental partnerships draw support from World Bank funding) and additional *public* financing (94% of environmental partnerships) to facilitate partnerships for sustainability. The figure takes into account that a single partnership can be funded with participation of multiple sources and actors. As we saw in the cases of climate finance partnerships, donor countries have often financed new governance initiatives through a proliferating number of Bank-managed trust funds (more than 75% of all environmental partnerships received financing through trust funds), which have been leveraged in a number of cases with nonstate contributions. While a variety of nonstate actors participate in World Bank partnerships, a relatively small share of them rely on contributions by private businesses, charitable foundations, or NGOs (Figure 4.6). This finding once again reflects the entrepreneurial role of the World Bank leadership to facilitate the creation of new instruments of soft public finance as a way to stimulate programs for global public goods in alliance with external actors.

---

[94] World Bank Operations Evaluation Department 2001; World Bank Development Committee 2007.

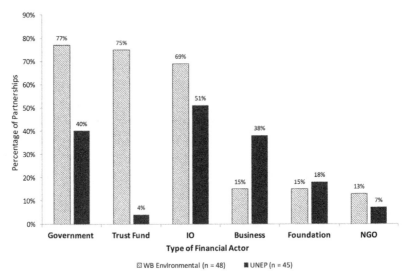

Figure 4.6 Financial partners of UNEP and World Bank environmental partnerships

The landscape of financial partners looks quite different in the case of UNEP. For an organization that has been traditionally starved of public resources, business contributions have been important in supporting some 38% of its partnership activities, keeping in mind that due to a lower degree of institutionalization, financial information is not available for about 18% of the UNEP partnership portfolio (Figure 4.6). While public financing has remained the most important single source in support of UNEP's partnership activities, only about 51% of the UNEP partnerships have relied on direct government support or new instruments of public financing such as trust funds (4%). These figures suggest that a relatively large proportion of UNEP partnerships are likely to involve a diverse set of private, societal, and expert actors, as illustrated in the cases examined here, and reflect the traditionally diverse engagement of the organization with environmental actors across multiple domains.

Conclusion

Global partnerships have introduced new institutional means for UNEP and the World Bank to pursue governance objectives related to the environment and sustainability. It is rather remarkable and counterintuitive from state-centric perspectives that the World Bank convened coalitions of governance entrepreneurs for climate finance partnerships to advance the implementation of the flexible mechanisms of the Kyoto Protocol, even as the U.S., the Bank's most powerful principal, abandoned the treaty. It is through the practice of partnerships, including the clean energy partnerships fostered as part of UNEP's programs, that ideas of carbon-lean and climate-resilient development have entered the development discourse. The relative agency autonomy, expertise, and policy networks of the two organizations have facilitated the entrepreneurial coalitions for new forms of governance. This chapter documents the great variety of coalitions between organizational entrepreneurs, proactive governments, and external actors, which have been the driving wheels behind the life cycle of institutional change and the rise of sustainability partnerships, as argued in the theoretical chapter. Global partnerships in turn have allowed UNEP and World Bank to expand their work on sustainability in ways that would not have been conceivable on the basis of classic intergovernmental politics.

As a consequence of their entrepreneurial dynamic and organizational embeddedness, partnerships have often targeted narrow and context-specific objectives, for example, preparedness and prevention of chemical risk across a number of local communities, diffusing life cycle methodologies to stimulate sustainable management, policy support for specific renewable technology, and the like. Such fragmentation of governance into a subset of problems related to larger issues captures the concern that their contribution is likely to be insufficient for addressing global environment problems. Furthermore, because of their entrepreneurial and necessarily opportunistic character at least initially, partnerships can falter, and their success and institutionalization cannot be assumed. While the UNEP Safer Production partnerships and REN21 are notable for going through multiple cycles of experimentation, broader uptake, and institutionalization, other partnerships, for example many of the initiatives endorsed by the Johannesburg Summit on Environment and Sustainable Development, have not generated a political following and successful implementation and diffusion.[95] Such observations on the nature of global partnerships

---

[95] See Pattberg *et al.* 2012.

raise questions about their cumulative effect on sustainability governance. Is the governance contribution glass of partnerships half full, or is it even altogether empty, as skeptics may charge, if such initiatives represent a diversion of the real business of broad intergovernmental regulation?

This study has advanced the understanding of the political origins of global partnerships as a new form of governance in the multilateral system rather than defining and examining their effectiveness, which is the next research question. Nonetheless, it provides some hard empirical evidence with respect to the debate on the role of collaborative initiatives in global environmental governance. Thus, if comprehensive regulation is the standard against which the contribution of partnerships is judged, the glass of partnership contribution may appear altogether empty. The global partnership portfolios of the World Bank and UNEP indeed barely produced new rules, standards, or any form of legalized and binding regulation. Yet this is hardly the right benchmark for assessing public–private governance. Global partnerships rarely have the authority to fulfill regulatory governance functions that rest primarily with intergovernmental bodies. A more relevant criterion is assessing their added value in creating governance in those areas that intergovernmental regimes have not been able to reach directly.

The data from UNEP and World Bank partnerships shows that such arrangements have enabled these organizations to advance seemingly impossible policy missions across a range of pressing issues. Global partnerships have furthermore mobilized new constituencies for advancing sustainability goals. They have created significant pockets of implementation capacity, new awareness and ideas, and extraordinary reach across appropriate scales of action, as documented in this chapter. These outcomes may be said to rival in practical sustainability impact the outcomes of some more formal institutions such as the interministerial dialogue on institutional governance within UNEP or traditional loan projects of the World Bank. The variation in partnership outcomes invites the extension of this research agenda to explore the relative effectiveness of different instruments of partnership governance and the pathways toward a more coordinated institutional framework for sustainability.

5 | *Partnerships for Children and Health*

Introduction

The well-being of children and efforts to improve global health are compelling international objectives. UNICEF and the WHO are the principal multilateral institutions that manage these policy spheres. They are governed by distinct sets of instruments but are highly inter-dependent in their normative and functional ends. The fulfillment of children's rights and potential begins with survival, adequate nutrition, and good health provision, especially for newborns, children, and adolescents, those vulnerable groups vital for the future of societies. This chapter examines the political conditions and entrepreneurial strategies of IOs and other actors that have led to global partnerships taking on an increasingly prominent role in the governance of health and children's issues. It analyzes how these partnerships have produced outcomes quite different than we would have expected from traditional international organizations by creating mechanisms to engender strong international commitments on neglected issues such as infant and mater-nal mortality, access to medicines, nutrition, and the fulfillment of rights, among others.

The institutional arenas of UNICEF and the WHO represent in many ways a most likely case of the theory of governance entrepre-neurship and dynamic institutional change. There is relatively high intergovernmental consensus on the goals of better health and well-being of children, but differences remain regarding priorities and means to advance unfulfilled commitments. Given the high reliance of cooperation on evolving scientific knowledge, medical innovation and on-the-ground implementation, states as intergovernmental prin-cipals have delegated highly specialized functions to the two agencies, with considerable scope for expert autonomy.[1] From the 1990s, as development organizations, advocacy groups, expert networks, and

---

[1] Cooper 1989; Haas E. 1990; Jolly 2014.

charitable foundations started to focus attention on the health problems of the poor and the most vulnerable, the organizational environments of UNICEF and WHO became increasingly turbulent and ripe for experimentation and change. Multiple studies document the reconstitutions of health governance to include new governors and forms.[2] At the same time, the highly normative mandates of these two organizations made the legitimacy risks of such engagement highly salient. Organizational entrepreneurs had to straddle with caution the boundaries between public objectives and private contribution and influence.

The objective of this chapter is to place the analytic spotlight on the *processes* and iterative cycle of governance entrepreneurship through which multilateral institutions have embraced far-reaching collaboration with a variety of external actors for children and health. The comparative perspective on UNICEF and the WHO is particularly valuable, because the two agencies vary considerably in structure, mandates, and organizational culture with respect to private-sector interactions. The chapter examines the dynamic changes within these institutions and case studies that illuminate the life cycle of specific partnerships. Similar to the other empirical chapters, it relies on expert interviews, archival research, text analysis, and new comparative data on global partnerships in the multilateral system. The analysis of the two organizations and their partnerships proceeds in parallel fashion to capture first the distinctive structures and sources of influence of UNICEF and the WHO, respectively, and how these characteristics and organizational contexts shaped the development of partnerships. These features, as the theoretical framework anticipates, have had a significant imprint on the life cycle of experimentation, diffusion, and institutionalization of partnership collaboration. At the same time, the WHO and UNICEF participate jointly in a substantial number of global partnerships. Drawing on the Global Partnerships Database, the chapter analyzes how partnerships have contributed to greater coordination by the two agencies over specific outcomes for health and children. It examines what types of issues have been tackled through partnerships and what kinds of

---

[2] Szlezák *et al.* 2010; Brown, Cueto and Fee 2006; Kickbusch 2009; Lee, Buse and Fustukian 2002; Lee 2003; Kickbusch and de Leeuw 1999; Jönsson 2010; Rosenberg *et al.* 2010; Moon *et al.* 2010; Youde 2012; Buse, Hein and Drager 2009; McInnes and Lee 2012; Clinton and Sridhar 2017.

instruments and resources partnerships have brought in. The new data and qualitative analysis present evidence on the expected imprint of IO priorities and expertise on the rise and outcomes of partnership governance. It presents new evidence on contentious debates regarding the continuing role of states and the negotiation of collaborative boundaries with private, advocacy, and epistemic actors.

Partnerships: At the Heart of the UNICEF Mandate

Agency Decentralization, Advocacy and Initiative

Of the five international agencies examined in this book, UNICEF has the longest-standing and most diverse experience of collaboration with civil society and the private sector. As one UNICEF document summarizes, "Partnerships are at the heart of the UNICEF mandate."[3] The organization's contemporary engagement with global partnerships is best analyzed through the prism of its capacity for advocacy and decentralized innovation and in the context of its history of pragmatic alliances to advance specific causes for children.

UNICEF's decentralization and single-minded focus on children are sources of substantial agency autonomy. Since its very creation, UNICEF has operated with a strong advocacy identity and multiple levels of decentralization that are unique in the UN system. The UN General Assembly established the organization as a temporary fund in 1946 to support the rehabilitation of children in post–World War II Europe. The work of the fund was context specific, reaching out to volunteers and local structures for timely delivery of milk, immunization, and other assistance. As Europe recovered, UNICEF "survived," according to historian Richard Jolly, despite "opposition from all major donors and from the specialized agencies within the UN."[4] A speech by the representative of Pakistan at the UN General Assembly helped turn the tide by eloquently making the case that a permanent agency was needed to mobilize action to improve the plight of children in developing countries, where living conditions were no better than they had been in war-torn Europe. The new agency received overwhelming support from the Social Commission of the General

---

[3] UNICEF 2012a, p. 2.
[4] Jolly 2014, p. 16.

Assembly. In the words of another historian of UNICEF, Maggie Black, "a principle of postwar international relations had been agreed upon: children were above the political divide."[5]

In terms of structure, UNICEF headquarters in New York provides policy direction and oversight alongside a decentralized network of country and regional offices with the autonomy to work directly on specific issues with members of national parliaments, NGOs, and municipal authorities. The organizational culture puts strong emphasis on testing ideas and approaches in local contexts before they are adopted at policy level.[6] Moreover, the agency generates an important share of its funding from nonpublic resources in a decentralized manner. In 2015, for example, 29% of UNICEF's income came from private-sector and nongovernment sources, mostly through UNICEF National Committees, which raised US$1.15 billion of the total private-sector revenue of US$1.46 billion.[7]

UNICEF also has a strong advocacy identity with a focus on outcomes for children. Black describes UNICEF's advocacy as pragmatic and non-confrontational, based on delivery of concrete benefits and efforts to "leverage certain principles and practice."[8] Organizational theories of IOs rarely discuss advocacy as a source of agency autonomy and initiative. Indeed, if specialized knowledge is the main currency of bureaucratic influence, advocacy could be seen to undermine the credibility and impartiality of expert authority.[9] And yet sociological studies have documented that IOs engage in actively "teaching" and socializing states, thus in effect advocating a set of norms under the rubric of expertise.[10]

The degree of operational and advocacy autonomy of different branches of UNICEF has enabled considerable scope for organizational initiative, as anticipated by Proposition 1 of the theoretical framework. Operationally, important innovations have included the bottom-up creation of UNICEF National Committees as nongovernmental organizations in industrialized countries; the diversification of

---

[5] Black 1996, p. 7.
[6] Interviews with Kate Rogers, UNICEF, July 2010, New York; Hiba Frankoul, Private Fundraising and Partnerships, UNICEF, July 2014, New York.
[7] UNICEF Annual Report 2015, accessed via www.unicef.org, November 2016, p. 45, 52.
[8] Black 1996, p. 137.
[9] Mitchell *et al.* 2006.
[10] Finnemore 1996; Haas P. 1989; Finnemore and Sikkink 1998; Sikkink 1986.

fundraising, be it through these committees, through the sales of greeting cards, or through fundraising initiatives by private individuals; and, since 1984, the appointment of celebrities as Goodwill Ambassadors to speak on behalf of children. It was UNICEF advocacy, with active leadership by then Executive Director James Grant that paved the way politically for the adoption of the 1989 UN Convention on the Rights of the Child. This unprecedented recognition of the universal human rights of children was subsequently ratified by 194 member states.[11] In the wake of the 2008–2009 financial crisis, the UNICEF Executive Director Anthony Lake advanced strong organizational advocacy for reducing global inequalities and focusing on issues that touch the most vulnerable and marginalized children.

However, UNICEF's scope for autonomous initiative does not mean that member states have taken a back seat. State principals have two primary means of control. First, the Executive Board, which consists of thirty-six members elected by the Economic and Social Council of the UN General Assembly, directly oversees the organization and approves its programs, policies, and the annual budget. Second, states also exercise influence with hold on the purse strings, as UNICEF's income depends entirely on voluntary contributions. While fundraising with National Committees and private entities has diversified UNICEF's budget and increased the scope for agency discretion, it has also attributed to the general public a more direct status of principals compared to most IOs. Both hierarchical and decentralized mechanisms of accountability can thus be activated with respect to the work of the agency, which is keenly aware of the extent to which its legitimacy and resources depend on advancing its normative purpose and on delivering results for children.[12] Agency initiative has thus gone hand in hand with the ability to secure the support of political coalitions, as anticipated by the dynamic model of institutional change elaborated in Chapter 2.[13]

---

[11] Black 1986, 1996; Jolly 2014; Holzscheiter 2010.

[12] Hawkins and Jacoby 2006; Grant and Keohane 2005; McCubbins and Schwartz 1984.

[13] For example, James Grant launched major programs for child survival in the 1980s and later advanced the Convention on the Rights of the Child only after active solicitation of financial and political backing by the Executive Board and with a strategy to mobilize support from developing countries and civil society.

Unlike other IOs examined in this book, for which public–private collaboration is a relatively recent phenomenon, UNICEF's unique scope for decentralized innovation has resulted in several streams of collaborative initiatives throughout its history. UNICEF documents speak not of public–private partnerships in general but of different types of arrangements: with civil-society organizations, private-sector partnerships, and more recently about global program partnerships.[14] The rise and diffusion of these partnering streams is analyzed in turn.

Decentralized Entrepreneurship of Collaborative Alliances

UNICEF has historically functioned in the context of partnerships as a consequence of the nature of its mandate and the substantial scope for practical, decentralized alliances. The development of collaborations between UNICEF and civil-society organizations such as the Red Cross, Save the Children, and local groups goes back to its original mission. UNICEF was established as an operational agency, supporting programs on the ground. The early discourse emphasized functionality and delivering outcomes – medicine, milk, and relief to the most vulnerable. It needed partners at the local level. Following decolonization and an increasingly intense focus on children and development, demand for UNICEF involvement soared. The number of NGOs with which UNICEF collaborated subsequently expanded greatly, locally and transnationally. Over time, partnerships with the private sector increasingly developed.[15]

Text analysis of UNICEF Annual Reports reveals that until 1997, the organization used the language of "working together" rather than partnerships to highlight its collaboration with civil society and with UNICEF National Committees, but also with a host of other subnational groups such as parliamentarians, mayors, religious leaders, and intergovernmental organizations.[16] The initiative of UNICEF country offices has been particularly important for such engagements. The strong emphasis on practicality and accomplishing specific ends for

---

Jolly (2014, p. 60) describes the entrepreneurship and expansion of the child survival programs as follows: "To this end Grant first mobilized UNICEF and then action by well over 100 developing country governments, most donor countries, and a host of civil society organizations, including churches and mosques, Rotarians, and NGOs like Save the Children."

[14] UNICEF 2009b, 2012a.

[15] Black 1996. Interview with Kate Rogers, UNICEF, July 1010, New York.

[16] See UNICEF Annual Reports 1989–2014, accessed via www.unicef.org, November 2014.

affected children has remained relevant, even as UNICEF has advanced to a more strategic and norm-driven collaboration with NGOs including, as we shall see later in the chapter, through broader global program partnerships.

UNICEF's collaboration with the private sector is another dimension of its partnering activities. Until 1997, the organizational discourse referred primarily to private-sector alliances, which captured varying degrees of coordination for different purposes. The traditional approach to the private sector was resource driven and philanthropic.[17] By the 1980s, UNICEF Committees and country offices had started experimenting with fundraising initiatives around specific sectors and themes. The Change for Good Alliance is an example of the entrepreneurial and bottom-up nature of such partnerships. The initiative was launched in 1987 by the UNICEF National Committee in the UK and international airlines. It was inspired by the journalist Howard Simons and his article "Giving a Little Change Could Go a Long Way," published in the *Wall Street Journal*. Today the Change for Good Alliance is one of the best-known corporate partnerships committed to raising resources for UNICEF causes at airports, on flights, through the company websites and private events, and in some instances through logistics support in humanitarian emergencies. By 2014, passengers had contributed more than US$130 million to the delivery of programs for children, with the participation of twelve airlines.[18]

As global companies started to adopt corporate social responsibility (CSR) strategies, UNICEF engaged increasingly in alliances that touched on corporate behavior and targeted specific objectives for children. Private-sector partnerships became a prominent terminology. UNICEF created the Private Sector Division in 1997, later renamed the Private Fundraising and Partnerships Division, dedicated to expanding corporate partnerships. Collaboration with the private sector still involves the donation of resources, but the structuring of the relationship has become more strategic in that it seeks to advance a specific issue related to the rights or well-being of children and how they relate to the core operations of companies.[19]

---

[17] Interview with Anne-Marie Grey, former Chief, International and Corporate Alliances, Private Sector Division, UNICEF; June 2007; see also O'Brien 2008; UNICEF Annual Reports 1989–2014, accessed via www.unicef.org November 2014.

[18] UNICEF 2008; U.S. Fund for UNICEF 2015; Spano 2012.

[19] O'Brien 2008; UNICEF 2014a.

The entrepreneurship of partnerships around CSR and children's issues has typically proceeded in a highly decentralized manner, taking cues from UNICEF's earlier experiences. A case study of a series of partnerships between UNICEF and IKEA aptly illustrates this dynamic of decentralized entrepreneurship of partnership approaches.[20] In 1998, IKEA approached UNICEF and Save the Children to learn more about the Convention on the Rights of the Child and the problem of child labor. The company had adopted a prohibition of child labor in its supply chain as part of its CSR strategy and as a response to advocacy scrutiny. It had introduced a private certification Rugmark for carpets produced without child labor. However, the strategy had backfired, as certification was inherently difficult to verify and only scratched the surface of a complex social problem. IKEA's motivation to seek a partnership is elaborated in an insightful case-study by Bartlett, Dessain and Sjoman, quoting the company's business manager for carpets: "The more we learned, the more we understood we had to tackle child labor as a much larger problem... It involved changing mindsets of whole communities, not just the behavior of our suppliers. Once we recognized that, we knew we would need to work in partnership with experts on community involvement."[21]

In 2000, the UNICEF office in India and IKEA launched a program on childhood education in Uttar Pradesh, the heart of India's carpet belt. UNICEF accepted IKEA's funding with some hesitation and after consideration of its CSR record. According to Bartlett, Dessain and Sjoman, "Beyond the funding, they acknowledged that IKEA could also bring the credibility and clout of a major buyer of carpets in the region, and this could be of great help in gaining local cooperation."[22] The initial three-year community development project covering 400 villages provided the opportunity for 24,000 children to attend school and was subsequently extended to include self-help groups for women and spread to 500 villages.

As anticipated by the theoretical framework on the cycle of governance entrepreneurship, the successful experimentation and achievement of specific results in Uttar Pradesh became a stimulus for the diffusion of partnering practices. The programs in India expanded to include

---

[20] Bartlett, Dessain and Sjoman 2006.
[21] Bartlett, Dessain and Sjoman 2006, p. 3.
[22] Ibid., p. 3.

projects across fifteen states on objectives related to the rights, survival, growth, and development of children. By 2012, the UNICEF–IKEA collaboration had contributed more than US$100 million toward projects in India on schools, families, nutrition, hygiene, and newborn health, affecting the lives of some 74,000 children.[23] In 2014, the IKEA Foundation committed an additional US$31.5 million and extended the partnership to countries such as Afghanistan, China, India, Pakistan, and Rwanda in support of UNICEF's new strategic focus on reaching the most vulnerable children.[24]

The UNICEF–IKEA partnership reveals the key role of entrepreneurial coalitions between governments, local branches of the agency, and business actors in the life cycle of corporate partnerships that achieve substantial uptake as organizational practice. A mapping document of UNICEF partnerships estimates that the organization engages in active collaboration with more than 600 companies worldwide at any given point in time.[25] These range from funding arrangements and cause marketing campaigns to more integrative partnerships, which involve country or regional offices, as well as national committees and headquarters divisions. Over time, UNICEF has become more selective, targeting collaborations that contribute innovative products or processes for results on specific issues such as nutrient deficiency, tetanus immunization, hygiene, access to sanitation and water in emergencies, or the use of mobile technologies for health monitoring, birth registration, and data collection.

The organization has gradually adopted a more proactive advocacy approach, particularly under the leadership of Executive Director Anthony Lake, in seeking to engage innovations and, where appropriate, corporate practices as agents of change in advancing children's causes. In 2011–2012, UNICEF, Save the Children, and the UN Global Compact led a process of consultation with business, civil society, and academia, which resulted in the formulation of the *Children's Rights and Business Principles*. The document specifies a set of voluntary standards for business, which draws on the Convention on the Rights of the Child, International Labor Organization (ILO) Conventions, and the UN Guiding Principles on Business and Human Rights as they

---

[23] See UNICEF 2012c.
[24] See UNICEF 2014b.
[25] UNICEF 2009a, p. 11.

relate to supporting the rights of children in business practices.[26] In effect, it introduces a new soft-law normative instrument in the hitherto pragmatic interaction between UNICEF and the private sector, seeking to promote specific commitments and practices not only through but also beyond partnership agreements.

Global Program Partnerships

Global program partnerships are a more recent modality of UNICEF's public–private collaborations, many of which have led to groundbreaking responses to major social issues such as nutrition, education, HIV, or unacceptable mother and child mortality rates. They typically unite UNICEF departments, other IOs, units of national governments, local or regional UNICEF offices, and private-sector, civil-society, or expert organizations around a set of programmatic objectives.[27] While traditional alliances with civil-society organizations and the private sector often emerged bilaterally and in a decentralized manner, global program partnerships have relied on more expansive multistakeholder networks and interagency coordination. The Global Partnerships Database reveals that the entrepreneurship and diffusion of this type of collaboration is a relatively recent phenomenon for UNICEF (Figure 5.1). The database includes eighty-nine partnerships identified via desk research as global program partnerships in which UNICEF participates rather than the hundreds of decentralized collaborations with CSOs and private actors for which systematic data is not available.[28] This partnering modality is furthermore the most comparable with the global partnerships of other IOs examined in this book. Indeed, more than 70% of UNICEF's global program partnerships in the database involve collaboration with the WHO for a more concerted and high-impact action on issues related to child survival, health, and development.

What political factors contributed to the development and diffusion of global program partnerships across the portfolio of work of

---

[26] UNICEF 2012b.

[27] UNICEF 2009b; UNICEF Evaluation Office 2009.

[28] The Global Partnerships Database, Graduate Institute, Geneva is the source of data for all figures in this chapter; see Annex 1 on its methodology. The analytical term "global partnerships" used throughout this book refers, in the case of UNICEF, to the global program partnerships recorded in the database.

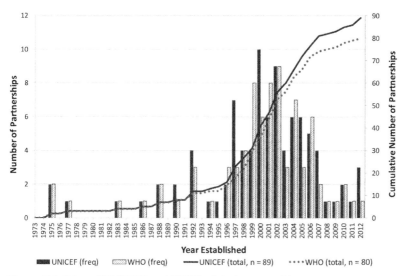

Figure 5.1 Rise of UNICEF and WHO global partnerships

UNICEF? Historically the organization participated in a limited number of global arrangements such as the Special Program for Research and Training in Tropical Diseases (1975), the Standing Committee on Nutrition (1977), or the Consultative Group on Early Childhood Care and Development (1983). These programs coordinated activities primarily among international agencies but also involved support from foundations and arrangements with the private sector or scientific institutions on research and product development.

The expansion of global program partnerships has picked up since the second half of the 1990s, a pattern that is similar for the WHO. Figure 5.2 provides information on the types of governance entrepreneurs behind this trend, keeping in mind that each partnership is typically convened by several actors.

The data confirms the theoretical expectation of leadership and facilitation by international agencies, which was also evident in the cases of the private-sector partnerships discussed earlier. The majority (87%) of the global program partnerships in which UNICEF participates are initiated by one or several IOs.[29] National governments have taken the lead in some 38% of these initiatives, which indicates the

---

[29] UNICEF 2009a, 2010; UNICEF Evaluation Office 2009.

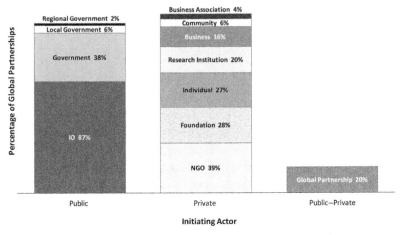

Figure 5.2 Initiating actors of UNICEF global program partnerships

substantial scope for autonomous agency initiative with respect to public–private collaborations. However, we shall see in subsequent sections and in more detailed cases that government backing (explicit or tacit), financing, and implementation efforts have been critical components in propelling the full entrepreneurship cycle of collaborative arrangements. As anticipated by the theoretical framework, tacit coalitions between agencies and supportive governments have been a core element of the dynamic change toward more integrative collaborative governance.

A variety of nonpublic actors have coinitiated global program partnerships with UNICEF. This is not surprising and reflects a long tradition with decentralized alliances and a degree of permeability between the different types of partnering modalities of the organization. NGOs have taken part in establishing a large share (39%) of the global program partnerships recorded in the Global Partnerships Database. Foundations have also been prominent players, often advancing advocacy on specific issues (for example, addressing problems related to nutrition, education, immunization, trachoma, polio, etc.) in co-founding 29% of these partnerships (Figure 5.2). UNICEF's singular focus on children and its capacity for decentralized innovation have provided for such external actors a field for governance entrepreneurship that is compelling in terms of its normative ends and possibilities to achieve measurable results (vaccines delivered, lives saved, education attained, etc.).[30] At the same time, given its historical experience with diverse alliances, the agency has greater capacity and autonomy for experimentation with external actors compared to most IOs, as stipulated by Propositions 3 and 4 of the theoretical framework.

For example, Rotary International, a transnational network of civic clubs, approached WHO and UNICEF in 1984 with the idea of supporting an immunization campaign to eradicate polio. It was prepared to provide financing and make available its network of volunteers. The then Executive Director of UNICEF James Grant responded with enthusiasm to the proposal, which corresponded closely to UNICEF's work on child survival and illustrates its greater leeway to develop external alliances. The WHO leadership, on the other hand, was more reticent and initially viewed the campaign as a diversion from its focus on horizontal approaches to healthcare strengthening. Following the intermediation of research institutes and the involvement of the U.S. Centers for Disease Control (CDC), the WHO ultimately endorsed and convened, in 1988, the Global Polio Eradication Initiative together with UNICEF.[31]

UNICEF's alliances with NGOs and the private sector have often provided experimentation for larger global partnerships. It was a localized fundraising campaign by the U.S. Fund for UNICEF and the Becton & Dickinson medical technology company that put on the agenda the issue of leveraging innovative technologies to expand tetanus immunization, which subsequently provided important support for the global Maternal Neonatal Tetanus Elimination Initiative. Nonetheless, corporate alliances have remained relatively separate from UNICEF's global program partnerships, of which only 16% are directly initiated by business actors (Figure 5.2).

UNICEF's growing engagement with global program partnerships has also responded to changes in its organizational environment. In the late 1990s, donor countries became increasingly interested in multistakeholder initiatives to tackle pressing social and development issues and their contestation by the antiglobalization movement. Failure to attain goals on improving child survival rates and well-being often became a major focus of concern over avoidable suffering and other

---

[30] Interview with Andrea Gay, United Nations Foundation, January 2008, Washington, DC.

[31] Telephone interview with Dr. Robert Scott, retired Chair, Rotary International Polio Plus Committee, November 2014.

social ills as economic globalization was gaining momentum. A case in point was mother-to-child transmission of HIV/AIDS. The stark reality of babies born with and orphaned by the virus amplified the urgency and the humanitarian dimension of the pandemic for political leaders in industrialized countries.[32] The creation of partnership platforms within the UN, such as the United Nations Foundation and UNFIP, further facilitated programmatic collaborations around issues of children's rights and development, with some 20% of the UNICEF global program partnerships being facilitated by such platforms (Figure 5.2).[33]

In sum, UNICEF's engagement in partnerships has taken a different path historically compared to the other four agencies examined in this book. It started with on-the-ground collaboration with NGOs, subsequently developed private-sector fundraising and cause-related corporate alliances, and more recently included global program partnerships with other IOs and multiple nonstate constituencies. The capacity for bottom-up and top-down innovation reflects, as anticipated by the theoretical discussion, the substantial scope for on-the-ground autonomous initiative of the agency, its relatively consensual mandate among principals, and substantial clustering of external actors with interest and resources for collaboration for children.

The case of a series of partnerships for maternal, newborn, and children's health illustrates these driving factors and the cycle of governance entrepreneurship through which global program partnerships have diffused and influenced the agenda for children, health and development.

Partnerships for Women and Children's Health

The Partnership on Maternal, Newborn and Child Health has successfully reached beyond national boundaries to raise political commitments for improved health and reduced mortality rates for mothers, newborns, and children. Together with sister initiatives – such as Countdown to 2015 and A Promise Renewed – partnerships have

---

[32] Interview with John Lange, former U.S. Ambassador to Botswana (1999–2002) and focal point for the UN Foundation global health diplomacy, July 2014. See also Szlezák 2012.

[33] See Chapter 3 and Andonova 2010.

pushed women's and children's issues up the international political agenda and instigated billions of dollars in funding.

The Partnership on Maternal, Newborn and Child Health was created in 2005 by pooling together the Partnership for Safe Motherhood and Newborn Health (hosted by the World Health Organization), the Healthy Newborn Partnership (hosted by Save the Children USA), and the Child Survival Partnership (hosted by UNICEF).

The core entrepreneurs of the integrated global program partnerships included the governments of Canada, India, and Ethiopia along with experts in UNICEF, WHO, and advocacy and professional organizations. They reacted to the slow progress in reducing maternal and early childhood mortality, which remained an orphan issue on domestic political agendas due to the neglect of the relation between the status of women and child welfare.[34] The new global partnership introduced an integrated health approach, the *continuum of medical care*, to treat women from pregnancy to birth and care for newborns and children in an effort to reduce avoidable mortality.

The partnership functions with a secretariat hosted by the WHO and its main innovation is to bring together actors that traditionally focus on different aspects of the continuum of care: health facilities, NGOs, professional associations of pediatrics, obstetricians, and nurses, developing country governments, communities, and public and private donors. The initiative advocates for an integrated focus on medical care and advances knowledge on specific interventions and practices that reduce the risk of maternal and childhood mortality. Its influence has materialized primarily through the rapid diffusion of partnership consultation across key developing countries and increased participation by different global constituencies, achieving a membership of 650 organizations by 2014.[35]

The diffusion of the integrated approach of women's and child care advocated by the Partnership for Maternal, Newborn and Child Health also benefited from coordination with related initiatives such

---

[34] Interview with Dr. Andres de Francisco, Executive Director a.i., Partnership for Maternal, Newborn and Child Health, WHO, November 2014, Geneva.

[35] The partnership works with twenty partner countries where prevalence of maternal and early childhood mortality is high. Approximately half of its membership consists of NGOs; the rest is divided across research and training organizations, professional associations, donors, IOs, and, most recently, private-sector entities. See Partnership for Maternal, Newborn and Child Health 2016.

as Countdown to 2015 and A Promise Renewed. While Countdown to 2015 tackles "coverage levels for health interventions proven to reduce maternal, newborn and child mortality,"[36] A Promise Renewed is a UNICEF initiative, which started from the premise of unacceptable suffering that is preventable:

Every year, 6.9 million children under five die from [disease] and other causes. 19,000 every day...Even crueler is the geography of fate. A child in sub-Saharan Africa is over 14 times more likely to die before reaching her or his 5th birthday than a child in the United States... Increasingly, innovations – new products, new technology and new applications of existing technology – help us reach the most disadvantaged communities and the most vulnerable children quickly and inexpensively.[37]

These partnerships elicit and monitor specific commitments to accelerate progress on newborn, child, and maternal survival, growing into a movement with commitments from 174 countries and more than 400 civil-society and faith-based organizations.[38]

The partnership experimentation, consolidation, networking, and diffusion across geographical boundaries and constituencies have succeeded in highlighting issues of women and children like no other single organization before. As anticipated theoretically, this process has propelled a cycle of dynamic and crucially important change leading to the institutionalization of new commitments and funding. In 2010, the UN Secretary-General presented UN Members with the Global Strategy for Women and Children's Health, which was not based on an intergovernmental mandate but on broad multistakeholder consultation while still involving governments and facilitated by the Partnership for Maternal, Newborn and Child Health. The multistakeholder initiative Every Woman, Every Child was created to rally support for the implementation of the Global Strategy. A new Global Financing Facility for women's, children's, and adolescents' health was announced at a high-level meeting during the 2014 UN General Assembly. Hosted by the World Bank, the facility would leverage some US$4 billion in new donor grants and World Bank concessional financing to support commitments to "improve reproductive, maternal, newborn, child and adolescent health."[39] This level

---

[36] Countdown to 2015 2015.
[37] Lake and Shah 2013, p. 1; A Promise Renewed 2016.
[38] Ibid.
[39] World Bank 2014.

of political commitment and institutionalization of resources for women and children became possible largely through the back door of governance entrepreneurship, diffusion, and expansion of partnership movements and their concerted interplay with intergovernmental decision making.

Institutionalization of UNICEF Partnerships

UNICEF was the first agency to adopt in 2001 specific *Guidelines and Manual for Working with the Business Community*, placing it ahead of the game compared to most IOs.[40] The advocacy identity of the agency and its sensitivity to legitimacy risks, associated with expanding corporate alliances, accounts for the early institutionalization of normative principles and due diligence process with respect to the private sector.[41] The former Executive Director of UNICEF Carol Bellamy is often quoted on the ethical dilemmas of corporate partnerships:

... [I]t is dangerous to assume that the goals of the private sector are somehow synonymous with those of the United Nations, because they most emphatically are not... But in coming together with the private sector, the UN must carefully, and constantly, appraise the relationship... without due diligence, one runs the risk of becoming associated with companies whose past records suggest that they may not be the best partners.[42]

The Guiding Manual introduces both positive and exclusionary criteria for cooperation with the private sector. UNICEF is to collaborate only with companies that have demonstrated a commitment to CSR. Companies engaged in arms production or trading, pornography, violation of UN sanctions, corruption or in violations of the International Code of Marketing of Breast-milk Substitutes are not eligible for collaboration; limitations are imposed for tobacco and alcohol companies. Partner selection is subject to a due diligence process and approval by a coordination committee overseen by the Executive Director. A written agreement specifies roles, responsibilities, and limitations on the use of UNICEF's name and emblem in compliance with the "no endorsement" and "no exclusivity" principles.[43]

---

[40] UNICEF 2001; Witte and Reinicke 2005; Interview with Gawaher Atif, Chief of Office/Secretary to the Advisory Board, UNFIP, June 2007, New York.
[41] Andonova and Carbonnier 2014.
[42] UNICEF 1999.
[43] UNICEF 2001.

As corporate alliances diversified and a substantial portfolio of global program partnerships developed, UNICEF took further steps toward institutionalizing its collaborative activities. This entailed considerable learning as the organization reflected on the evolving relations with a multitude of partners and the capacity to steer them.[44] At the request of the Executive Board, the organization commissioned a mapping document of collaborative activities and a Study of UNICEF Engagement in Global Program Partnerships (GPPs), conducted by the Evaluation Office. The evaluation characterizes these initiatives as significant innovation: "GPPs are expanding the current system of international cooperation from being primarily intergovernmental to being tripartite (state, business, and civil society)."[45] It also invites greater institutionalization within the intergovernmental mandate of UNICEF by recommending more hierarchical oversight from senior management and clarification of "what constitutes the authorizing environment" for partnerships and the adoption of explicit policies and baselines for evaluating results.[46]

In 2009, the Executive Board approved the UNICEF Strategic Framework for Partnerships and Collaborative Relationships, which formalizes the support by the intergovernmental body and the different modalities of partnerships, including with civil society organizations, corporate partners, knowledge partners, media, and global program partnerships. The document engages the characteristic for UNICEF discourse focused on "results for children" to establish the organizational commitment to public–private collaboration, stating that "Partnerships and collaborative relationships are the way of doing business. It has become clear that the UNICEF cooperative approach has enabled much better results for children than UNICEF could have achieved on its own."[47] The Strategic Framework explicitly situates collaborative activities within the normative intergovernmental framework of the Convention on the Rights of the Child. In 2012, the Executive Board of UNICEF endorsed the Organization's Report on the Implementation of the Strategic Framework for Partnerships and Collaborative Relationships, which goes even further in clarifying that partnership activity is anchored in the intergovernmental nature of the organization. It identifies several governance functions of partnerships

[44] UNICEF 2010.
[45] UNICEF Evaluation Office, 2009, p. 1.
[46] UNICEF Evaluation Office, 2009, p. 17.
[47] UNICEF 2009b, pp. 13–15.

in terms of policy advocacy, program implementation, the advancement of knowledge, and mobilization of resources and society for children's causes. Compared to the WHO and other organizations examined in this book, UNICEF's engagement in collaborative alliances has proceeded throughout its history. Nonetheless, these initiatives have followed comparable cycles of innovation from within and experimental adoption, expansion, and institutionalization grounded in the normative and task-specific objectives of the agency.

Partnerships for Global Health

WHO: Epistemic and Normative Authority

The WHO is often characterized as an expert organization par excellence.[48] The scope of its influence in international life has been rooted therefore in its epistemic authority and associated mandate to coordinate standards and norms related to health. Created in 1948, the agency built on a history of international cooperation for the containment of contagious disease and the adoption of sanitary standards as part of the International Sanitary Conferences (1851, 1938), the Office International d'Hygiène Publique (1907), the Pan American Sanitary Bureau, and the League of Nations Health Organization (1920). Unlike its predecessors, the WHO has a broad normative mandate in addition to strong scientific and technical specialization. Its normative work ranges from the elaboration of standards for medical technologies, products, diagnostics, and treatment procedures to taking the initiative in proposing conventions, agreements, and regulations on health matters. The WHO Constitution advances the objective of "attainment by all peoples of the highest possible level of health," whereby health is defined broadly as "state of complete physical, mental and social well-being and not merely the absence of disease or infirmity."[49]

The normative authority of the WHO and its position as a source of consensual knowledge underpin the scope of its agency autonomy and strategies in the governance of health, as anticipated by the theoretical framework.[50] The WHO relies on extensive collaboration

[48] Haas E. 1990; Cooper 1989.
[49] WHO Constitution, Article 1 and preamble.
[50] Haas E. 1990; Cooper 1989; Moon 2013; Szlezák 2012; Chorev 2012.

with professional organizations such as national health authorities, scientific institutes and laboratories and, in some instances, with private-sector researchers. The majority of WHO staff are medical professionals, who engage in research and in the coordination of information related to pandemics and health policy. Unlike UNICEF or the World Bank, the WHO does not have direct implementation functions; it works with countries through training and as "the key source of authoritative advice on health through the production of norms, standards and guidelines."[51]

Along with its substantial epistemic capacity and expert autonomy, the WHO also has a strong intergovernmental identity. The World Health Assembly convenes 194 states, represented primarily by their public health officials, each with an equal vote. The Assembly sets the overall policy direction of the organization and has the authority to adopt regulations and standards. It appoints the Director-General and elects the thirty-four members of the Executive Board, who are qualified health experts that represent member states, often seconded by ministries of health. With expert members serving on both the Executive Board and the General Assembly, this structure in effect reduces the informational asymmetry of the agency and makes the WHO structure potentially one of the most accountable and representative in the multilateral system.[52] Donor countries, in reality, still exercise significant informal influence via earmarked financing and coalescing behind specific agendas.

The coexistence of substantial expert autonomy and strong mechanisms for accountability to political and epistemic audiences has been overlooked by international relations theories of IOs. This is so because principal–agent approaches view organizational expertise largely as a source of opportunistic influence beyond the mandates of member states, while sociological theories tend to focus on how the internal workings of the bureaucracies shape policy choices. The theoretical framework of this book argues for a dynamic conceptualization of the relations between international bureaucracies, member states, and external audiences, precisely to capture the interplay between intergovernmental and organizational politics and the resulting implications for pathways to institutional change. Such

[51] WHO 2011b, A64/4, p. 8.
[52] Kiewiet and McCubbins 1991; Bawn 1995; Krehbiel 1992; Hawkins *et al.* 2006.

perspective is supported by a recent sociological study by Nitsan Chorev who characterizes the WHO as, on the one hand, dominated by geopolitics and on the other as an agency with substantial capacity "to restructure global ideational regimes that member states impose... to fit their own institutional culture [and to] protect their interests in the face of external demands."[53]

The capacity of the organization to negotiate the space between its expert mandate and the policy frames favored by principals has shaped its institutional approaches to health and, subsequently, its engagement with partnerships. In its early years, the WHO saw a prevalence of a biomedical perspective and the development of control programs against malaria, tuberculosis, and parasitic and viral diseases as well as nutrition and sanitation. In 1979, the then Director-General, Halfdan Mahler, led the work of the agency toward more horizontal strengthening of public health systems with the adoption of the declaration on *Health for All in the Year 2000*. Shortly after, however, a group of donor agencies proposed a modified focus on "selective" primary care that prioritized cost-effective interventions and attributed a growing role to agencies with implementation functions such as UNICEF and the World Bank.[54]

By the early 1990s, the WHO saw its authority diminished amid competition for turf with other agencies and by growing legitimacy challenges associated with the leadership of Director-General Hiroshi Nakajima. Its regular budget was frozen as a consequence of financial austerity in industrialized countries. A series of articles in the *British Medical Journal* accused the Nakajima administration of poor management, highlighting allegations of corruption, low staff morale, and inability to advance the WHO mandate.[55] The legitimacy challenge from epistemic communities coupled with policy scrutiny and budgetary pressures from principals produced a perfect organizational storm. The international system for managing health issues was ripe for change. Global partnership became a quintessential feature of that transformation.

---

[53] Chorev 2012, p. 2.
[54] Cassels, Smith and Burci 2014; Hoffman and Rottingen 2014; Chorev 2012; Brown, Cueto and Fee 2006.
[55] Godlee 1994, 1995; Bull and McNeill 2007; Yamey 2002a; Youde 2012.

Entrepreneurs of Partnerships for Health and Development

It was agency initiative with the support of political coalitions rather than intergovernmental design that led the WHO to develop more extensive collaboration with external actors. Gro Harlem Brundtland, who became WHO Director-General in 1998, worked actively to create institutional space for the entrepreneurship of global partnerships. The new leadership responded to pressures associated with resources and legitimacy by capitalizing on epistemic networks and selective support by principals. A cycle of dynamic institutional change was set in motion.

Collaborative initiatives became part of the agency strategy to assert its centrality in international health governance. This strategy responded to growing advocacy by a variety of actors about the relative neglect of diseases of the poor and their impact on development and reached out to other IOs and external actors to leverage resources and expertise. Brundtland spoke to the organization's principals in these terms:

As I took up this position in July 1998, I said that the global health agenda is too big for any one entity. To work effectively, we need to pull together. Since then, we have reached out to different parts of government, civil society, professional associations, the research community, foundations and bilateral agencies, encouraging intensive and focused partnerships.[56]

Access to health and development became the leading frame for the WHO's engagement in collaborative initiatives. Renowned as the Chair of the World Commission on Environment and Development (1983–1987), Brundtland was no stranger to reframing a global issue and its development implications. Collaboration with private actors on specific objectives was not entirely new for the WHO either (Figure 5.1). Since its early years, the organization had worked on disease-control programs such as malaria or tuberculosis treatment with the Rockefeller Foundation, the ICRC, and specialized NGOs, among others. For example, the Special Program for Research and Training in Tropical Diseases (TDR), established in 1975, is a notable example of a platform for collaboration between the WHO, UNDP, the World Bank, and UNICEF, which also involved collaboration with

---

[56] Brundtland 2001, A54/3, p. 4.

foundations, private companies, research institutes, and more recently with other partnerships on product development, drug donation, and funding.

The WHO leadership was nonetheless taking a risk in allowing more extensive collaboration with private actors. Unlike UNICEF's history of pragmatic alliances around operational objectives, the WHO had maintained a relation of caution and even distrust of the private sector. Dr. Adetokunbo Lucas, a former Head of TDR, characterizes the approach to the pharmaceutical sector as follows: "JCB [Joint Coordinating Board] kept a watchful eye on TDR's links with industry, assuring the sponsors and other interested parties that in all the contracts and joint activities, the public interest was well protected."[57] At the core of this tension is the WHO's identity and legitimacy as an expert and normative organization. Many within the agency and among its external audiences share the view that it should avoid close relations with entities that may be also the subjects of its standard-setting work.[58] Public–private collaboration could become associated with real or perceived conflicts of interest and thus undermine the credibility of the agency's normative authority.

The WHO leadership justified its strategy, as had other organizational entrepreneurs discussed in earlier chapters, as a response to multiple sources of internal and external pressures and situated it within the broader organizational mandate. Three main lines of discourse and justification emerge in agency documents. First, the global health agenda was no longer just about health. Health was recognized as essential for development, and a wide array of actors had a role to play in advancing that nexus. Second, access to medicines and to innovative diagnostics and treatment had become an urgent imperative with a humanitarian face. The WHO required new institutional mechanisms to engage both the private sector as a source of innovation but also advocacy actors, affected communities, and states. Third, the WHO recognized that international health had been globalized, whereby an increasing number and variety of organizations were

---

[57] Lucas 2002, p. 22. See Reich 2002; Muraskin 1998, 2002, on approach to the private sector.
[58] Interview with Ilona Kickbusch, Director Global Health Program, Graduate Institute, October 2014, Geneva. See also Buse and Walt 2002; Reich 2002; Roberts, Breitenstein and Roberts 2002.

claiming governance roles.[59] Partnerships became part of the strategy
for the WHO to claim centrality in the new *global* governance of
health.

The Corporate Strategy for the WHO Secretariat, which Brundtland
presented to the Executive Board, centered on the nexus between
health, development, and new strategic interventions on specific health
conditions, including through public–private partnerships. It advanced
the position that in order for the WHO to "respond effectively to a
changing international environment," the organization needed to
adopt "a broader approach to health within the context of human
developments, humanitarian action and human rights, focusing particularly on the links between health and poverty reduction. . ."[60] The
organizational discourse referred to the emerging informal norms on
access to medicines as essential for the fulfillment of the broad mandate
of the WHO, as well as of basic human rights and development.[61] The
advocacy movement of the 1990s had placed the HIV/AIDS pandemic
and its development and humanitarian implications at the center of the
international agenda. The creation of UNAIDS as a new agency with a
collaborative structure was largely interpreted as a no-confidence vote
for the WHO. The contestation of the Agreement on Trade-Related
Aspects of Intellectual Property Rights (TRIPS), which implied longer
restrictions to lifesaving technologies, further heightened the urgency
of finding new institutional solutions and the kind of actors that need
to be involved therein.[62] Brundtland argued that the WHO needed to
respond to new health imperatives more quickly to bring industry to
bear as well as affected communities. This was not possible to accom-
plish within the standard institutional structure because of its arms-
length relation with external actors. Partnerships became platforms

---

[59] These arguments transpire in many reports of the WHO Secretariat to the
Executive Board and World Health Assembly. See Brundtland 2001; WHO
1999a, 1999b, 1999c, 1999d (EB105/3; EB105/8; A52/6; A52/26); WHO
2000a, 2000b (EB 107/7; EB 105/R11). I am also grateful for the discussion on
these processes with Gian Luca Burci, Legal Counsel, WHO, October 2014,
Geneva. See also Hanrieder 2015.
[60] WHO 1999a; EB105/3, p. 3.
[61] Hein and Moon 2013; Clapham *et al.* 2009.
[62] See, among others, Busby 2010; Hein, Bartsch and Kohlmorgen 2007; Bartsch
and Kohlmorgen 2007; Sell 2003; Sell and Prakash 2004; Morin 2011; Lee,
Buse and Fustukian 2002; Lee 2003; Szlezák 2012; Hein and Moon 2013;
Youde 2012.

through which more dynamic collaboration with industry, funders, and all relevant communities could be tested.

The WHO leadership not only took the initiative but also actively expanded the organizational capacity for institutional change, as anticipated by Proposition 3 of the theoretical framework, by tapping into internal and external epistemic networks.[63] Tore Godal, who was a former head of TDR and a prominent public health figure from Norway, became Brundtland's cabinet adviser and an influential proponent of global partnerships. A study by Jon Lidén documents the experience, ideas, and epistemic networks through which Godal facilitated major partnerships such as the Medicines for Malaria Ventures and, later on, the Global Alliance for Vaccines and Immunization (GAVI). According to Lidén:

> Brundtland and the people around her had already been strongly influenced by the thinking of the authors of the 1993 World Development Report, such as Dean Jameson and Chris Murray, as well as by the (then) head of Mexico's National Institute of Public Health, Julio Frenk, the director of the Health Economics and Financing Program at the London School of Hygiene & Tropical Medicine, Anne Mills; and (then) Harvard professor Jeffrey Sachs.[64]

The Commission on Macroeconomics and Health, established by WHO and chaired by Professor Jeffery Sachs, played a particularly prominent role in advancing scientific backing and advocacy for health as a cornerstone to economic development. The Commission's report argued for political attention and financing for a set of diseases, in particular HIV/AIDS, malaria, tuberculosis, and childhood infections preventable by vaccination, which were "responsible for a high proportion of the health deficit" and required urgent scaling up of action.[65]

As anticipated by the theoretical framework on dynamic institutional change, the relative autonomy and epistemic capacity of the agency, coupled with strong leadership at the top, favored a

---

[63] See the seminal work of Ernst Haas 1990 on WHO's capacity for learning and change through epistemic networks.

[64] Lidén 2013, p. 17. Jon Lidén's study presents rich, firsthand evidence and discussion on the variety of coalitions, actors, and individuals that engaged in the entrepreneurship of some of the best-known global partnerships.

[65] Commission on Macroeconomics and Health 2001, p. 16.

strategy for learning and institutional experimentation in response to internal pressures on resources and legitimacy and external turbulence associated with the rising prominence of new actors and norms. Governments and national experts in health and development played central roles in the political coalitions for new global health initiatives. Widespread concerns over legitimacy risks associated with private-sector interactions required substantial communication with both the Executive Board and the Health Assembly. Dr. Brundtland had to strategize to overcome the traditional split between those who emphasized primary health care and the normative mandate of the organization and those advocating high-impact interventions on specific diseases. She undertook both. Professor Ilona Kickbusch, a public health and governance expert, pointed out in an interview: "Brundtland had a certain amount of trust and credibility. With these credentials behind her, she had the reputation to convene political and epistemic support for new governance and public–private partnerships."[66] As the WHO opened up more to public–private partnerships, the Director-General nonetheless advanced the agency's normative work and decisively took on the tobacco industry with the groundbreaking adoption of the Framework Convention on Tobacco Control.

Diffusion of Partnerships for Health

Global partnerships have replicated and diffused rapidly since the 1990s, influencing significantly the structure of global health governance (Figure 5.1).[67] Figure 5.3, which maps the initiating actors behind the growth in numbers, shows that majority of partnerships are initiated by the WHO and other IOs, along with other entrepreneurial actors. Partnerships became platforms not only to reinvent relations with nonstate actors but also to coordinate strategies among international agencies. Organizational entrepreneurs such as Tore Godal (WHO) and Richard Feacheim (World Bank) purposely sought to move away from bureaucratic turf battles toward a "systems-based" and "problem-based" approach in the facilitation of some of the early and highly influential partnerships such as GAVI and the

---

[66] Interview with Ilona Kickbusch, Director Global Health Program, Graduate Institute, October 2014, Geneva.
[67] See also studies by Widdus and White 2004; Lidén 2013, Bull and McNeill 2007; Buse and Harmer 2004; Buse and Tanaka 2011; Widdus 2001.

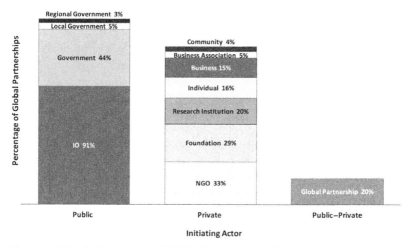

Figure 5.3 Initiating actors of WHO global partnerships

Global Fund.[68] However, the dramatic expansion of partnerships for health in number, size, reach, and resources would not have been possible without the substantial support of governments and private foundations, working in broad coalitions with NGOs, research organizations, and business entities (Figure 5.3).

Governments took initiative in some 44% of the partnerships in the WHO portfolio. The influence of the development and finance agencies of donor countries with active agendas in global health and development such as the UK, Norway, the U.S., and France was particularly palpable both politically and through substantial financing. Increasingly, emerging and developing countries such as Brazil, China, Chile, India, Russia, and Ethiopia have also supported the diffusion of partnership initiatives with financial support and leadership.[69] While donor governments have most often backed initiating coalitions, the uptake of partnerships by developing countries has been the key to their practical implementation and hence for the diffusion and legitimacy of this model of governance. At the heyday of the expansion of global partnerships, Brundtland emphasized in a speech at the World Health Assembly the different but equally essential roles of donors and

---

[68] Lidén 2013, p. 38; Bull and McNeill (2007) underline the high-level coordination by the heads of the WHO (Gro Harlem Brundtland), the World Bank (James Wolfensohn), and UNICEF (Carol Bellamy) in the creation of GAVI.

[69] The Global Partnership Database 2015.

implementing countries in realizing new mechanisms in health governance: "Developing country governments **are** in the lead, changing their
spending to give higher priority to their people's health. But the bulk of
the new resources required must come from the wealthy world."[70]

Several studies have told the story of the political struggles and
coalitions that led to the creation of the Global Fund for HIV/AIDS,
Tuberculosis and Malaria. This partnership has been particularly influential in health governance through the sheer increase of resources that
it has made available to developing country governments and societies
for tackling these diseases and for the impact achieved.[71] A detailed
account by Jon Lidén on the first round of Global Fund financing
illustrates vividly its founding as a governance experiment backed by
donor governments and the critical role of developing countries for
implementation, diffusion, and evolving institutional design:

> The developing-country governments felt rather bemused by all this activity
> supposedly on their behalf... By February, the first call for applications had
> been issued. And instead of a few dozen envelopes arriving in response to the
> call, the small Global Fund secretariat had to clear out a whole office to stack
> the hundreds of applications – many several folders thick – it received in
> response. In April, the first $550 million were awarded for 'Round 1', and by
> December, the first three grant agreements had been signed and disbursement
> had been readied for Haiti, Ghana and Tanzania...What the Global Fund
> basically said to about 145 eligible countries was 'let us know what it will
> take to deal with these pandemics and we will see if we can finance it.' The
> demand-driven funding model did two major things to the world of global
> health and development assistance: it shifted the attention from the relatively
> abstract theoretical 'needs' figures...to a measure of a much more concrete
> 'fundable demand'; and it created a more real and feasible case for raising the
> necessary funding.[72]

This case, similar to other partnerships examined in the book, illustrates how moderate divergence of state preferences with respect to the
means of achieving global objectives can provide both incentives and
space for entrepreneurial coalitions of new governance. Over time, the
institutional structure of the Global Fund evolved through the process
of learning by doing and through the diffusion of collaborative

---

[70] Brundtland 2001, A54/3, p. 14. Emphasis in the original.
[71] Hein, Bartsch and Kohlmorgen 2007; Szlezák 2012; Youde 2012; Bartsch 2007;
Jönsson 2010.
[72] Lidén 2013, p. 39.

practices across states and society at the global and domestic levels. Subsequently, it was recognized as a legally incorporated public–private institution with a substantial degree of autonomy and resources, setting an important organizational precedent in international governance.

Finally, Figure 5.3 also provides evidence of the substantial role of nonstate actors in the initiation and diffusion of partnerships for health, which could be expected given the diversity of advocacy and expert and private actors in the organization's environment that pushed for the search for new governance solutions. In addition to research institutes, which are a traditional constituency of WHO and participated in the creation of some 20% of health partnerships, NGOs have taken an active role in leading some 33% of them. This speaks of the close collaboration between the WHO and UNICEF on many partnerships related to children's health but also more broadly on the rising role of advocacy in the international health agenda.[73] Transnational networks such as the Medecins Sans Frontieres, Save the Children, Care, Oxfam, Rotary International, the International Federation of the Red Cross and Red Crescent Societies (IFRC), the American Red Cross, and religious organizations have participated in the convening of partnerships on a range of issues – from access to treatment to vaccination, disease eradication, and humanitarian coordination. The leading role of issue-specific movements – for example, the International Federation of Anti-Leprosy Associations, the Iodine Network, Sight and Life, International Agency for the Prevention of Blindness, or the International Water and Sanitation Centre – also speaks of the substantial advocacy component in partnerships for health.

In comparison to NGOs, business entities have been initiating actors for just 15% of the WHO collaborative initiatives in the database, primarily in cases when drug donation or specific technology is the central component of collaboration. While many large health partnerships target the behavior of the private sector and involve its representation through business associations, the limited role of commercial companies in initiating coalitions reflects on the one hand their aversion to the risks of public commitments and on the other hand WHO's tradition of distancing and caution. This is despite the fact that some

[73] Hein and Moon 2013; Busby 2010; Sikkink 1986; Bartsch and Kohlmorgen 2007; McCoy and Hilson 2009; Morin 2011.

partnerships such as Roll Back Malaria were devised to provide separate platforms to bring business actors to the table, something the WHO could not do within its traditional structure. As we shall see later, despite their limited role in the foundation of global partnerships, business actors have supported financially, including through drug donation, a substantial share (40%) of partnerships for children and health (Figure 5.7).

Foundations have coinitiated about a third (29%) of the WHO partnerships directly (Figure 5.3). Prior to the 1990s, private and charitable foundations such as Rockefeller or Edna McConnell Clark Foundation (Clark Foundation) influenced public health chiefly by supporting research and product development. Global partnerships have provided venues for more direct impact on the health agenda through foundation-led advocacy and partnership programs for intervention on specific issues. The size of foundation financing has changed as well, particularly with the significant impact of the Bill and Melinda Gates Foundation as the largest private advocate and financier for global health.[74]

The cases of the International Trachoma Initiative and its sister partnership, the WHO–led Alliance for the Elimination of Blinding Trachoma by 2020, illustrate the evolving role of a multitude of private, public, advocacy, and epistemic actors in the entrepreneurship and broad diffusions of partnerships for access to treatment and eradication of diseases. The Clark Foundation had supported research on tropical diseases for decades including with WHO programs when it created, along with the pharmaceutical company Pfizer, the International Trachoma Initiative in 1998. Trachoma is a bacterial infection leading to millions of cases of blindness in tropical regions. The partnership was motivated by an opportunity to leverage a grant of US$3.2 million from the Clark Foundation matched by equal funding from Pfizer, plus the company's commitment to donate the Zithromax antibiotic, worth approximately US$60 million, for the treatment of the disease.[75] The Expert Committee, which advises the work of the International Trachoma Initiative, included prominent medical and public

---

[74] Birn 2014; Muraskin 1998; Bull and McNeill 2007; Owen, Lister and Stansfield 2009.
[75] See an excellent case analysis of the partnership by Barrett, Austin and McCarthy 2002, p. 56.

health professionals from research institutes and universities, as well as from the WHO and NGOs.

The International Trachoma Initiative started with an experimental pilot project in Morocco before it expanded its work to twenty-nine countries.[76] It also supports the work of the WHO Alliance for the Elimination of Blinding Trachoma by 2020 by advancing a specific component of the WHO–recommended SAFE strategy for trachoma control (surgery, antibiotic treatment, facial cleanliness, and environmental improvement). As a measure of success, Morocco was the first country to be certified as trachoma-free by the WHO.

The entrepreneurship and expansion of the International Trachoma Initiative and the Alliance for the Elimination of Blinding Trachoma are interesting examples because they capture several patterns of partnership diffusion in the governance of health. First, global health partnerships are typically convened by *diverse* networks of medical experts, advocacy organizations, and public and private organizations from developed and developing countries, in addition to the funding partners. Second, partnerships for health tend to diffuse quickly across jurisdictions and across relevant actors. Qualitative information from the Global Partnerships Database indicates that the majority of health partnerships aim to reach all countries where a particular health problem is prevalent, and their success depends on broad and meaningful participation.[77] While some sixteen organizations participated in the 1996 convening of the Global Alliance for the Elimination of Trachoma, its 2013 meeting gathered some seventy-two partners, with a large representation from scientific institutes and developing countries.[78] The International Trachoma Initiative expanded from its core initiating coalition to work with some forty-four formal partners as of 2014, aiming to reach forty-two of the fifty-nine countries where the disease is considered endemic.[79] The majority of WHO partnerships have adopted deliberate strategies of widening participation, including through networks of local implementation and through partners' forums and constituency representation.

---

[76] International Trachoma Initiative 2015.
[77] Global Partnerships Database 2016.
[78] WHO 2013.
[79] See International Coalition for Trachoma Control 2016; International Trachoma Initiative 2015.

Third, and as anticipated by the life cycle of institutional change, successful experimentation with new governance initiatives has been important for the replication and diffusion of the partnership model. The results of the International Trachoma Initiative pilot project in Morocco were closely followed by the expert committee and policy institutions to inform the development and expansion of the partnerships and of the Global Alliance for the Elimination of Trachoma. Similarly, the early success of other initiatives such as the Stop TB Partnership (launched in 1998) to improve the access and effectiveness of treatment for multi–drug-resistant tuberculosis (TB) led to its rapid expansion by the year 2000. In 2001, the Global Drug Facility (GDF) for TB was created as a new partnership to support the implementation of the Stop TB initiative, followed by even larger financial facilities such as the Global Fund and the International Drug Purchase Facility (UNITAID).[80] According to the website of the Stop TB partnership, by 2014, it had "more than 1200 partners who are a collective force transforming the fight against TB in more than 100 countries. They include NGOs, civil society and community groups, international and technical organizations, government programs, research and funding agencies, foundations and the private sector."[81] Over time, partnerships for health grew not only in number but also horizontally across geographies and constituencies and through networks of interplay with each other and with public policy and scientific institutions. They became a method of health governance.

Institutionalization

The institutionalization of partnerships within the intergovernmental structure of the WHO followed the cycle of their experimentation and diffusion. The WHO has often taken on the hosting of partnership secretariats and programs to assert its organizational centrality, while UNICEF, by contrast, has assumed diverse roles in partnerships depending on the specific functionality that helps reach children. At the same time, the engagement of the WHO with partnerships has remained much more critically debated than has been the case for UNICEF, the World Bank, or UNEP. Greater contestation and deliberation thus became an important element in the reverse

[80] Matiru and Ryan 2007, p. 1.
[81] See Stop TB Partnership 2016.

institutionalization of WHO partnerships, which followed their development by entrepreneurial coalitions and *de facto* consolidation in the governance of health.

Critical questions about the accountability of partnerships and institutional implications came from external audiences and subsequently from within the organization. Many NGOs advocating for attention to specific diseases and access to medicines have found greater influence through partnerships.[82] Yet other groups felt that the WHO has become too close to the private sector. The People's Health Movement, which convenes several health advocacy networks, charges that funding from private sources and foundations gives "undue importance to private profit-making bodies" with insufficient safeguards for the public interest. The World Alliance for Breastfeeding Action similarly qualifies partnerships as the deregulation of health and legitimation of big business.[83] The movement has also focused on the invitation of Bill Gates and Melinda Gates as speakers at the World Health Assembly as a lightning rod to question how the large share of Gates Foundation contributions to the annual budget of the WHO might exert undue influence on public priorities and on the accountability of the organization to member states versus an unelected private actor.[84]

Members of the scientific community, a critically important audience for the WHO, have raised questions about potential contradictions between the standard-setting functions of the agency and collaboration with the private sector, as well as about the influence of private funders and the crowding of the health agenda. The work of Kent Buse and his colleagues, for example, has made an important contribution in analyzing partnerships for health and raising questions about uneven participation by developing countries in the convening of partnerships and, more broadly, about their legitimacy and potential contradictions related to private influence on public health priorities.[85] Many of these questions have resonated within the WHO, including the agency and some of its member states. An article by the then WHO Legal Counsel

---

[82] Hein and Moon 2013.
[83] People's Health Movement 2014; World Alliance for Breastfeeding Action 2011, p. 1.
[84] People's Health Movement 2014.
[85] Buse 2004; Buse and Walt 2002; Buse and Harmer 2004; Buse and Tanaka 2011. See also Richter 2004; Yamey 2002b, 2004; Storeng 2014; Asante and Zwi 2007; Van de Pas and Schaik 2014.

Gian Luca Burci summarizes eloquently the dilemmas associated with the growing prominence of partnerships for health:

It has been felt that, besides financial support, involvement of the private sector brings a business mindset focused on strategic planning, driving for results and targeted progress evaluation, which may benefit the activities of the partnership. At the same time, in view of the essentially public nature of the functions of partnerships and their direct impact on corporate interests, the issue of management of conflicts of interest could not be ignored.[86]

This discussion reveals that in the structure of the WHO, multiple "fire alarms" can be activated to demand accountability and clarification on how the organization is managing the interface between its public, normative purpose and private involvement through partnerships. It shows that the organization is beholden to multiple audiences including a strong activist movement, a professional epistemic community, and internal procedures that staff and member states can activate. The institutionalization of global partnerships, therefore, required in this case stronger procedural measures to define channels of internal accountability as well as a broadly deliberative process on the nature of institutionalization as part of the World Health Assembly.

Responding to such organizational concerns, the then Director-General, Margaret Chan, introduced the issue of partnership governance and institutional fit to the Executive Board in 2008. One important issue for the Secretariat and for a number of member states was the *de facto* existence of "parallel systems of governance" or "dual accountability," whereby the secretariats of hosted partnerships are directly accountable to their hybrid management boards and at the same time to the Director-General of the WHO and its intergovernmental bodies. The organization made the case that the priority of WHO rules and system of accountability needed to be made more explicit, especially for hosted initiatives. In addition, the transaction costs associated with multiplicity of partnerships had compounded both for the WHO and for implementing countries, thus requiring greater rationalization and capacity.[87] The reverse nature of partnership institutionalization by

---

[86] Burci 2009, p. 371.
[87] Burci 2009; Interview with Isa Matta, Legal Department, WHO, November 2014; Geneva; Schäferhoff 2014. A study by Rosenberg *et al.* (2010, pp. 26–28) illustrates how, for example, some thirty-five organizational players worked on HIV/AIDS in Tanzania in 2004, including NGOs, IOs, civil society organizations, donor agencies, global partnerships, and private associations.

intergovernmental bodies, *after* their facilitation from within the agency, and the organizational imperatives behind the processes are evident in the commentary of Isa Matta of the WHO Legal Department:

Initially, partnerships were new, experimental structures; the WHO was gaining experience with them. Over time, it became clear that some public–private partnerships control substantial funds and have visible activities. There were concerns that partnerships are indirectly influencing the WHO agenda, in a way that may not be entirely aligned with the priorities of member states. An even greater concern is that by interpreting WHO norms or standards in their implementation practices, public–private partnerships may be shaping the normative work of the organization, which is vested strictly within the WHO and should not be influenced by private actors.[88]

The agency actively engaged its bodies of principals to justify greater oversight over partnerships and to address such organizational concerns. Similarly to other processes of reverse institutionalization documented in this book, the Secretariat presented a series of reports informing the Executive Board and the World Health Assembly on different types of partnership arrangements.[89] As in the case of UNICEF's institutionalization of global program partnerships, the WHO reports affirmed the partnership outcomes for health: "Overall, global health partnerships have contributed much. Significant outcomes include enhanced predictability of large-scale, new funding; introduction of new ways of working, with greater participation of civil society and the private sector; consensus and coordination on key technical and operational strategies, with accelerated progress in their implementation; support for global public goods; economies of scale; and increased innovation."[90] They also highlighted the concerns that the process of institutionalization was seeking to address, including "competing accountabilities, high transaction costs for member states due to having to serve on multiple boards, and the need to consider more consistent policy positions across partnerships" as well as "increasing, and at times unpredictable, demands for the organization to scale up the provision of technical support to countries in response to rapidly increasing partnership financing."[91]

---

[88] Interview with Isa Matta, Legal Department, WHO, November 2014, Geneva.
[89] WHO 2007 (EB122/19), WHO 2008a, 2008b (EB123/6, EB123/6 Add. 1), WHO 2009a, 2009b (EB124/23, A62/39); WHO 2010a (A63/44); WHO 2011a (EB130/5 Add.4); WHO 2012 (EB132/INF./2).
[90] WHO 2007 (EB122/19), p. 2.
[91] WHO 2007 (EB 122/19), p. 3.

In 2009, the Secretariat proposed Draft Policy Guidelines for consideration by the Executive Board and the World Health Assembly.[92] Subsequently, World Health Assembly resolution WHA63.10 titled *Partnerships* endorsed the *Policy on WHO's Engagement with Global Health Partnerships and Hosting Arrangements*. The policy envisages that the activities of hosted partnerships will be consistent with WHO policies, rules, and accountability framework and that partnerships are responsible for mobilizing resources to cover the costs of their own secretariats and related activities. It furthermore makes explicit that "public health goals take precedence over the special interests of the participants" and outlines a decision tree for assessing the criteria and fit for WHO engagement.[93] The resolution, moreover, entails elements of explicit intergovernmental endorsement and legitimation by requesting the Director-General to:

...continue collaboration with concerned organizations of the United Nations system, international development partners, international financial institutions, nongovernmental organizations, representatives of communities affected by diseases, and private-sector entities in implementing the Medium-term strategic plan 2008–2013 in order to advance the global health agenda contained in the Eleventh General Program of Work, 2006–2015.[94]

The World Health Assembly Resolution 63.10 completed an important step in the institutionalization process of public–private initiatives within the intergovernmental mandate of the organization. However, the debate on cooperation between the WHO and nonstate actors did not end there. The issue of public–private cooperation became part of the broader organizational reform undertaken between 2011 and 2015. The reform sought to delineate the leading functions of the WHO in health governance and to increase the control by the World Health Assembly over voluntary and heavily earmarked financing, the share of which has increased progressively from about 45% of the organization's budget compared to assessed financing in the mid-1990s to more than 75% by 2013, of which some 25% came from nonstate sources.[95] A draft Framework of Engagement with Non-State Actors

---

[92] See WHO 2009a (EB124/23) and WHO2009b (A62/39).
[93] WHO 2010b, WHA63/2010/REC/1.
[94] WHO 2010b; WHA63/2010/REC/1, p. 17.
[95] WHO 2006a (WHO/PRP/06.1); WHO 2014c; WHO 2014b (A67/43, pp. 5–6 for 2013 calculations).

was included in the package of institutional reforms the Secretariat submitted to the World Health Assembly in 2014.[96] The twenty-six-page document, which is the most extensive treatment on the subject in the multilateral system, outlines four separate sets of operational procedures to guide the work of the organization with NGOs, private-sector entities, philanthropic foundations, and academic institutions, respectively. In addition, a new Committee of the Executive Board provides another tier of supervision charged with regular reporting and review of collaborative arrangements. In 2016, the World Health Assembly adopted in resolution WHA 69.10 the final text of the Framework on Engagement with Non-State Actors.[97] Global partnerships have thus evolved from experimental initiatives to established and universally recognized institutional practice in the WHO. But they are not taken for granted; their outcomes and steering have been debated and institutionalized in ways that seek to reconcile a sensitive public mandate with the governance of a truly multistakeholder issue domain.

Partnership Outcomes for Children and Health

Partnerships have contributed some striking results on a broad range of issues related to health and children. The number of people receiving antiretroviral therapy for HIV/AIDS increased exponentially from about 100,000 in 2003 to approximately 17 million in 2015, of which approximately 13 million live in low- and middle-income countries.[98] By 2014, the cost of first-line antiretroviral therapy in low- and middle-income countries had been reduced to US$100 per person per year for first-line formulations from approximately US$10,000 per person per year in these same countries in the mid-1990s.[99] The number of people affected by trachoma fell from some 360 million cases in 1985 to an estimated 80 million in 2006.[100] According to the WHO, in 2015 alone, "... more than 185,000 people received surgical treatment for advanced disease, and 56 million people were treated with antibiotics

---

[96] WHO 2014a (A67/6).).
[97] WHO 2016b, WHA69/2016/REC/1.
[98] See Asante and Zwi 2007, p. 178, for 1990 figures; and UNAIDS 2016a, 2016b, pp. 1–2.
[99] UNAIDS 2013b, 2015.
[100] See WHO 2006b.

for trachoma."[101] GAVI reported support for the immunization of 580 million additional children in seventy-seven countries by 2013, contributing to the prevention of 8 million additional deaths from infectious disease.[102] Polio has been eradicated in most endemic countries, while strong commitment remains to tackle the remaining pockets of the disease in difficult contexts such as Nigeria, Cameroon, Pakistan, Afghanistan, and Somalia. The urgent need to improve the continuum of care for maternal, neonatal, child, and adolescent health gained political prominence and new institutional and financial support.

Such dramatic outcomes of partnership activity, on a scale unprecedented in other issue areas, align with the theoretical expectation that the organizational fields of UNICEF and WHO exemplify a most likely arena for new hybrid initiatives. It also prompts several questions: What are the broader outcomes of partnerships, beyond the most visible cases that have been at the center of public and scholarly attention? What is the range of issues on which collaborative initiatives have focused? What governance instruments have they leveraged and what kind of financial partners have supported them? The Global Partnerships Database allows us to discern these larger patterns. The analysis of these patterns links to the theoretical discussion and inquires how expertise of IOs and the entrepreneurial coalitions that facilitated collaborative initiatives have shaped their outcomes. It focuses primarily on the subset of partnerships that are coordinated between UNICEF and WHO, which cover more than 70% of the initiatives in the portfolio of each agency, while also considering the rest of the sample to illuminate partnership interventions that may be specific to each agency.

The Global Partnerships Database reveals that public–private collaboration has targeted a much broader spectrum of issues than recognized in the current literature (Figures 5.4 and 5.5).[103] To be sure, issues such as HIV/AIDS, malaria, and tuberculosis, around which the nexus between health, development, and human rights was focalized, have drawn a lot of partnership activity. Similarly, a

---

[101] WHO 2016.

[102] GAVI 2015, p. 9.

[103] The issue focus of partnerships is coded based on the language of their mission statements or comparable documents. A single partnership can identify one or several related issues as primary foci.

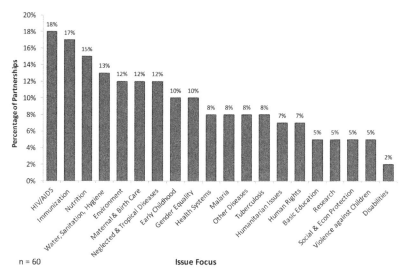

Figure 5.4 Issue focus of WHO and UNICEF joint global partnerships

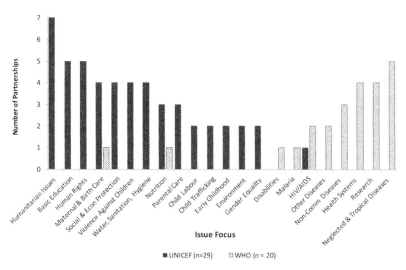

Figure 5.5 Issue focus of UNICEF and WHO partnerships that are not coordinated across the two organizations

large number of immunization partnerships are associated with the desire of public and private entrepreneurs to contribute to compelling and measurable results in health, with a clear impact on preventing disability and premature mortality of children.[104] Beyond these often-cited areas of collaborative activity, however, partnerships have targeted a wide range of conditions underpinning health and child survival such as nutrition, water and sanitation, environmental factors, maternity and birth, early childhood care, and gender equality (Figure 5.4). Such concerns lie precisely in the intersection between core programs of UNICEF and the WHO while also responding, as discussed earlier, to wide-ranging advocacy by NGOs and private actors.

Furthermore, the qualitative analysis behind the data reveals a considerable diversity of issues tackled within the categories of Figure 5.4. In relation to nutrition, for example, some partnerships focus on specific micronutrients such as iodine, vitamin A, vitamin D, or iron and their impact on health; others take cross-cutting approaches to nutrition as an essential condition for maternal health, child survival, or better schooling and educational attainment. Partnerships that advance immunization often correspond to long-standing programs of UNICEF and the WHO related to measles, tuberculosis, neonatal tetanus, meningitis, intestinal parasites, cholera prevention, polio, and so on. For many of these programs, public–private collaboration has facilitated access to new products and technologies through the private sector, greater reach through NGO networks, and fundraising by charitable foundations to stimulate improved vaccination coverage. In some instances, nonstate entrepreneurs, such as the Bill and Melinda Gates Foundation or Rotary International, have actively shaped the agenda on immunization by advancing initiatives respectively for new and underused vaccines (GAVI) and polio eradication.

The tendency of governance entrepreneurs to prioritize issues in which concrete and measurable improvements for children and health could be achieved has resulted in a greater share of disease-specific partnerships compared to those that support the strengthening of

---

[104] Interviews with Andrea Gay, United Nations Foundation, January 2008, Washington, DC; and with Eelco Szabó, Director, Legal Department, GAVI, November 2014, Geneva.

health systems. This is a common critique in the health literature, as the tension between disease-focused and health systems–focused intervention remains highly relevant in the organizational context of the WHO. However, implementation challenges have persuaded an increasing number of partnerships, such as the Global Fund and GAVI, to introduce health systems–strengthening components. GAVI's decision to direct 15 to 25% of its annual expenditure for health systems strengthening reflected the realization that if there was no adequate system to administer the vaccines, the initiative was unlikely to achieve adequate coverage rates; its objective could fail.[105] Nonetheless, the question of the appropriateness and adequacy of systems-strengthening programs remained intensely debated both within the partnership and its donor and epistemic communities.[106]

If we consider the issue focus of the subset of partnerships that are not shared across WHO and UNICEF (Figure 5.5), we see increasing attention to health systems in WHO partnerships in particular and even greater diversity of issues UNICEF advances in collaboration with external partners, including humanitarianism, children's rights, education, and the social and economic protection of children.[107]

In sum, the systematic data analysis reveals that the reality of partnering is considerably more diverse than recognized in the debates focused on large partnership institutions. WHO and UNICEF have facilitated initiatives that reflect their extensive mandates and approaches. Public–private collaboration has touched many different conditions, rights, and interventions that pertain to the well-being of children and to health.

The governance instruments of global partnerships shed light on the question of *how* they approach problems related to children and health. Figure 5.6 shows that the large majority of partnerships (92%) that involve both the WHO and UNICEF use information to influence the governance of specific issues. Advocacy, capacity building, and monitoring also play important roles in advancing outcomes for children and health, keeping in perspective that typically a single

[105] Interview with Eelco Szabó, Director, Legal Department, GAVI, November 2014, Geneva.
[106] Storeng 2014.
[107] Because a small share of global partnerships in the WHO and UNICEF portfolios are not shared across the two organizations, the data in Figure 5.4 is presented in absolute numbers rather than as a percentage of a small sample.

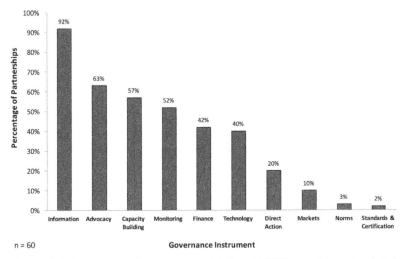

Figure 5.6 Governance instruments of joint UNICEF and WHO global partnerships

partnership is built around several instruments. These patterns reflect the convening roles of WHO and UNICEF, as well as the strong role of advocacy in the work of UNICEF and entrepreneurial coalitions for health and development, described earlier in the chapter. The participation of WHO in global initiatives is almost always connected to the knowledge, information systems, and application of expertise-based standards that it harbors. UNICEF's work in turn relies on connecting information, advocacy, and capacity between global concerns, local conditions, and the implementation of specific programs. As we saw in the cases discussed in this chapter, information, advocacy, and capacity building are often primary instruments when partnerships leverage public and private knowledge on diagnostics, treatment, populations affected by certain problems, research on new products and processes, and the roles of relevant domestic actors and their concerns in addressing them.

By contrast, the partnerships in which both WHO and UNICEF participate engage to a very limited extent with regulation and norm setting. These are competencies of multilateral institutions, in which states and IOs have primary and often exclusive legal authority, and, as anticipated by the theoretical framework, they allow limited scope for experimentation with hybrid mechanisms. The WHO is particularly careful to maintain the distance between its regulatory work and its interaction with private actors. The agency has voiced concerns that large partnerships could affect regulatory developments indirectly via their practices and agendas; one of the objectives of the institutionalization process, as discussed earlier, was to delineate regulation as largely a public function. In the subset of partnerships that are *not* shared with WHO, UNICEF engages more frequently in initiatives that advance soft, nonlegalized norms and standards, for instance by formulating guidelines on internet safety for children or by advancing the Guidelines for the Alternative Care of Children (the Better Care Network partnership).[108]

Some 40% of the partnerships in which both WHO and UNICEF participate leverage new financing and technologies (medicines, diagnostics, or other medical and information technologies) to advance objectives for health and children. Finance is thus one of multiple instruments of partnership governance on these issues. At the same time, the data on finance and technology should be interpreted cautiously concerning the sheer scale and modalities of large financial partnerships and hence their broader influence.

Initiatives such as GAVI and the Global Fund were explicitly targeted to scale up the resources and efforts in health and development. The entrepreneurs of the Global Fund acted on the argument that "billions, not millions" are necessary to turn around the rising toll of HIV/AIDS, malaria, and tuberculosis in terms of preventable deaths, disability, and poverty.[109] Indeed, by 2014, the Global Fund had raised more than US $31 billion and disbursed more than US$26 billion (investing about US $4 billion per year) to help national programs in some ninety countries to support better to access lifesaving technologies.[110] GAVI is often described as the brainchild of Tore Godal, of the WHO, and the financial child of the Bill & Melinda Gates Foundation, which contributed a US$750 million five-year pledge toward its establishment. It was set up to deal with a specific set of market failures related to limited access to new vaccines (initially the hepatitis B vaccine) in developing countries. There were initial concerns by professional audiences that the narrow focus on new vaccines could undermine the objective of

---

[108] See International Telecommunications Union 2016; Better Care Network 2016.
[109] Lidén 2013.
[110] See The Global Fund 2016, accessed November 2016 at https://www.the globalfund.org/en/portfolio/. The annual budget of the WHO for all its programs 2012–2013 was similarly about US$4 billion (WHO 2014c, p. 8).

universal baseline vaccination. Over time, however, GAVI mobilized significant new resources (US$7.4 billion for the period 2011–2014 and a new pledge of US$7.5 billion for the period 2016–2020), through which it increased support for eight underused or new vaccines by 2014. Importantly, this includes the development and introduction of a vaccine for the pneumococcus virus, which causes pneumonia, otitis, meningitis, and bacteremia and is a leading vaccine-preventable cause of early childhood mortality in developing countries.

Large financial partnerships have influenced the broader sample also by introducing innovative financial instruments and supporting a host of related partnering activities. GAVI, for instance, has experimented with several different methods to increase the availability of funding for vaccines. These include advanced market commitment to accelerate development of new commodities such as the pneumococcal vaccine, a matching fund to increase incentives for private contributions to GAVI, and the International Finance Facility for Immunization, created in 2006 with the support of then UK Chancellor Gordon Brown. The Facility uses long-term sovereign pledges from donor governments to raise money by issuing "vaccine bonds" in the capital markets, contributing some US$2.5 billion to the work of the partnership by 2014. In turn, GAVI has supported a host of other partnerships that use vaccines to decrease disability and preventable disease and mortality.

The International Drug Purchase Facility (UNITAID) is another partnership that introduced innovative financial instruments such as an airfare tax levy to raise a stream of large-scale and predictable funding for HIV/AIDS, tuberculosis, and malaria. The funding is used to influence markets and leverage price reductions of quality drugs and diagnostics. According to its latest financial reports, UNITAID's investments have contributed to price reductions of 80% for pediatric HIV medicines, 80% for the high-quality malaria treatments, and 40% for tuberculosis tests.[111] The Executive Director of the Global Fund, Mark Dybul, describes UNITAID as an upstream financing initiative that pushes innovation and affordability of essential commodities and thus allows other partnerships (the Global Fund, Stop TB, etc.) to better support access by affected populations.[112]

Who are the primary financial partners of global partnerships for health and children? Figure 5.7 demonstrates the significance of private

[111] UNITAID 2014.
[112] UNITAID 2013, p. 18.

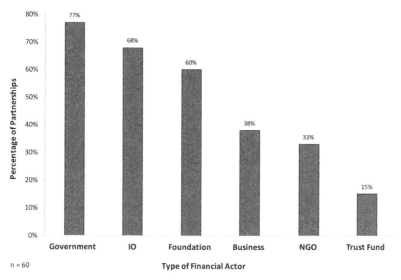

Figure 5.7 Financial partners in WHO and UNICEF joint global partnerships

actors, including foundations, which support some 60% of the initiatives in the sample of initiatives in which both the WHO and UNICEF participate, but also business actors (38%) and NGOs (33%). The share of the nonstate contribution is thus significantly higher and more substantial compared to partnerships in other arenas such as human rights or environmental sustainability (Chapters 3 and 4). This can be accounted for, to some extent, by the longer tradition of investment in research and advocacy for health and children by foundations and NGOs. On the other hand, these figures also reflect the all-out efforts of advocates and governance entrepreneurs to emphasize the need for substantial scaling up of resources and interventions that involve expensive technology and innovation to tackle global pandemics. The scaling up of resources for global health and children's issues has clearly targeted the interests of private actors to leverage technology and resources through partnerships in order to mitigate public pressures and the reputational risks resulting from global market and institutional failures. As anticipated by the theoretical framework articulated in Chapter 2, the cycle of global partnerships for health and children involved the interplay of political incentives linked to resource pressures and legitimacy challenges on international agencies (and the capacity of organizational entrepreneurs to engage the growing density of transnational actors pushed to reconcile market-based incentives and public objectives related to health, development, and human rights.

However, the financing of partnerships for health and children has not been a purely or even a largely private affair. Similar to portfolios of partnerships for other issue areas examined, a larger share of UNICEF and WHO initiatives rely on public funding (Figure 5.7). The substantive investment by large governmental donors such as the UK, the U.S., Norway, Germany, France, the EU, Canada, and Australia has been significant, both as direct entrepreneurs of global partnerships and through targeted multilateral financing.[113] The Bill & Melinda Gates Foundation is perhaps the only private actor with contributions that are comparable in some initiatives to those of the large sovereign donors. In the case of GAVI, for example, the UK is the largest contributor as of 2015, followed by the Bill & Melinda Gates Foundation, the U.S., and Norway, with financing also from most of the industrialized countries and increasingly from emerging-market countries such as China and Russia. Indeed, about 75.5% of the 2011–2015 budget of GAVI came from public sources, while 23% comes from the Bill & Melinda Gates Foundation and 1.5% from other actors.[114] Other partnerships with large financial arms such as the Global Fund, the Global Financing Facility (for maternal, neonatal, children's, and adolescents' health), and UNITAID similarly rely on donor financing for a large share of their resources and, in some instances, on innovative instruments such as the air travel tax for UNITAID, initiated by France, Brazil, Chile, Norway, and the United Kingdom.[115] This kind of public investment provides additional evidence on Proposition 2 of the theoretical framework, which emphasizes the role of agent–principal coalitions as political belts behind the cycle of governance entrepreneurship of global public–private partnerships.

Conclusion

The analysis of UNICEF's and WHO's engagement with partnerships provides strong evidence for the argument of dynamic institutional change facilitated by IOs. Public–private initiatives for children and

---

[113] Global Partnership Database 2016. See also Lidén 2013; UNICEF 2009a.
[114] Data for 2011–15 from GAVI 2016.
[115] See UNITAID 2016.

health were driven by coalitions, which included alliances between proactive principals, the core international agencies, and private and advocacy entrepreneurs. The partnerships diffused rapidly across countries and constituencies through domestic implementation efforts and expanding networks and financing. The role of multilateral intergovernmental bodies became salient primarily in the process of institutionalization *after* substantial partnership activity became a reality.

Moreover, the comparison between UNICEF and WHO illuminates particularly well how organizational mandates, episteme, and principal–agent relations shape the nature of new collaborative activities. There is a striking variation across the two agencies in the paths toward greater collaboration with external actors despite their shared participation in many global partnerships. One important observable implication of the theory of dynamic institutional change is that organizational entrepreneurs respond to a set of stimuli and constraints that are characteristic for their environment and tend to project organization-specific priorities and expertise via new experimental governance. Indeed, UNICEF and the WHO have approached partnering from dramatically different positions. The WHO faced a barrage of financial, legitimacy, and advocacy pressures to reinvent itself as globalization brought about changing perceptions over the right to health, its core mandate. It sought innovative approaches to respond to resource and legitimacy pressures and to regain centrality by capitalizing on advocacy for health and development. Its engagement with public–private partnerships was driven from the top by the leadership of Gro Harlem Brundtland, who addressed the organization's principals in a discourse on globalization, health, and development and who actively sought the support of epistemic networks and donor countries.

UNICEF's partnering practices, by contrast, have been long-standing, diverse, and initiated largely from the bottom-up, reflecting the decentralized structure of the organization and its substantial autonomy and normative activism. By developing new global program partnerships, organizational entrepreneurs within UNICEF were not responding to specific legitimacy or resource pressure but rather to new opportunities to develop more integrative partnerships and to leverage new types of resources, innovation, and advocacy for children. In the case of UNICEF, guidelines and restrictions on collaboration with the private sector were institutionalized early on by organizational entrepreneurs due to the ethical sensitivity of the agency's mission with respect to a wide range of audiences including states, publics, and NGOs.

Partnering was thus adapted to organizational imperatives, norms, and, gradually, to internal systems of accountability across the two institutional contexts. In both cases, however, the rise of global partnerships proceeded through supportive agent–principal coalitions and relied on these organizations' substantial capacity for autonomous initiative and networks with a growing diversity of external actors. The empirical analysis of this chapter documents the anticipated cycle of dynamic institutional change at the level of the two institutions, as well as in the context of multiple partnering initiatives and alliances. When the literature speaks of global partnerships as a generic phenomenon or as the privatization of the multilateral system, it misses both essential variations across institutional fields and the central role of IOs in shaping collaborative practices.

The chapter reveals that a unique feature of global partnerships for health and children's well-being is the substantial coordination of activity across international agencies and with a multitude of transnational and national actors. Institutional change has gone further in these issue areas in achieving more expansive collective action and in monitoring its outcomes than in other spheres of partnership activities. In a move that would not be anticipated by theories that emphasize principal control or agency drift, staff of the WHO, UNICEF, and the World Bank working on partnerships actively mobilized to learn from each other and to create a community of practice that would support their organizational capacity. Such initiative reflects concerns about transaction costs, associated with expanding forms of governance, as well as the need to address issues of institutionalization.

While the chapter focuses on questions of institutional change and partnership outcomes, it also reveals that the legitimation of partnership governance is an ongoing process that is crucial for the future of public–private collaboration. This process reflects, on the one hand, scrutiny by multiple audiences and, on the other hand, efforts to establish the fit with organizational mandates, to limit contradictions, and to clarify channels of accountability. Given their extensive scope and outcomes, so far unmatched in any other arena of international governance, partnerships for children and health provide an ideal area for further systematic research on their effects and accountability mechanisms.

6 | Conclusion

Institutional Diversity and Global Partnerships

The governance of international issues has been transformed in less than two decades by the development of global partnerships. This book sheds light on the politics of creating new spaces for public–private collaboration in a system that is often perceived as tightly controlled by states and mired in bureaucracy. It offers a comparative perspective on the rise and rapid diffusion of partnerships across issues ranging from environmental sustainability to health, children, and human rights. Critically, it asks what impact the growing agency of nonstate actors and the diversification of governance arrangements has had on the multilateral system.

The theoretical contribution of the book lies in the conceptualization of the politics and processes through which multilateral institutions have evolved to include new instruments of governance in direct collaboration with nonstate actors. The argument stipulates that such processes of institutional change are considerably more dynamic than previously recognized and at least partially endogenous to the multilateral system. Partnerships have not resulted from a punctuated equilibrium and a grand bargain between powerful states emphasized by classic international relations theories. The organizational capital of the multilateral system itself has enabled change stimulated by certain circumstances and conditions. Global partnerships grew out of the organizational turbulence that shook IOs in the last decade of the twentieth century, caused by the globalization of economic and social relations. The analysis emphasizes the subsequent role of governance entrepreneurs in bringing together structural stimuli and political agency to establish new global partnerships.

The theory of dynamic institutional change elaborated in Chapter 2 relies on a more fine-grained conceptualization of the structure of IOs compared to theoretical perspectives that focus either on mechanisms of state control or primarily on their bureaucratic structure and expertise. While we observe a clear vertical hierarchy of authority and delegation of variable autonomy from states to international agencies, it is also important to recognize the opportunities for coalition building horizontally between agents and principals on the one hand and external constituencies on the other. Such a dynamic understanding of principal–agent interactions and their contextual embeddedness allows us to anticipate an iterative cycle of change in the multilateral system, whereby entrepreneurial coalitions can start small by proposing experimental initiatives. Those experiments that are perceived as successful can unlock the processes of replication, diffusion, and expanding political support that facilitate the institutionalization of new governance. Thus dynamic change and its political acceptance are not inevitable. Organizational entrepreneurs have had to navigate formal mandates in order to justify experimentation with new governance, as we have seen in multiple cases of global partnerships. They have been forced to learn from contention and obliged to expand the political base of those initiatives that won more permanent acceptance.

The analysis challenges the notion that the growing collaboration between IOs and nonstate actors amounts to the "privatization" of international governance. It does so by theorizing the political agency behind such institutional change and by documenting the rise of global partnerships as well as their patterns of governance using new data and primary research. The empirical research presented across the chapters reveals greater yet more subtle differences in the structure and epistemic capacity of IOs than previously documented in international relations literature, which have played a pivotal role in forging coalitions, through their dynamic interactions with state principals. This variation, in turn, has left a clear imprint on the entrepreneurship of new governance across institutional domains. The following sections reflect on the main findings of the book and their implications for recurrent debates about global partnerships and their future.

IOs and Diversity of Global Partnerships

The very organizational characteristics of the UN Secretariat, UNEP, the World Bank, UNICEF, and the WHO have profoundly influenced their approach to partnerships and their eventual outcomes. As anticipated by the dynamic theory of institutional change, the specific sources of agency autonomy and capacity as well as the nature of principal–agent coalitions forged have shaped in important ways the development of global partnerships and their variable characteristics across agencies. Table 6.1 summarizes some of the main elements of variation in IO structures and in their entrepreneurship and subsequent institutionalization of public–private collaboration.

A broad comparison on the sources of agency autonomy suggests that its organizational impact on international life goes beyond the boundaries defined by formal state control mechanisms. Leadership, epistemic capacity, discursive strategies, and a variety of entrepreneurial coalitions between agents, principals, and external actors have shaped the scope of agency initiative and its outcomes. These characteristics and dynamics are summarized in columns 2 through 4 of Table 6.1, and their implications are discussed comparatively in this section.

The office of the UN Secretary-General has the least formal agency autonomy of the five IOs examined in this book. It is tightly influenced by its intergovernmental bodies and the Security Council in particular. However, the broad humanitarian mandate of the Office of the Secretary-General has allowed proactive leaders to take the initiative in finding ways to advance the UN mission and in seeking political support. The leadership of Kofi Annan and the subsequent policies of Ban Ki-moon were decisive factors in opening the UN to public–private cooperation. Strategies of argumentation, experimental change, and diversifying political support created institutional space in which, for example, the UN could establish partnership platforms to raise questions about business responsibility and human rights or to push ahead with commitments addressing issues of maternal, newborn, children's, and adolescent health.

The comparative analysis of UNEP and the World Bank shows that both organizations have acted with a degree of autonomy to partner with nonstate actors on environmental governance. However, the sources of their agency autonomy and initiative have varied considerably (Table 6.1). UNEP was created with a highly technical mandate and capacity to advance consensual scientific knowledge as a basis for new environmental agreements, but its role in intergovernmental politics was curbed from the end of the 1980s when treaty negotiations were moved beyond its remit and its resources limited. The World

Table 6.1 Diversity of IOs and partnership approaches

	Principal bodies	Sources of autonomy	Organizational entrepreneurs	Partnership strategy	Partnership institutionalization – key elements
UN Secretariat	Security Council, UN General Assembly (UNGA)	Interpretation of broad mandate, authority to propose initiatives	UN Secretary-General (Kofi Annan, Ban Ki-moon), Office for Policy Coordination and Strategic Planning	Experimental adoption, normative framing, supportive political coalitions	Guidelines on Cooperation between the United Nations and the Business Community (2000, 2009); United Nations Office for Partnerships (2009) UNGA resolutions affirming commitment to partnerships and recognizing the UN Global Compact
World Bank	Board of Directors, Board of Governors	Financial management, economic expertise	World Bank Presidents (James Wolfensohn, Robert Zoelik), specialized units	Global public goods framing, development grant facility, experimental Initiatives, trust funds	World Bank Department on Global Partnership and Trust Fund Operations; Vice Presidency for Concessional Finance and Global Partnerships (later incorporated in the Development Finance [DFi] Vice Presidency) Reviews of the World Bank's Involvement in Global Partnerships presented to the Board of Directors by the Independent Evaluation Group
UNEP	Governing Council, UN Environment Assembly (2014)	Environmental expertise	Specialized units, Head of UN DTIE Jacqueline Aloisi de Larderel, UNEP Executive Director Achim Steiner	Experimental initiatives	UNEP Policy on Partnerships and Guideline for Implementation, approved by UNEP's Senior Management Team (2009)
UNICEF	Executive Board, UNGA	Advocacy mandate, operational decentralization, financial decentralization	UNICEF country offices, specialized units, UNICEF national committees, since 2010 Executive Director Anthony Lake	Task delivery arrangements, fundraising, cause-related marketing, issue-specific alliances, global program partnerships, results for children and equity framings	UNICEF Guidelines and Manual for Working with the Business Community (2001) Strategic Framework for Partnerships and Collaborative Relationships (2009) and Report on the Implementation of the Strategic Framework for Partnerships and Collaborative Relationships (2012), both endorsed by the Executive Board
WHO	Executive Board, World Health Assembly (WHA)	Expertise, epistemic networks	Director-General and Cabinet (Gro Harlem Brundtland, Margaret Chan)	Health & development framing, WHO centrality framing, supportive political coalitions, large experimental initiatives	Policy on WHO's Engagement with Global Health Partnerships and Hosting Arrangements, endorsed by the Executive Board and by a WHA resolution (2010) Framework of Engagement with Non-state Actors (2016)

Bank, in contrast, can marshal agency influence thanks to its substantial financial clout and associated economic expertise. The impact of the World Bank on environmental issues, however, has been contested because of the primacy of neoliberal economics and infrastructure projects in its portfolio. Developing countries, moreover, demonstrated limited interest in borrowing for global issues. Both organizations engaged in the entrepreneurship of partnerships as a new means to extend their environmental work, but as documented in Chapter 4, they responded to different organizational concerns and projected very different governance instruments through such activities.

The World Bank approached partnerships from the top when its President, James Wolfensohn, took the lead in soliciting new grant-based financing from its major public donors to support issues providing global public goods, which were later leveraged with non-state contributions. UNEP engaged in partnerships motivated partly through financial weakness and partly through its substantial capacity for bottom-up experimentation in its technical fields of specialization – energy, chemical safety, biodiversity, green economy, or sustainable production and consumption.

The other pair of IOs examined in the book, UNICEF and the WHO, brings into analytical focus their substantial agency autonomy coupled, interestingly, with multiple channels of accountability to principals and external audiences. The coexistence of broad agency autonomy and clear lines of top-down and horizontal accountability challenges standard assumptions about IOs. It reinforces the theoretical argument that the interactions between IOs and a variety of political principals are more complex than a relationship of unidirectional control, agency drift, or bureaucratic influence. Both UNICEF and WHO engage in partnerships with diverse sets of actors, but such new approaches to governance depend heavily on continued political vetting by state principals.

The comparative analysis of global partnerships across four specialized agencies thus provides consistent support for the theoretical expectation that IO structure, mandates, and knowledge significantly shape the process and outcomes of incremental institutional change. All organizations have relied to a great degree on information, specialized knowledge, and epistemic networks to forge new experimental governance. The World Bank has used a range of financial instruments to advance its environmental work through partnerships, while UNEP has adopted a more diverse approach combining information with focus on technologies, eco-efficiency processes, and advocacy.

UNICEF led the way in experimenting with various forms of alliances that arose primarily from its decentralized structures. Starting with the joint implementation of operational tasks with NGOs, it has developed private fundraising, cause-related marketing, integrative partnerships around corporate social responsibility issues, and, most recently, larger global program partnerships. Its partnering modalities often involve bottom-up initiatives around specific tasks or normative causes for children. The WHO, by comparison, has been highly sensitive about possible conflicts of interest associated with direct interaction with the private sector due to the normative and standard-setting nature of its mandate. It advanced partnerships in the late 1990s as new institutional platforms to allow targeted collaboration with a variety of actors. This was a strategic innovation from the top, responding to organizational exigencies and a need to reaffirm the central role of the WHO in tackling health-and-development challenges, a role undermined by globalization and uneven access to life-saving medical technologies (Table 6.1). In sum, the strategies of IOs as entrepreneurs of global partnerships vary greatly and reflect their specific circumstances, the nature of their authority and, importantly, some risk taking and leadership to convene supportive coalitions. As a consequence, partnerships have often emerged as opportunistic structures relying on agency autonomy and the capability of IO staff to exercise initiative and coalesce with proactive principals and external actors.

Broadening Participation

Who are the *partners* in global public–private initiatives? Unlike most multilateral institutions, global partnerships do not seek to achieve universal support. The cycle of governance entrepreneurship has often proceeded with the adoption of experimental initiatives, involving a core group of public and private supporters. The theoretical discussion of dynamic institutional change stipulates, however, that broader diffusion of partnerships adoption and political vetting are likely to be important conditions for the recognition and subsequently greater institutionalization of new, experimental governance. The data on initiating actors and financial partners shows a much greater diversity of involvement behind public–private cooperation than recognized in prior studies. The participation in collaborative initiatives has also evolved over time as they have diffused across countries and issues. The new empirical material of the Global Partnerships Database and of the case studies thus challenges the intuitive assumption of partnerships as "governance by a few" in several ways.

To start with, the data defies the notion of the "privatization" of the multilateral system. The analysis of a wide range of initiatives follows the theoretical proposition that IOs have taken a central role in facilitating the large majority of collaborative initiatives in the multilateral sphere. Evidence of the steering role by international agencies emerges in the process and documents on the creation of partnerships and their institutionalization, in the statistical patterns revealed by the Global Partnerships Database, and in the substantive imprint of IO mandates and toolkits on the governance instruments and focus of global partnerships. In addition, this research has revealed greater interagency coordination as a consequence of global partnerships, particularly for issues related to children, health, humanitarianism, and clean energy. They have stimulated the emergence of communities of practice across agencies' partnership staff and have fostered learning and capacity to address the early underinstitutionalization of new governance.[1]

Governments and, in particular, donor countries such as the UK, Germany, France, the U.S., Norway, and Canada, have been similarly critical players in the creation of a large number of global partnerships. Financial contributions by private actors have often, although not always, followed political and financial commitments by public institutions. This is particularly evident in global partnerships for health and children, where the exponential rise of resources to address specific conditions and alleviate inequalities in access to health technologies would not have been possible without the ratcheting up of public effort. In sum, the central role of public organizations in global partnerships cannot be underestimated.

Second, the data on the patterns of partnership participation speaks of a much greater variety of nonstate partners than suggested by existing case studies mainly of large, prominent partnerships. Overall, NGOs have taken part in initiating coalitions to the greatest extent compared to other categories of nonstate actors. They have contributed

---

[1] UNICEF, WHO and the World Bank 2010.

to the entrepreneurship of about 40% of UNICEF's global program partnerships and 33% of WHO's partnerships, while on environment issues, NGOs have led 20% of UNEP's and 20% of the World Bank's initiatives.[2] It is important to clarify that the NGO category in the Global Partnerships Database does not include business groups or associations, for which a separate category exists. Issue-specific and advocacy NGOs have also played an important indirect role in stirring organizational turbulence and putting pressure on IOs to seek change (as in the case of the World Bank and the environment or on HIV/AIDS and access to health). Furthermore, they have provided issue-specific expertise and on-the-ground implementation and advocacy. Expert organizations are similarly an important constituency of partnerships across organizational fields but particularly in the collaborative work of UNEP and the WHO, for which strong scientific capacity and epistemic networks are core organizational characteristics.

The private sector plays a relatively limited direct role in global partnerships as revealed, somewhat surprisingly, by the data. Business entities have led, along with other actors, between 13% and 15% of the global programmatic partnerships in which WHO and UNICEF participate and only 9% of the World Bank environmental partnerships. This pattern reflects the relative aversion of the private sector to engaging with broad public issues and bureaucratic organizations, as well as the sensitivity of IOs, such as the WHO, in keeping at arms length actors that may be subject to its norm-setting functions.

The Global Compact and UNICEF are two noteworthy exceptions, among others, to the overall trend of relatively low business participation across partnership initiatives. The Global Compact was specifically designed to engage business around the recognition and voluntary implementation of a set of UN norms. Related partnership activities of the Global Compact and the UN Secretary-General on issues such as climate change, water, or, more recently, gender equality and children's rights have maintained a high-profile involvement of corporate actors. UNICEF has a wide range of alliances with the private sector around fundraising, cause-related marketing, and specific issues and technologies to improve the lives of children.

---

[2] These and all figures cited hereafter are based on data presented in Chapters 3, 4, and 5 of the book and quantitative analysis drawing on the Global Partnerships Database.

The variation across initiatives and organizations suggests that business tends to coordinate with IOs primarily on partnerships that focus explicitly on issues related to corporate social responsibility (for example the Global Compact, IKEA–UNICEF cooperation on child labor, or the UNEP partnerships related to industrial externalities and sustainable production) or around specific corporate contributions such as innovative technologies, processes, or fundraising. The private sector is less likely to participate in partnerships related to broad global objectives. For example, UNEP has worked with the private sector in advancing some 38% of its environmental partnerships, while the share of private participation in the World Bank partnerships for the environment, as noted earlier, is limited to 9%. At first glance this is surprising given the market orientation of the World Bank. However, the patterns keenly reflect the different kinds of environmental concerns targeted by the two organizations via public–private collaboration. The World Bank has built its partnerships around problems framed as global public goods, primarily by raising additional soft *public* finance. At UNEP, the Division of Technology, Industry and Economics, which was created in the 1970s to interface with industrial sectors and associations on environmental issues, spearheaded partnerships around the work of its departments related to specific industries, economics, and new technologies (chemical safety, refrigeration, industrial risk, sustainable production, sustainable tourism, clean energy technology, green economy, etc.).

Private and charitable foundations are among the private actors that have played a particularly prominent role in global partnerships, again with important variations across issue domains. Foundations are financial partners in some 60% of the global initiatives for health and children, which involve both the WHO and UNICEF. A considerably smaller share of partnerships for the environment is supported by foundations. They are listed as financial partners in 18% of UNEP's initiatives and in 15% of the World Bank environmental partnerships according to the Global Partnerships Database. Indeed, the arena of health research and product development has been influenced by actors such as the Rockefeller Foundation throughout the twentieth century. Since the late 1980s, the presence and scope of the programs of major funders including the Rockefeller Foundation, the Clark Foundation, the Rotary Foundation, the Bill & Melinda Gates Foundation, the Carter Foundation, the Clinton Foundation, and others have taken larger and more expansive dimensions. Importantly, foundations also exercise influence through the support of partnership platforms such as the United Nations Foundation and the United Nations Fund for International Partnerships, as well as through large partnerships such as GAVI, which in turn support a broader network of partnering activities.

Overall, global partnerships have entered the multilateral sphere through the involvement of a broader base of actors than previously recognized and through variable constellations of entrepreneurial coalitions. These dynamics make it difficult to qualify partnerships as the capture of international institutions by private interests because of the steering roles of public organizations in the large majority of the initiatives and the diversity of norms, public ends, and private objectives that are typically negotiated in their creation.

Finally, the participation in global partnerships has become more extensive over time in the course of their implementation and diffusion across jurisdictions, within societies, and through networks of interplay. Developing countries and subnational actors (units of government, professional organizations, civil societies, or business associations) have been the most important belt in that process, a critical link without which the implementation and subsequently the greater legitimation of hybrid initiatives would not have been possible. Partnerships depend on expanding uptake and recognition by states before they can be institutionalized as features of multilateral institutions. Bottom-up initiatives, such as UNEP's programs on industrial risk and chemical safety, first took root in a few developing countries before they expanded to other policy contexts with the active participation of national administrations and tailoring to reflect the specificity of domestic industrial structures. Other UNEP initiatives, such as REN21 on renewable energy, expanded through global networks, which nonetheless elicited growing national and subnational interest. By broadening its participation base and with the support of the UNEP platform, REN21 became one of the best-recognized sources of authoritative information on cleaner energy systems and policy.[3] Equally, many global partnerships for health have expanded from a few pilot countries to target the large majority of populations where a particular health issue is prevalent.

---

[3] See Stadelmann and Castro 2014; UNGA 2011b.

More contentious global initiatives, such as the Global Compact or the World Bank climate funds, have needed to reach a broader swath of relevant actors and take root in developing countries to ensure political survival. For example, the World Bank Prototype Carbon Fund became the target of criticism for its uneven activities, favoring large emerging economies and industrial offsets, with a virtual lack of participation from the group of least developed countries. The carbon finance partnerships quickly multiplied to experiment with offsets from forests and community-based projects. Subsequently, the Carbon Investment Funds also introduced a focus on technology diffusion, adaptation, and coordination with regional development banks to better reflect the development concerns of countries in their activities. Although the World Bank's involvement in climate policy remains contested by a variety of audiences, climate finance has become, via experimentation and substantial expansion of national, subnational, and institutional participation, a recognized feature of development cooperation. By contrast, environmental partnerships such as many of those adopted at the World Summit on Sustainable Development in 2002, which overlooked the exigencies of implementation and expanding uptake in the global South, have largely failed to sustain political support and continuity.[4]

It is therefore important to recognize that developing countries and actors in these societies play critical roles in the processes of implementation, uptake and diffusion of collaborative practices, upon which the larger cycle of incremental institutional change depends. Sociological theories of organizations indeed point to processes of replication, mimicking, isomorphism and the emergence of fields of like – or related – organizations as precursors of change and the social legitimation of new structures.[5] Global partnerships have diffused in these ways both across the institutions of the multilateral system and across and within states.

This poses a continuing dilemma for global partnerships. While the diversification of governance has brought new resources to domestic contexts, it has also increased transaction costs and placed a strain on capacities of public administrations, particularly in low-income countries. Moreover, the differential roles played by traditionally powerful

---

[4] Pattberg *et al.* 2012; Bäckstrand and Kylsäter 2014.
[5] DiMaggio and Powell 1983; Hannan and Freeman 1989.

actors, such as donor governments and transnational organizations, in the initiation of global partnerships and the critical importance of developing countries in the domestication and implementation of partnerships raises valid concerns about the reproductions of preexisting power relations through new forms of governance.[6] The cycle of institutional change does not therefore develop in a smooth, unidirectional, or normatively neutral or taken-for-granted way. It involves contestation precisely because it entails a rearrangement of roles in global governance and questions about the power structures behind such rearrangements. The next section considers what we have learned about the lines of contestation of global partnerships and the processes of their institutionalization and legitimation.

Institutionalization, Contestation and Legitimation of Partnerships

The institutionalization of global partnerships formalized their recognition as a feature of multilateralism. It has placed partnerships in a more direct interface with intergovernmental bodies of IOs. As anticipated by the organizational theory of dynamic institutional change, the process took on a reverse sequence – from experimentation with new governance to formal intergovernmental institutionalization. The empirical material in Chapters 3 through 5 and the comparative Table 6.1 reveal that partnership policies were adopted predominantly around 2009 or later, following the rise of a critical mass of initiatives and their diffusion. The creation of experimental, often time-bound partnerships initially found justification in advancing the normative or operational mandates of IOs and in supporting organizational capacity to address sources of organizational turbulence. However, they also introduced an incremental diversion from a strictly intergovernmental view of the multilateral system. New sources of authority and influence became directly relevant in multilateral affairs, which inevitably raised concerns about the extent to which the primacy of states and public goals may be undermined. Multiple forms of deliberation and contestation have thus accompanied the rise of global partnerships.

Partnerships created tensions between different views on the nature of IOs and the compatibility between intergovernmental and nonstate

[6] Jönsson 2013; Newell 2012; Woods 2006.

authority. Internal skeptics raised questions about the risk of introducing undue private influence in inherently intergovernmental mandates and potential conflicts of interest; others within IOs struggled with the departure from standard procedures or were concerned about resource diversion. External contestation came primarily from advocacy movements that protested globalization and the rise of corporate power. The role of NGOs in global partnerships is differentiated between those that advocate for specific issues and have found greater influence through partnerships and those that have become watchdogs guarding the entrance to the global public domain. Several advocacy networks such as Amnesty International, Save the Children, the World Resources Institute, Greenpeace, and others have taken a dual approach. They have prioritized advocacy and normative coherence, on the basis of which they have lent support to some partnerships, but simultaneously have scrutinized specific features of these initiatives and, in some instances, have withdrawn from them.

Intergovernmental contestation of partnerships was limited by several factors. Organizational entrepreneurs were strategically careful not to overstep the mark of agency autonomy in advancing initiatives largely *implementing* elements of their mandate, as anticipated by the scope conditions for change from within outlined in the proportions of the theoretical framework.[7] The comparative data in Chapters 4 and 5 shows that very few partnerships engage with regulatory or policy instruments even of the informal kind, while the majority deploy different packages of information, capacity building, or technology toward the implementation of specific objectives. Leadership initiatives such as those of the UN Secretary-General, the President of the World Bank, or the Director-General of the WHO employed explicit political justification and framing around the mandates of the organizations and their advancement in a globalized context (see summary of strategies in Table 6.1). Bottom-up initiatives typically have proceeded from the premise of implementation or on-the-ground change involving local and governmental actors. The fact that influential governments took important roles in entrepreneurial coalitions as well as the subsequent expansion of partnerships across jurisdictions further consolidated political support, as discussed earlier.

---

[7] Similar patterns are also identified by the study of Tallberg *et al.* 2013 on the formal opening of IOs to access by nonstate actors.

The degree of contention and the processes of legitimation and institutionalization of global partnerships have nonetheless varied considerably across IOs. Indeed, the partnering activities of UNEP and UNICEF have faced relatively limited contestation. Both UNEP and UNICEF have histories of task-specific coordination with external actors. UNEP has a formalized relation with industrial sectors through its Department for Technology, Industry and Economics, as well as a tradition of cooperation with NGOs and scientific organizations. Many of UNEP's partnerships grew out of sector-based or local-level programs and were thus viewed largely as an extension of its work. They brought much-needed resources to those programs and were often legitimated tacitly via their results and expanding interest by governments. Some of UNEP's partnering activities were called into question later on and from the top down, when a 2011 audit by the UN Office of Internal Oversight Services recommended more explicit oversight by senior management and procedures to safeguard against undue influence of private interests.[8] UNICEF has the longest history of pragmatic alliances with a variety of organizations as a result of its creation as an on-the-ground humanitarian agency and its decentralized structure. The expansion of public–private collaborations since the 1990s added new approaches to existing interactions that had to be managed in line with UNICEF's norms and ethical standards. UNICEF's strong advocacy identity and fundraising campaigns across societies have exposed it to widespread scrutiny. This has resulted in the early adoption of principles, procedures and limitations to guide its interaction with corporations in particular (see Table 6.1).

In the context of the UN Secretariat, we observe very different levels of contestation and strategies of legitimation across three examples of major partnerships: the Global Compact, the United Nations Fund for International Partnerships (UNFIP), and Every Woman Every Child. The UN's Global Compact boldly opened the door to large corporate actors while trying to socialize them according to key UN norms. Not surprisingly, it met with staunch opposition from the antiglobalization movement and a great degree of initial skepticism by developing countries despite the very careful positioning of the initiative within the core prerogatives of the

---

[8] See Chapter 4 for further discussion on the institutionalization of UNEP partnerships.

agency. The Global Compact has survived because it diffused quickly, albeit still unevenly, across emerging markets and other developing countries and demonstrated its utility to economic actors outside the industrial North. In addition, the introduction of measures for greater accountability of the signatories of the Global Compact, including the delisting of nonreporting companies, has been important for its greater legitimation. Advocacy scrutiny of the initiative persists. Indeed, the watchdog role of certain NGOs provides an essential element of external accountability and maintains pressure for the ongoing enforcement of the normative quality of the initiative.

In comparison, the creation and work of the UNFIP, later leading to the UN Office for Partnerships, provoked little concern either within or outside the UN. It was perceived largely as a facilitator and funder of UN agencies' initiatives to involve nonstate actors. The fact that UN agencies were at the helm and that it generated new resources to implement projects globally on development, sustainability, women, and health underpinned the subsequent formal approval of the partnership platform by the General Assembly. The partnership Every Woman, Every Child was also broadly endorsed. The partnership, convened by the UN Secretary-General Ban Ki-moon, sought to elicit greater commitments to policies and institutional funding for advancing women's, children's, and adolescents' health and wellbeing, including from UN member states. It evolved from a groundswell of action through a chain of partnerships involving UN agencies, NGOs, and other nonstate actors. In many ways, the Every Woman, Every Child movement has been the culmination of previous partnering and legitimacy gained on this issue.

The World Bank and the WHO are the two IOs that have faced the greatest scrutiny of new collaborative activities with nonstate actors, albeit by different audiences and for different reasons. The World Bank opened to partnerships for global public goods in consultation with its Board of Directors and by leveraging new grant-based financing. Early contestation came not so much from within the organization but from the antiglobalization movement. Global partnerships for health, in turn, have generated debates among multiple WHO constituencies on a range of subjects such as the prioritization of vertical intervention for specific diseases versus horizontal support of health systems, the need to maintain a clear distance between the standard-setting role of the agency and private interests, or the power of hybrid initiatives that command significant resources to influence the public health agenda. It was uniquely in the context of the WHO that both intergovernmental bodies – the Executive Board and the World Health Assembly – reacted to questions of the institutionalization of global partnerships (see Table 6.1). This degree of concern indicates the sensitivity of WHO's epistemic and normative authority to the legitimacy risks of real or perceived influence by private actors. However, it is also a response to the significant impact global partnerships have had over the last ten years on health issues and on the exponential increase of earmarked financing for global public health.

While questions of the legitimacy of global partnerships are not the central focus of the study, the systematic analysis of the process of change makes an inductive but important contribution to larger debates on the legitimation of new modes of governance.[9] It documents how the road to recognition of partnerships as a feature of multilateralism has been covered by the dialectic of contestation (real or anticipated) and evolving efforts at legitimation.

Legitimation of partnerships can thus be conceptualized as the process of seeking and/or gaining social approval and acceptance of authority to govern. When governance entrepreneurs in the multilateral system embark on new experimental initiatives with nonstate actors, they seek, at the very least, the explicit or tacit approval of governmental principals, who have the power to block change, along with normative justification within the broader intergovernmental constituency. To that end, they use organization-specific normative framing, argumentative strategies, or explicit linkages to organizational exigencies and tasks. The contestation of such initiatives is often proportionate to the perceived risk of undue influence or the lack of clear accountability processes as captured by the variation across IOs and across public–private initiatives. The capacity of organizations to anticipate and engage with internal and external debate and to adapt the features of new governance becomes an important element of the legitimation process.[10] While the normative aspects of legitimacy are critical for justifying initial adoption, the sociological processes

---

[9] See the work of Andonova and Carbonnier 2014; Bäckstrand 2006; Bexell and Mörth 2010; Bexell 2015; Dingwerth 2005; Buse and Walt 2002; Jönsson 2014, among others, on the legitimacy of public–private partnerships.

[10] Buchanan and Keohane 2006.

of replication, mimicking, recognition, and isomorphism become dominant during the diffusion of partnership practices.[11] The implementation of partnerships and the social vetting of their outcomes have indeed underpinned the political foundations behind their institutionalization.

Table 6.1 (column 6) examines comparatively the policies and procedures adopted across IOs to institutionalize partnerships shortly after the peak in their diffusion. These policies and resolutions start with a series of statements that endorse partnerships and their outcomes as advancing the purposes of the respective organization and then proceed with specifying principles for further engagement, accountability, and management. These decisions in effect grant some explicit degree of legitimacy to the *practice* of public–private collaboration before they establish more permanent institutional rules. The procedures, in turn, have varied in the degree of formality and involvement of intergovernmental bodies. UNEP and the World Bank adopted oversight of partnerships primarily at the level of the organizational management and, in the case of the World Bank, via reporting to the Executive Board by the Independent Evaluation Group. Within the UN Secretariat, various means of soft institutionalization have been employed with the elaboration by the Office of the Secretary-General of guidelines on partnerships, the creation of the UN Office for Partnerships, and the adoption of a series of resolutions by the UN General Assembly that affirm the commitment to partnerships.

It is UNICEF and the WHO – the two agencies with the greatest scope for agency autonomy based on strong expert specialization and degree of decentralization – that have adopted the most formal and detailed instruments to regulate the rationales, oversight, and accountability of global partnerships. This again relates to their sensitivity to possible ethical dilemmas associated with public–private interactions. In the case of WHO, the considerable involvement of both the Executive Board and the World Health Assembly since 2009 also reflects the growing concern within the organization about the potential impact of global partnerships on the health agenda and the need

---

[11] Normative and sociological approaches to gaining legitimacy are sometimes juxtaposed in analytical debates. For important theoretical contributions in elaborating these approaches, see Buchanan and Keohane 2006; Keohane 2011; Bernstein 2005, 2011; Hurd 1999. In practice, both normative and sociological processes have been important in the legitimation of global partnerships.

to ensure more explicit lines of accountability to public objectives and intergovernmental bodies. The strategies of institutionalization thus appear to be proportionate to the assessed ethical and legitimacy risks for IOs. Institutionalization itself becomes part of the broader social process of acquiring greater legitimacy and recognition of new mechanisms of governance.

The Future of Partnerships

Over the course of two decades, a veritable organizational ecosystem of global partnerships has emerged. The pages of this book trace the unfolding of this institutional development. The storyline captures the role of entrepreneurial actors and supportive coalitions, the expanding participation and the contentious debates around partnerships as they have diffused and, perhaps most interestingly, the tremendous variety of forms, instruments, and institutional outcomes. We observe a confluence of qualitative and quantitative change in institutional practices.

Partnerships have become a reality through the entrepreneurship of institutional change. What is their future? On its seventieth anniversary in 2015, the UN launched a set of Sustainable Development Goals for advancing human well-being. The formulation of these goals has been defined through intergovernmental talks conducted in parallel with consultations with private, societal, and expert actors. It is intended that public–private partnerships will be used to implement them in conjunction with more traditional instruments such as international treaties, domestic policies, and development assistance. Global partnerships have become part of the architecture of multilateralism, but how will they evolve?

The relatively recent and ongoing processes of institutionalization suggest that global partnerships are likely to move toward consolidation and internal development rather than continued expansion in numbers. In some instances, we observe efforts to link partnerships and more traditional multilateral mechanisms in cross-cutting efforts to advance specific intergovernmental policies. This has been the case, for example, in the regulation of transboundary pollution from mercury, in advancing policy and funding for maternal and childhood health, or in strengthening the financial mechanisms for climate cooperation under the UNFCCC. Another set of partnerships continues to develop activities internally, across jurisdictions, and with sister initiatives. Some collaborative initiatives may not succeed in their objectives or may have completed them. Institutional documents increasingly clarify the need for IOs to manage their engagement in ways that anticipate exit strategies and a more strategic approach to new collaborations. The organizational field of global partnership has moved toward a state of greater maturity. This has important implications for future research and its policy relevance.

The impact of partnerships at the domestic and community levels is a question ripe for new research. The findings of this book invite further analysis on the impact of partnerships on the ground, particularly in developing countries, by uncovering in greater detail the diversity of partnership effects across issues and jurisdictions. Important debates revolve around the implications of partnerships for public administrations and local communities. They concern the materialization of actual benefits as well as possible unintended effects such as the crowding out of alternative agendas, the strain on public institutions, or the limited accountability to local constituencies. Legitimation claims are often based on reference to partnership outcomes in terms of numbers of people reached, resources provided, programs advanced, or policy objectives supported. Such debates cannot be adequately addressed without further analytic work and comparative data at the subnational level, which also captures the diversity of partnering initiatives. This book has painted a shifting picture of the rise and emerging landscape of global partnerships in the multilateral system. It sets the tone for a broader research agenda in which social science may cast further light on the symbiosis of public institutions and private actors in addressing global issues and improving human well-being.

Annex
Constructing the Global
Partnerships Database

The Global Partnerships Database is a new source of data, constructed for the purposes of this book. It includes four data documents on the partnership portfolios of UNEP, the World Bank, the WHO, and UNICEF, respectively. The database is, to our knowledge, the largest and most comprehensive source of information on the patterns of partnership governance across several institutional domains in the multilateral system. It provides the basis for a systematic analysis on partnership governance across time and organizational fields, including the specific patterns of partnership emergence, participation, clustering, and outcomes. It is also a source of empirical material to assess some of the observable implications of the organizational theory of institutional change formulated in the book, along with the qualitative methods that were employed and documented in the chapters. The creation of the database involved, first, the collection of representative data on partnerships across the four institutional fields and second, the implementation of a coding scheme which enables a systematic comparative analysis. The collection and coding of data was undertaken with support by the Swiss National Science Foundation research grants 100017_134884 and 100017_146513 by a team including Liliana Andonova (Principal Investigator), Manoela Assayag (main PhD Research Assistant), and Defne Gonenc (PhD Research Assistant in the last semester of the project) at the Graduate Institute for International and Development Studies, Geneva.[1] The methodologies of data collection and of the coding scheme are discussed in turn.

[1] The author Liliana Andonova is grateful to Manoela Assayag and Defne Gonenc for the fruitful collaboration and for multiple discussions and cross-verification on the data collection, coding scheme, and coding results. I am also much obliged for additional research assistance by Zuzana Hudáková, Kathryn Chelminski, Elena Zheglova, and Diana Jack with data verification and updates in different stages of the project.

212

Generating Data on Global Partnerships

The Global Partnerships Database collects information on a range of characteristics of partnerships in which a given IO (UNEP, World Bank, UNICEF, WHO) participates as a leading actor, as a member, and/or as a donor. Partnerships are thus the units around which the data is organized. Global partnerships are defined in Chapter 1 of this book as: "voluntary agreements between public actors (IOs, states, or substate public authorities) and nonstate actors (NGOs, companies, foundations, etc.) on a set of governance objectives and norms, rules, practices, or implementation procedures and their attainment across multiple jurisdictions and levels of governance." According to this definition, such initiatives entail coordination between at least one public and at least one nonstate actor around an explicit public purpose.[2] The term "global" refers to those partnerships that operate within the broad frameworks of the multilateral system and connect diverse sets of actors across jurisdictions in response to problems with global dimensions. The set of partnerships included in the database ranges from large partnerships with wide geographical presence to smaller initiatives, which are often present in a few countries, as long as they relate to an existing intention to impact the management of global issues. Previous studies on public–private partnerships have highlighted the challenge of capturing the larger patterns and significance of such collaboration because of its diversity, its spread across institutions, jurisdictions, and time and the often limited detail on partnership activities.[3] The Global Partnerships Database has sought to address such concerns by focusing on a specific institutional domain (the multilateral system) and by recording systematically detailed information based on publically available documents on the creation of collaborative initiatives and a host of their characteristics.

The data collection and parallel coding proceeded from September 2011 to December 2014. The fact that global partnerships had reached a degree of organizational maturity in the multilateral sphere by 2009–2010 helped the research process in several ways. All four IOs

---

[2] See Andonova, Betsill and Bulkeley 2009 and Bulkeley *et al.* 2014 on the expectation of an explicit public purpose in qualifying a transnational initiative as governance.

[3] Andonova 2010; Börzel and Risse 2005; Biermann *et al.* 2007; Pattberg *et al.* 2012.

had adopted their internal definition of partnerships, which conceptually aligned with the broader academic definition advanced in the book. This implied that we could meaningfully identify a set of governance initiatives in the multilateral system as global partnerships. Moreover, some of these IOs had started to conduct internal mapping and evaluations of their partnering activities, which was very helpful for the data collection effort.

The World Bank list of partnerships in the Global Partnerships Database has been adapted from a survey and evaluation report titled *The World Bank's Involvement in Global and Regional Partnership Programs*, published in 2011.[4] The lists of UNEP and WHO partnerships were compiled entirely by the research team. We identified the existing UNEP and WHO partnerships, respectively, after an extensive research of UNEP and WHO documents, their websites, partnership websites (including PDF documents and presentations of partnerships available via their websites), and articles available through academic search mechanisms. In the various searches, we used terms such as "UNEP" or "WHO," "partnership," "PPP," "project," "initiative," "intraagency," "partner" to identify a set of initiatives that correspond to the conceptualization of the term "global public-private partnership" adopted in this book. UNICEF had conducted a mapping study of global program partnerships (GPPs) and an evaluation of its involvement in such activities in 2009. The Global Partnerships Database used a 2010 list of "Active GPPs in which UNICEF participates" as its baseline for its UNICEF partnerships list.[5] The UNICEF list was further updated during the period of data collection (September 2013–September 2014) with additional partnerships in which UNICEF is listed as participant (in various capacities) on the basis of desk research of publically available sources.[6] We used the same search methodology for updating the UNICEF list as for the collection of data on WHO and UNEP partnerships. In the process of the identification of partnerships in which the four IOs participate, our team discovered that a number of global partnerships in the portfolio of UNICEF, the WHO, and the World Bank have shared participation by these organizations.[7]

---

[4] Independent Evaluation Group 2011.
[5] UNICEF 2010.
[6] These include, for example, mention of the organization as "partner," "participant," member of scientific committees of partnerships, or member of partnership boards.
[7] See also UNICEF, WHO and World Bank 2010.

Table A1 *Global partnerships data*

Data	Number of observations	Sources
UNEP public–private partnerships	45	Survey of UNEP website; of partnership websites; UN reports; secondary literature
World Bank public–private partnerships	133	Independent Evaluation Group 2011; partnership websites
UNICEF global program partnerships	89	UNICEF 2010; UNICEF Evaluation Office 2009; survey of partnership websites and documents
WHO public–private partnerships	80	Survey of WHO website; of partnership websites; WHO reports; secondary literature

These partnerships appear in the data documents for each organization. The comparative analysis, however, takes into account such coordination of activity. The desk research for all four IOs was complemented by a series of interviews, including with managers of specific partnerships or staff that have been involved in the development of partnership policies, which increased our understanding and confidence in the adequacy of data. Table A1 summarizes the number of observations collected in the data documents for each organization.

The diversity and nature of global partnerships is such that it is not possible to assert that any particular set of data represents a complete list of initiatives. For example, when organizations produce lists of partnerships in which they are involved, these lists can change over time depending on the significance that a particular organization attributes to its engagement in specific partnerships, on differing views within the organizations about what partnership engagement entails, or as a result of the discontinuation of some partnerships. Our methodology, including the extensive survey of institutional and partnership websites, coupled with cross-checks with secondary literature and primary documents, increases our confidence that the Global Partnerships Database provides representative data on partnerships in the institutional spheres of UNEP, the World Bank, UNICEF, and the WHO at a particular snapshot in time. It is, to our knowledge, the only and most comprehensive source of data presently available that allows for systematic and comparative analysis of public–private partnerships in the multilateral system.

Coding of Data

Once a comprehensive and representative set of global partnerships was identified, the documents and websites of each partnership were hand coded for key characteristics. The methodology of coding built on earlier datasets focusing on transnational governance[8] while refining and adjusting the methodologies to correspond to the particular sphere of governance examined in this book. The coding categories in the dataset were chosen with two objectives in mind. First, the new data seeks to contribute to a better understanding of the nature of partnership governance and the extent of its correspondence to the norms, tools, and objectives of the multilateral system. Second, the coding categories are chosen so as to allow for systematic assessment of the observable implications of the theory of incremental institutional change toward global partnerships. The following sections describe the main categories of variables and their analytic rationales as they relate to the main questions and themes pursued in the book *Governance Entrepreneurs*.

The coding category *Initiating/Lead Actors* (Table A2), provides systematic data on the nature of the entrepreneurial coalitions behind the creation of a specific initiative. The database also records the year of the partnership's founding. This data complements the qualitative process tracing and archival analysis in the empirical chapters to consider the evidence related to core theoretical hypotheses on the leading role of IOs as organizational entrepreneurs and the nature of supportive coalitions with proactive principals and external actors. Unless otherwise indicated, the coding of variables in the database is binary (for example, 1 if one or more IOs have participated in initiating coalitions of a particular partnership, 0 otherwise, etc.).

The coding category *Participating Actors* (Table A3), in turn, provides information on the nature of participation in global partnerships at the time of the data collection (2012–2014) and the extent to which a variety of transnational and substate actors are involved across

---

[8] See Andonova and Levy 2003; Bulkeley *et al.* 2014.

Table A2 *Entrepreneurship of global partnerships*

Coding Category	Variables	Rationale for category and variable description
Initiating/Lead Actors		*What types of actors have engaged in the establishment of global partnerships?*
	Individual_L	Individual(s)
	IO_L	One or more IOs, regional or global
	Government_L	National government (s)
	R government_L	Regional government(s)
	L government_L	Local government (s)
	Business P_L	Business for-profit organizations
	Business A_L	Business association or nongovernmental organization
	NGO_L	Nongovernmental societal organization
	Community_L	Community-based organization
	Foundation_L	Foundation
	Research_L	Research organization
	PPP_L	Public–private partnership

industrialized and developing countries. Since the majority of partnerships recorded in the database were established between the second half of the 1990s and 2009 (with a peak around the turn of the millennium; see Chapter 1, Figure 1.1), the data on *initiating actors* (Table A2) and that on *participating actors* (Table A3) provides an important intertemporal perspective on partnership diffusion and the evolution of participation. The two coding categories were often complemented with qualitative information, where such was available, for example including the names of initiating actors and organizations, funders, or participating governments. The qualitative data on participating actors has been an essential tool, together with the documentary and process tracing methods, for the analysis on the cycle of governance entrepreneurship of global partnerships.

The category *Financial Partners* (Table A4) indicates what types of actors have supported global partnerships with resources.

The coding categories *Initiating/Lead Actors*, *Participating Actors*, and *Financial Partners* allow us to provide a more comprehensive view on the agency behind institutional change toward global partnership

Table A3 *Participation in global partnerships*

Coding Category	Variables	Rationale for category and variable description
Participating Actors		*Who participates in global partnerships (2012–2014)? How are actors in the global North and global South engaged in global partnerships?*
	IO	IO(s), global or regional
	NGO	NGO(s)
	Business	Business for-profit organization(s)
	Business_A	Business association or nongovernmental organization(s)
	Research	Research institute(s)
	Foundation	Foundation(s)
	Government	Government(s) participation
	Num_country	Number of country members
	Gov_li	Country members from low income (use WB classification)
	Gov_mi	Country members from middle income (use WB classification)
	Gov_BRISCAM	BRISCAM country members
	Gov_ind	Country members from industrialized countries
	R government	Regional government(s)
	L government	Local government (s)
	PPP	Participation and/or collaboration with other global partnerships

and, importantly, on the nature of public and private involvement. Typically, each partnership is initiated by several types of actors, involves participation of an even greater variety of actors, and more often than not involves financial contributions from several sources. A number of questions on the nature and legitimacy of public–private partnerships revolve, in part, around questions of the agency behind their creation and funding and the patterns of participation. An important contribution of the Global Partnerships Database is that it provides systematic data across many fields and issues of governance and thus sheds new light on these debates.

Table A4 *Financial support for global partnerships*

Coding Category	Variables	Rationale for category and variable description
Financial Partners		*What kind of actors and organizations have contributed to the financing of global partnerships?*
	IO_F	Financing from IO(s), global or regional
	Gov_Ind_F	Financing from industrialized country government(s)
	Gov_LMI_F	Financing from low- and middle-income country government(s)
	Business_F	Financing from a private for-profit entity(ies)
	Foundation_F	Financing from foundation(s)
	NGO_F	Financing from NGO(s)
	Trust_F	Financing from trust fund(s)

Another set of coding categories focuses on the governance activities of global partnerships The category *Issue Focus* (Table A5) indicates the range of global problems that partnerships seek to affect via governance interventions, keeping in mind that a single partnership may target one or several related issues. For example, while a single partnership may focus largely on education, on nutrition, or even more narrowly on the supply of specific micronutrients; other partnerships can have more integrative foci on education, nutrition and preventing child labor. The issue–category variables were derived inductively from the information on the activities of individual partnerships, as well as on the basis of the mandates of participating IOs. Partnership websites and documents list explicitly the principal issues that they seek to address in mission statements and in rubrics such as "about," "activities," and "history," which we examined as the primary sources of data and coding. Keeping in perspective the issues that fall within the mandates of the IOs whose partnership activities were being analyzed was also important. It allows an assessment of the degree of correspondence (or lack thereof) between partnership activities and the different issues that fall in the purview of institutional mandates. Following the research design and comparative analysis of Chapters 4 and 5, respectively, two different sets of issue categories

Table A5 *Issue focus of global partnerships*

Coding Category	Rationale for category
Issue focus	*What is the substantive focus of global partnerships? What kinds of issues and global problems have been prioritized by global partnerships?*

Variables	
Environment & Sustainable Development	Children & Health
Agriculture	Basic education
Biodiversity	Gender equality
Climate (mitigation + adaptation)	Parental care
Air pollution	Violence against children
Desertification	Human rights
Disaster preparedness	Humanitarian issues
Sustainable energy	Child trafficking
Forests	Child labor
Fresh water	Water and sanitation
Minerals and mining	Hygiene
Mountains	Nutrition
Oceans/fisheries	Environment
Chemicals	Early childhood
Tourism	Health (one or more of the following):
Environment and health	*Immunization*
Urban	*Malaria*
Sustainable production	*Tuberculosis*
Sustainable consumption	*Maternal and birth care*
Waste	*Disabilities*
	Noncommunicable diseases
	Neglected diseases
	Health systems
	Health research
	Air pollution
	Other diseases
	Social and economic protection

Table A6 *Governance activities of global partnerships*

Coding Category	Variables	Rationale for category and variable description
Governance Instruments		*How are governance functions carried out by global partnerships? What specific instruments and approaches are deployed to affect outcomes?*
	Advocacy	Awareness raising, advocacy, and advancement of specific issue(s) and/or governance approaches
	Information	Sharing of information and specialized knowledge as a basis of governance
	Capacity	Capacity building
	Finance	Provision of new finance or financial mechanisms to advance specific objective
	Markets	Market-shaping activities, market certification, other market-based instruments
	Technology	Transfer of or access to technology
	Direct action	Direct intervention to help address a specific problem or objective
	Norms	Formulation a set of norms related to specific global issues
	Reg_Law	Formulation of a soft-law framework
	Reg_Standard	Setting or diffusing standards or certification
	Reg_Rule	Setting of specific rules
	Regulation	Regulation_Law OR Regulation_Standard OR Regulation_Rule
	Monitoring	Mechanisms of monitoring

were established for partnerships for environment and sustainable development in which UNEP and/or the World Bank participate (left column of Table A5) and for partnerships for children and health in which UNICEF and/or the WHO participate (right column of Table A5).

The coding category *Governance Instruments* inquires how partnerships carry out governance functions (Table A6). Following earlier methodologies for analyzing transnational governance,[9] the Global Partnerships Database considers a range of instruments through which

[9] Andonova, Betsill and Bulkeley 2009; Bulkeley *et al.* 2014.

partnerships exercise governance functions: i) advocacy of issues and governance approaches; ii) using information, financial instruments, or market-based mechanisms to steer governance outcomes; iii) the building of capacity, facilitating access to technology, and using direct action to support the implementation of governance objectives; and finally, iv) the adoption of different means of soft regulations (norms, standards, soft laws, or specific rules). While a few partnerships may focus on a single instrument (for example, information on clean energy policy and technology or the transfer or access to specific technology), the majority of partnerships typically employ more than one instrument to advance their governance objectives. The websites and documents of individual partnerships were the primary sources of data and coding for this category. The theory on quasi-endogenous and incremental institutional change anticipates greater scope for the entrepreneurship of new partnership initiatives around implementation mandates and instruments, where IOs may have a greater degree of autonomy and advantage in specialization. By contrast, the hypotheses imply that regulative activities are more likely to be kept under tighter control by intergovernmental bodies. The data on governance instruments provides new systematic evidence in relation to the observable implication of the theoretical framework.

In sum, the categories *Issue Focus* and *Governance Instruments* provide new information on the ends and means of partnership governance. As discussed in the empirical chapters, such fine-grained data on the issues pursued by a variety of global partnerships allows us for the first time to have a more comprehensive understanding of the multitude of governance objectives of public–private collaboration. The data is also an analytical tool to examine observable implications of the organizational theory of institutional change, which suggests important variations in the clustering of global partnerships across certain organizational mandates but not others and in the instruments they bring to the table. The Global Partnerships Database has served to generate new insight on global partnerships as incremental institutional change and their governance activities. Following the publication of the book, the data can be used by policy institutions in their assessment of partnering activities as well as for further academic inquiry.

Bibliography

Bibliography of UN and Other Primary Documents

Aloisi de Larderel, Jaqueline. 2002. Speech at the WSSD Roundtable – Private Sector and Civil Society Contributions to Sustainable Development. Accessed November 2016 at www.uneptie.org/Media/speeches/copenhagen_wssd.pdf (also on file).

Amnesty International, The Ethical Globalization Initiative, Global Witness, Human Rights First, International Save the Children Alliance, and Oxfam. 2004. Statement by NGO Participants in the Global Compact Summit. *Civil Society Observer*, 1:3. New York: United Nations Non-Governmental Liaison Service.

Annan, Kofi. 1999. Secretary-General Proposes Global Compact on Human Rights, Labour, Environment, in Address to World Economic Forum in Davos. Press Release, United Nations Office of the Secretary-General, 1 February 1999 (SG/SM/6881), New York. Accessed March 2015 at www.un.org/press/en/1999/19990201.sgsm6881.html.

    2000. *"We the Peoples": The Role of the United Nations in the 21st Century*. New York: United Nations. Accessed March 2015 at www.unmillenniumproject.org/documents/wethepeople.pdf.

    2009. Problems without Passports. *Foreign Policy*, Special Report. Accessed March 2015 at http://foreignpolicy.com/2009/11/09/problems-without-passports/.

    2013. Public Lecture at the Graduate Institute of International and Development Studies and the University of Geneva, March 26.

A Promise Renewed. 2016. A Promise Renewed. Accessed November 2016 at www.apromiserenewed.org/.

Arce, Maria and Ama Marston. 2009. Are Climate Pilots Building towards the Right Climate Architecture? *The Bretton Woods Update*, 66. Accessed July 2009 at www.brettonwoodsproject.org/art-564928.

Bern Declaration. 2007. Clean Words, Dirty Business: Corporate Social Responsibility: The Disconnect between Rhetoric and Reality. *Bern Declaration Magazine*, Special Issue. (Citation on page 7).

Better Care Network. 2016. Home. Accessed November 2016 at www.bettercarenetwork.org/.

Brundtland, Gro Harlem. 2001. Address by Dr. Gro Harlem Brundtland, Director-General, to the Fifty-Fourth World Health Assembly. 54th World Health Assembly, Agenda Item 3, May 14 (A54/3), World Health Organization, Geneva.

Carbon Partnership Facility. 2016. Carbon Partnership Facility. Accessed October 2016 at http://cpf.wbcarbonfinance.org/.

Chen, Lincoln, C., Mary Oakes Smith and Franklin A. Thomas. 2006. *Public–Private Partnerships at the United Nations: UNF/UNFIP: A Story of Generosity, Thoughtfulness and Accomplishment.* New York: United Nations.

Commission on Macroeconomics and Health. 2001. *Macroeconomics and Health: Investing in Health for Economic Development.* Geneva, Switzerland: World Health Organization. Accessed March 2015 at http://whqlibdoc.who.int/publications/2001/924154550x.pdf.

CorpWatch. 2000. Coalition Letter to Kofi Annan on the Global Compact. Accessed March 2015 at www.corpwatch.org/article.php?id=961.

    2001. Alliance for a Corporate-Free UN Campaign Profile. Accessed April 2013 at www.corpwatch.org/article.php?id=927.

Countdown to 2015. 2015. Home. Accessed January 2015 at www.countdown2015mnch.org/. From Commitment to Action:

Dossal, Amir A. 2004a. UNFIP: Partnerships beyond Borders. *UN Chronicle*, 41:1.

    2004b. UN Partnerships: Working Together for a Better World. Presentation at Columbia University, New York, June 18.

Fall, Papa Luis and Mohamed Mounir Zahran. 2010. *United Nations Corporate Partnerships: The Role and Functioning of the Global Compact.* Report of the Joint Inspection Unit, JIU/REP/2010/9. Geneva, Switzerland: United Nations.

GAVI (The Vaccine Alliance). 2014. Progress Report 2013. Accessed February 2015 at www.gavi.org/results/gavi-progress-reports/.

GAVI. 2015. The Vaccine Alliance Progress Report 2015. Accessed November 2016 at www.gavi.org/library/publications/gavi-progress-reports/gavi-progress-report-2015/.

    2016. Key Figures: Donor Contributions & Pledges. Accessed November 2016 at www.gavi.org/funding/donor-contributions-pledges/.

Human Rights up Front. 2016. Human Rights up Front: A Summary for Staff. Accessed October 2016 at www.un.org/News/dh/pdf/english/2016/Human-Rights-up-Front.pdf.

Independent Evaluation Group. 2006. *2006 Annual Report on Operations Evaluation.* Washington, DC: World Bank.

    2011. *The World Bank's Involvement in Global and Regional Partnership Programs: An Independent Assessment.* Washington, DC: World Bank.

International Coalition for Trachoma Control. 2016. International Trachoma Initiative. Accessed November 2016 at www.trachomacoalition.org/about-ictc/members/international-trachoma-initiative.

ISO (International Organization for Standardization). 2011. ISO Survey 2011. Accessed February 2015 at www.iso.org/iso/iso-survey.

International Telecommunications Union. 2016. COP Guidelines. Accessed November 2016 at www.itu.int/en/cop/Pages/guidelines.aspx.

International Trachoma Initiative. 2015. About ITI: How ITI Works. Accessed December 2014 at http://trachoma.org/how-iti-works.

Ki-moon, Ban. 2013. Renewing Our Commitment to the Peoples and Purposes of the United Nations. Speech by the UN Secretary-General, 22 November. Accessed October 2016 at www.un.org/sg/en/content/sg/speeches/2013-11-22/renewing-our-commitment-peoples-and-purposes-united-nations-scroll.

——— 2016. Letter dated 24 December 2015 from the Secretary-General addressed to the President of the General Assembly. United Nations General Assembly, 70th Session, Agenda Items 20, 34, 72, 116 and 112 (A/70/656), New York.

Kirby-Zaki, Jane. 2009. Global Partnerships. Presentation to World Bank Group Donor Forum, Paris, 26 May 2009.

Lake, Anthony and Rajiv Shah. 2013. A Promise Renewed: A Great Global Ambition and Every Father's Dream. *The Huffington Post*. Accessed April 2015 at www.huffingtonpost.com/anthony-lake/children-preventable-disease_b_3447592.html.

Lock, Karen. 2006. Statement on Behalf of the Group of 77 and China by Ms. Karen Lock, Permanent Mission of South Africa to the United Nations, on Agenda Item 117: The United Nations Fund for International Partnerships (UNFIP). Fifth Committee of the General Assembly, New York, 9 November 2006. Accessed September 2014 at www.g77.org/Speeches/110906B.html.

Marques, Tomas. 2011. UNEP's Portfolio of Programmes on Safer Production and Industrial Risk Reduction. Presentation at the OECD Working Group on Chemical Accidents Meeting 7 October 2011, Paris.

O'Brien, Philip. 2008. UNICEF Collaboration with the Corporate Sector: An Evolution. Remarks at the United Nations System Private Sector Focal Points Meeting: Exploring the Challenges and Opportunities of Collaboration throughout the Partnership Life Cycle, Geneva, 2 October 2008.

OECD (Organization for Economic Cooperation and Development). 2013. OECD Creditor Reporting System (CRS) Database. Last accessed February 2015 at http://iif.un.org/content/oda-flows.

Partnership for Maternal, Newborn and Child Health. 2016. Members and Constituencies. Accessed November 2016 at www.who.int/pmnch/about/members/en/.

People's Health Movement. 2014. Bill Gates Invitation to World Health Assembly. News Release. Accessed December 2014 at www.phmovement.org/en/node/72.

Robinson, Mary. 1999. Building Relationships That Make a Difference. Statement at Business for Social Responsibility Conference on Profitable Partnerships, San Francisco, CA, 3 November 1999. Accessed March 2015 at www.unglobalcompact.org/newsandevents/speeches_ and_statements/san_francisco_conference_on_profitable_partnerships .html.

Social Accountability Accreditation Services. 2012. SA8000 Certified Organizations. Accessed December 2012 at www.saasaccreditation.org/certfacilitieslist.htm.

Spano, Susan. 2012. Hey, Travelers, Got Any Spare Change?: Now I Know What to Do with My Jar of Turkish Liras, Cambodian Riels and Irish 50-Pence Pieces. *Smithsonian Magazine*. Accessed May 2015 at www.smithsonianmag.com/travel/hey-travelers-got-any-spare-change-5411224/?no-ist.

Steiner, Achim. 2013. Sustainable Development Post Rio+20: In Search of a Shared Paradigm in a Divided World. Public Lecture at the Graduate Institute of International and Development Studies, Geneva, Switzerland, 8 May 2013. Accessed October 2016 at http://graduateinstitute .ch/events/_/events/corporate/2013/event_7802.

Stop TB Partnership. 2016. Our Partners. Accessed November 2016 at www.stoptb.org/about/partners_landing.asp.

The Global Fund. 2016. Grant Portfolio. Accessed November 2016 at www.theglobalfund.org/en/portfolio/.

The World Alliance for Breastfeeding Action (WABA). 2011. WABA Common Position Statement on Public–Private Partnerships. Accessed March 2015 at www.waba.org.my/whatwedo/advocacy/pdf/PPP2011 .pdf.

UNITAID. 2013. *Annual Report 2013: Transforming Markets, Saving Lives.* Geneva: World Health Organization. Accessed February 2015 at www.unitaid.org/media/annual_report/2013/UNITAID_ Annual_Report_2013.pdf.

   2014. Audited Financial Report for the Year End 2013. Accessed February 2014 at www.unitaid.eu/images/budget/2013%20Financial%20State ments.pdf.

   2016. About UNITAID. Accessed November 2016 at http://www.unitaid .eu/en/who/about-unitaid.

United Nations. n.d. The United Nations Charter: Chapter 15: The Secretariat. Accessed March 2015 at www.un.org/en/sections/un-charter/chapter-xv/index.html.

1945. Charter of the United Nations. Accessed September 2016 at http://treaties.un.org/doc/publication/ctc/uncharter.pdf.

2002. Monterrey Consensus of the International Conference on Financing for Development. In *Report of the International Conference on Financing for Development* (A/Conf.198/11, Sales No. E.02.II.A.7). Annex. International Conference on Financing for Development, Monterrey, Mexico, 18–22 March 2002.

2008. Honoring 60 Years of United Nations Peacekeeping. Accessed September 2015 at www.un.org/en/events/peacekeepersday/2008/60years.

2012. Consultative Status with ECOSOC. Accessed December 2012 at www.un.org/esa/coordination/ngo/about.htm.

2016. Sustainable Development Knowledge Platform. Accessed July 2016 at https://sustainabledevelopment.un.org/.

United Nations Children's Fund (UNICEF). 1999. Public, Private and Civil Society. Press Release, April 16. Accessed March 2014 at www.unicef.org/french/media/media_11989.html.

2001. *UNICEF Guidelines and Manual for Working with the Business Community: Identifying the Best Allies, Developing the Best Alliances.* Geneva: United Nations Children's Fund.

2008. UNICEF's Corporate Partnerships: Signature Partnerships: Change for Good. Accessed January 2015 at www.unicef.org/corporate_partners/index_25030.html.

2009a. *Mapping UNICEF Partnerships and Collaborative Relationships. Report to the UNICEF Executive Board.* Accessed January 2015 at www.unicef.org/about/execboard/files/09-11-mapping-ODS-English.pdf.

2009b. *UNICEF Strategic Framework for Partnerships and Collaborative Relationships.* Executive Board Annual Session 2009, 8–10 June 2009 (E/ICEF/2009/10). Accessed February 2011 at www.unicef.org/about/execboard/files/N0928210.pdf.

2010. UNICEF Engagement in Global Health Partnerships and Initiatives: A Background Note. Paper Presented at the UNICEF/World Bank/World Health Organization Workshop on Institutional Engagement in Global Program Partnerships: Improving Policy and Practice, 9–10 February 2010, Geneva.

2012a. *Report on the Implementation of the Strategic Framework for Partnerships and Collaborative Relationships.* Executive Board Second Annual Session 2012, 11–14 September 2012 (E/ICEF/2012/18).

Accessed January 2015 at www.unicef.org/about/execboard/files/
2012-18-Strategic_framework_for_partnerships-ODS-English.pdf.

2012b. *Children's Rights and Business Principles.* New York: UNICEF.
Accessed January 2015 at www.unicef.org/indonesia/child_rights_and_
business_principles.pdf.

2012c. IKEA, UNICEF Programmes Reach 74 Million Children in India.
Press Release, September 5. Accessed January 2015 at www.unicef.org/
media/media_65718.html.

2014a. Summary of UNICEF Private Fundraising and Partnerships Plan
2014–2017. Accessed April 2015 at www.unicef.org/about/execboard/
files/Private_Fundraising_and_Partnerhsips_Plan_2014-2017_summary
.pdf.

2014b. IKEA Foundation Contributes US$31.5 Million to UNICEF. Press
Release, November 18. Accessed January 2015 at www.unicef.org/
media/media_77940.html.

United Nations Children's Fund (UNICEF) Evaluation Office. 2009.
*Evaluation Working Paper: A Study of UNICEF Engagement in
Global Programme Partnerships.* New York: United Nations Children's Fund.

United Nations Conference on Trade and Development (UNCTAD). 2011.
Inward and Outward Foreign Direct Investment Flows, Annual, 1970–
2011. Last Accessed February 2015 at http://unctadstat.unctad.org/
TableViewer/tableView.aspx?ReportId=88.

United Nations Environment Program (UNEP). 2004. *Natural Allies: UNEP
and Civil Society.* Nairobi: United Nations Environment Program.

2009. *UNEP Policy on Partnerships and Guidelines for Implementation
Approved by UNEP Senior Management Team, August, 2009.* Nairobi:
United Nations Environment Program. Accessed August 2016 at
www.pnuma.org/sociedad_civil/reunion2013/documentos/STAKEHOLDER
%20PARTICIPATION/2009%20UNEP-PolicyonPartnerships.pdf.

2011. 25 Years of Local Level Preparedness and Environmental
Emergency Management. Background Document Prepared for
Global APELL Anniversary Forum, Beijing, China, 15–17 November 2011.

2016. Funding. Accessed September 2016 at www.unep.org/about/
funding/.

United Nations Foundation. 2008. *Building Bridges to Solve Global Problems.* Washington, DC: United Nations Foundation.

United Nations Foundation and UNFIP (United Nations Fund for International Partnerships). 1999. *Programme Framework on Biodiversity.*
Washington, DC: United Nations Foundation and United Nations Fund
for International Partnerships.

United Nations Foundation and UNFIP. 2001. *"Interim" Program Frame-work for Sustainable Energy/Climate Change.* Washington, DC: United Nations Foundation and United Nations Fund for International Partnerships.

United Nations Fund for International Partnerships (UNFIP). 2013a. *Children's Health Programme.* New York: UNFIP. Accessed February 2015 at www.un.org/partnerships/YPAChildHealth.htm.

2013b. *Environment Programme.* New York: UNFIP. Accessed February 2015 at www.un.org/partnerships/YPAEnvironment.htm.

2013c. *Population and Women Programme.* New York: UNFIP. Accessed February 2015 at www.un.org/partnerships/YPAPopulationAndWomen.htm.

United Nations General Assembly (UNGA). 1972. Resolution 2997: [Institutional and Financial Arrangements for International Environmental Cooperation]. 27th Session, 2112th Meeting. 15 December 1972 (A/RES/27/2997), New York.

1998. United Nations Fund for International Partnerships: Report of the Secretary-General. 53rd Session, Agenda Item 113: Programme Budget for the Biennium 1998–1999. 24 November 1998 (A/53/700), New York.

1999. United Nations Fund for International Partnerships: Report of the Secretary-General. 54th Session, Agenda Item 119: Programme Budget for the Biennium 1998–1999. 10 December 1999 (A/54/664), New York.

2000a. United Nations Fund for International Partnerships: Report of the Secretary-General: Addendum. 54th Session, Agenda Item 119: Programme Budget for the Biennium 1998–1999. 12 July 2000 (A/54/664/Add.1), New York.

2000b. United Nations Fund for International Partnerships: Report of the Secretary-General: Addendum. 54th Session, Agenda Item 119, Programme Budget for the Biennium 1998–1999. 2 March 2000 (A/54/664/Add.2), New York.

2000c. United Nations Fund for International Partnerships: Report of the Secretary-General: Addendum. 54th Session, Agenda Item 119, Programme Budget for the Biennium 1998–1999. 18 May 2000 (A/54/664/Add/3), New York.

2000d. Resolution Adopted by the General Assembly: United Nations Millennium Declaration. 55th Session, Agenda Item 60 (b). 18 September 2000. (A/RES/55/2), New York.

2000e. Ministerial Statement Adopted at the Twenty-Fourth Annual Meeting of the Ministers for Foreign Affairs of the Group of 77, New York, 15 September 2000. 55th Session. 6 October 2000 (A/55/459), New York.

2001a. Resolution Adopted by the General Assembly: Towards Global Partnerships. 55th Session, Agenda Item 173. 6 March 2001 (A/RES/55/215), New York.

2001b. Cooperation between the United Nations and All Relevant Partners, in Particular the Private Sector: Report of the Secretary-General. 56th Session, Agenda Item 39, Towards Global Partnerships. (Item 50 of the Provisional Agenda, 28 August 2001). 9 October 2001 (A/56/323), New York.

2001c. United Nations Fund for International Partnerships: Report of the Secretary-General. 55th Session, Agenda Item 117, Programme Budget for the Biennium 2000–2001. 5 February 2001 (A/55/763), New York.

2002a. Resolution Adopted by the General Assembly: Towards Global Partnerships. 56th Session, Agenda Item 39. 24 January 2002 (A/RES/56/76), New York.

2002b. United Nations Fund for International Partnerships: Report of the Secretary-General. 57th Session, Item 114 of the Preliminary List, Programme Budget for the Biennium 2002–2003. 2 July 2002 (A/57/133), New York.

2003a. Enhanced Cooperation between the United Nations and All Relevant Partners, in Particular the Private Sector: Report of the Secretary-General. 58th Session, Item 47 of the Provisional Agenda, Toward Global Partnerships. 18 August 2003 (A/58/227), New York.

2003b. United Nations Fund for International Partnerships: Report of the Secretary-General. 58th Session, Item 123 of the Provisional Agenda, Proposed Programme Budget for the Biennium 2004–2005. 18 August 2003 (A/58/173) New York.

2004a. Resolution Adopted by the General Assembly: Towards Global Partnerships. 58th Session, Agenda Item 46. 19 February 2004 (A/RES/58/129), New York.

2004b. United Nations Fund for International Partnerships: Report of the Secretary-General. 59th Session, Item 110 of the Provisional Agenda, Programme Budget for the Biennium 2004–2005. 23 July 2004 (A/59/170), New York.

2005a. Enhanced Cooperation between the United Nations and All Relevant Partners, in Particular the Private Sector: Report of the Secretary-General. 60th Session, Item 61 of the Provisional Agenda, Towards Global Partnerships. 10 August 2005 (A/60/214), New York.

2005b. United Nations Fund for International Partnerships: Report of the Secretary-General. 60th Session, Item 124 of the Provisional Agenda, Programme Budget for the Biennium 2004–2005. 15 November 2005 (A/60/327), New York.

2005c. Resolution Adopted by the General Assembly on 16 September 2005: 2005 World Summit Outcome. 60th Session, Agenda Items 46 and 120. 24 October 2005 (A/RES/60/1), New York.

2006. Resolution Adopted by the General Assembly: Towards Global Partnerships. 60th Session, Agenda Item 59. 29 March 2006 (A/RES/60/215), New York.

2007a. Enhanced Cooperation between the United Nations and All Relevant Partners, in Particular the Private Sector: Report of the Secretary-General. 62nd Session, Item 63 of the Provisional Agenda, Towards Global Partnerships. 14 September 2007 (A/62/341), New York.

2007b. United Nations Fund for International Partnerships: Report of the Secretary-General. 61st Session, Item 115 of the Provisional Agenda, Programme Budget for the Biennium 2006–2007. 20 April 2007 (A/61/189), New York.

2007c. Resolution Adopted by the General Assembly on 19 December 2007: Towards Global Partnerships. 62nd Session, Agenda Item 61. 11 March 2008 (A/RES/62/211), New York.

2008. United Nations Office for Partnerships: Report of the Secretary-General. 63rd Session, Item 121 of the Provisional Agenda, Programme Budget for the Biennium 2008–2009. 8 August 2008 (A/63/257), New York.

2009a. Enhanced Cooperation between the United Nations and All Relevant Partners, in Particular the Private Sector: Report of the Secretary-General. 64th Session, Item 61 of the Provisional Agenda, Towards Global Partnerships. 1 September 2009 (A/64/337), New York.

2010a. Resolution Adopted by the General Assembly on 21 December 2009: Towards Global Partnerships. 64th Session, Agenda Item 59. 25 March 2010 (A/RES/64/223), New York.

2010b. United Nations Office for Partnerships: Report of the Secretary-General. 65th Session, Item 131 of the Provisional Agenda, Programme Budget for the Biennium 2010–2011. 3 September 2010 (A/65/347), New York.

2011a. United Nations Office for Partnerships: Report of the Secretary-General. 66th Session, Item 133 of the Provisional Agenda, Programme Budget for the Biennium 2010–2011. 27 July 2011 (A/66/188), New York.

2011b. Resolution Adopted by the General Assembly: International Year of Sustainable Energy for All. 65th Session, Agenda Item 20. 16 February 2011. (A/RES/65/151), New York.

2012. Resolution Adopted by the General Assembly: Towards Global Partnerships. 66th Session, Agenda Item 26. 28 March 2012 (A/RES/66/223), New York.

2015. Resolution Adopted by the General Assembly (A/70/479): Toward Global Partnerships: A Principle-Based Approach to Enhanced Cooperation between the United Nations and All Relevant Partners. 70th Session, 22 December 2015, New York.

United Nations Global Compact (UNGC). 2007. UN Global Compact Annual Review 2007: Leaders Summit. Geneva, Switzerland: United Nations.

2009. *Annual Review 2008*. New York: United Nations Global Compact Office.

2010a. *Local Network Report 2010*. New York: United Nations Global Compact Office.

2010b. *Annual Review: Ten Years 2000–2010*. New York: United Nations Global Compact Office.

2010c. *2010 Global Compact Implementation Study*. New York: United Nations Global Compact Office.

2011. *Global Compact Trust Fund: Share of Country Contributions (Percentage of Total)*. New York: United Nations Global Compact Office.

2013a. Local Networks. Accessed January 2013 at www.unglobalcompact .org/NetworksAroundTheWorld/index.html.

2013b. Participants & Stakeholders: Participant Search by Date, Business and Non-Business with Breakdown by Type. Accessed January 2013 at http://www.unglobalcompact.org/what-is-gc/participants/.

2015. The Ten Principles of the UN Global Compact. Accessed September 2015 at www.unglobalcompact.org/what-is-gc/mission/principles.

2016. Global Compact Governance. Accessed November 2016 at https://www.unglobalcompact.org/about/governance.

United Nations Children's Fund (UNICEF), World Health Organization (WHO) and the World Bank. 2010. Improving Institutional Engagement in Global Program Partnerships: Policies and Practice Report of a UNICEF/World Bank/WHO Workshop. 9–10 February. Geneva, Switzerland.

United Nations Office of Internal Oversight Services. 2009. Audit Report: Management of the United Nations Fund for International Partnerships (UNFIP). Accessed July 2014 at http://usun.state.gov/sites/default/files/ organization_pdf/140716.pdf.

2012. Audit Report: Audit of Management of Partnerships at UNEP. Accessed July 2014 at http://usun.state.gov/sites/default/files/organ ization_pdf/206757.pdf.

United Nations Office of the Secretary-General. 1998. *Linking Universal UN Values with the Global Reach of Business. Strategy Note for Address by Kofi Annan to World Economic Forum in Davos*. New York: United Nations.

2000. *Guidelines on Cooperation between the United Nations and the Business Community*. New York: United Nations.

2009. *Guidelines on Cooperation between the United Nations and the Business Community*. New York: United Nations.

United Nations Office of the Special Adviser on the Prevention of Genocide. 2014. The Responsibility to Protect. Accessed August 2016 at www.un.org/en/preventgenocide/adviser/responsibility.shtml.

United Nations Program on HIV/AIDS (UNAIDS). 2013a. *Global Report: UNAIDS Report on the Global AIDS Epidemic 2013*. Geneva: UNAIDS. Accessed February 2015 at www.unaids.org/sites/default/files/sub_landing/files/UNAIDS_Global_Report_2013_en_1.pdf.

2013b. AIDS by the Numbers. Accessed February 2015 at www.unaids.org/sites/default/files/media_asset/JC2571_AIDS_by_the_numbers_en_1.pdf.

2015. UNAIDS Announces that the Goal of 15 Million People on Life-Saving HIV Treatment by 2015 Has Been Met Nine Months ahead of Schedule. Press Release, July 14. Accessed November 2016 at www.unaids.org/en/resources/presscentre/pressreleaseandstatementarchive/2015/july/20150714_PR_MDG6report.

2016a. Fact Sheet 2016: Global Statistics – 2015. Accessed November 2016 at www.unaids.org/sites/default/files/media_asset/UNAIDS_Fact Sheet_en.pdf.

2016b. Global AIDS Update 2016. Accessed November 2016 at www.unaids.org/en/resources/documents/2016/Global-AIDS-update-2016.

United Nations Secretariat. 2009. *Secretary-General's Bulletin: Organization of the United Nations Office for Partnerships*. 18 December 2009 (ST/SGB/2009/14), New York. New York: United Nations.

United States Fund for UNICEF. 2015. American Airlines: Change for Good. Accessed April 2015 at www.unicefusa.org/supporters/organizations/businesses/partners/aa/change-good.

Widdus, Roy and Katherine White. 2004. Combating Diseases Associated with Poverty: Financing Strategies for Product Development and the Potential Role of Public–Private Partnerships. Based on a Workshop of the Same Title Organized by the Initiative for Public–Private Partnerships for Health, 15–16 April 2004, London. Geneva, Switzerland: The Initiative on Public–Private Partnerships for Health. Accessed March 2015 at www.who.int/intellectualproperty/topics/ppp/en/CombatingDiseases-Abridged.pdf.

Witte, Jan Martin and Wolfgang Reinicke. 2005. *Business Unusual: Facilitating United Nations Reform through Partnerships*. New York: United Nations Global Compact Office. Accessed March 2015 at http://europeandcis.undp.org/guides/poverty/spd/ras/48_Business_UN usuall.pdf.

World Bank. 2005. *A Strategic Framework for the World Bank's Global Programs and Partnerships*. Washington, DC: World Bank.

——— 2006. *The Role of the World Bank in Carbon Finance: An Approach for Further Engagement*. Washington, DC: World Bank. Accessed December 2010 at http://wbcarbonfinance.org/docs/Role_of_the_WorkBank .pdf.

World Bank Development Committee. 2007. *Global Public Goods: A Framework for the Role of the World Bank*. Washington, DC: World Bank.

——— 2009. *Carbon Finance for Sustainable Development: Annual Report 2009*. Washington, DC: World Bank.

——— 2010a. World Bank Engagement in Global Health Partnerships and Initiatives: A Background Note. Paper Presented at the UNICEF/World Health Organization/World Bank Workshop on Institutional Engagement in Global Program Partnerships: Improving Policy and Practice, 9–10 February 2010, Geneva.

——— 2010b. *World Development Report 2010: Development and Climate Change*. Washington, DC: World Bank.

——— 2010c. *10 Years of Experience with Carbon Finance: Insights from Working with Carbon Markets for Development & Global Greenhouse Gas Mitigation*. Washington, DC: World Bank.

——— 2010d. *Climate Investment Funds*. Washington, DC: World Bank.

——— 2010e. *Innovative Finance for Development Solutions: Initiatives of the World Bank Group*. Washington, DC: World Bank.

——— 2014. Development Partners Support the Creation of Global Financing Facility to Advance Women's and Children's Health. Press Release, 25 September 2014. Accessed March 2015 at www.worldbank.org/en/news/press-release/2014/09/25/development-partners-support-creation-global-financing-facility-women-children-health.

World Bank Operations Evaluation Department. 2001. *Global Public Policies and Programs: Implications for Financing and Evaluation*. Proceedings from a World Bank Workshop. Washington, DC: World Bank.

——— 2004. *Addressing the Challenges of Globalization: An Independent Evaluation of the World Bank's Approach to Global Programs*. Washington, DC: World Bank.

——— 2005. *Strengthening the World Bank's Role in Global Programs and Partnerships*. Washington, DC: World Bank. Accessed March 2015 at http://documentsworldbank.org/curated/en/2006/05/6891692/strengthening-world-banks-role-global-programs-partnerships.

World Health Organization (WHO). 1999a. A Corporate Strategy for the WHO Secretariat: Report by the Director-General. Executive Board, 105th Session, Provisional Agenda Item 2. 10 December 1999 (EB105/3), Geneva.

1999b. Public–Private Partnerships for Health: Report by the Director-General. Executive Board, 105th Session, Provisional Agenda Item 2. 14 December 1999 (EB105/8), Geneva.

1999c. Roll Back Malaria: Report by the Director-General. 52nd World Health Assembly, Provisional Agenda Item 13. 14 April 1999 (A52/6), Geneva.

1999d. Collaboration within the United Nations System and with Other Intergovernmental Organizations: Report by the Secretariat. 52nd World Health Assembly, Provisional Agenda Item 18. 14 April 1999 (A52/26), Geneva.

2000a. Partnerships with Nongovernmental Organizations: Report by the Secretariat. Executive Board 107th Session, Provisional Agenda Item 3.4. 12 December 2000 (EB107/7), Geneva.

2000b. Stop Tuberculosis Initiative: Resolution of the Executive Board of the WHO. Executive Board 105th Session, Agenda Item 3.4. 27 January 2000 (EB105/R11), Geneva.

2006a. Program Budget 2004–2005: Performance Assessment Summary. (WHO/PRP/06.1). Accessed March 2015 at http://apps.who.int/iris/bitstream/10665/69406/1/WHO_PRP_06.1_eng.pdf.

2006b. Blinding Trachoma: Progress Towards Global Elimination by 2020. Press Release April 10. Accessed November 2016 at www.who.int/mediacentre/news/notes/2006/np09/en/.

2007. Partnerships: Report by the Secretariat. Executive Board 122nd Session, Provisional Agenda Item 6.3. 20 December 2007 (EB122/19), Geneva.

2008a. Global Health Partnerships: Progress on Developing Draft Policy Guidelines for WHO's Involvement: Report by the Secretariat. Executive Board 123rd Session, Provisional Agenda Item 6.1. 18 April 2008 (EB123/6), Geneva.

2008b. Global Health Partnerships: Progress on Developing Draft Policy Guidelines for WHO's Involvement: The GAVI Alliance: Report by the Secretariat. Executive Board 123rd Session, Provisional Agenda Item 6.1. 13 May 2008 (EB123/6 Add.1), Geneva.

2009a. Partnerships: Report by the Secretariat. Executive Board 124th Session, Provisional Agenda Item 7.1. 2 January 2009 (EB124/23), Geneva.

2009b. Partnerships: Report by the Secretariat. 62nd World Health Assembly, Provisional Agenda Item 19. 30 April 2009 (A62/39), Geneva.

2010a. Partnerships: Report by the Secretariat. 63rd World Health Assembly, Provisional Agenda Item 18.1. 22 April 2010 (A63/44), Geneva.

2010b. Resolutions and Decisions. 63rd World Health Assembly. 17–20 May 2010 (WHA63/2010/REC/1), Geneva. Accessed August 2016 at http://apps.who.int/gb/ebwha/pdf_files/WHA63-REC1/WHA63_REC1-en.pdf.

2011a. WHO Reform: Governance: Promoting Engagement with Other Stakeholders and Involvement with and Oversight of Partnerships: Report by the Secretariat. Executive Board 130th Session, Provisional Agenda Item 5. 27 December 2011 (EB130/5 Add.4), Geneva.

2011b. The Future of Financing for WHO: World Health Organization: Reforms for a Healthy Future: Report by the Director-General: Executive Summary. 64th World Health Assembly, Provisional Agenda Item 11. 5 May 2011 (A64/4), Geneva.

2012. WHO Hosted Partnerships. Executive Board 132rd Session, Provisional Agenda Item 5. 23 November 2012 (EB132/INF./2), Geneva.

2013. Report of the 17th Meeting of the WHO Alliance for the Global Elimination of Blinding Trachoma, 22–24 April 2013, Geneva. Accessed March 2015 at www.who.int/blindness/publications/GET 17Report_final.pdf?ua=1.

2014a. Framework of Engagement with Non-State Actors: Report by the Secretariat. 67th World Health Assembly, Provisional Agenda Item 11.3. 5 May 2014 (A 67/6), Geneva.

2014b. Financial Report and Audited Financial Statements For the Year Ended 31 December 2013. 67th World Health Assembly, Provisional Agenda Item 20.2. 17 April 2014 (A67/43), Geneva. Accessed March 2015 at http://apps.who.int/gb/ebwha/pdf_files/WHA67/A67_43-en .pdf.

2014c. Program Budget 2014–2015. Accessed March 2015 at www.who.int/about/resources_planning/PB14-15_en.pdf?ua=1.

2016a. Trachoma: Fact Sheet. Accessed November 2016 at www.who.int/mediacentre/factsheets/fs382/en/.

2016b. *Framework of Engagement with Non-State Actors*, WHA69.10, 28 May, Geneva: World Health Organization. Accessed July 2017 at http://apps.who.int/gb/ebwha/pdf_files/WHA69/A69_R10-en.pdf?ua=1

Wu, Junhui and Christian Rey, 2009. Trust Fund Portfolio Update & Progress on Implementation of New Management Framework. Presentation at World Bank Group Donor Forum 2009, 25 May 2009, Paris.

Bibliography of Academic Sources

Abbott, Kenneth W. and Duncan Snidal. 1998. Why States Act Through Formal International Organizations. *The Journal of Conflict Resolution*, 42:1, 3–22.

2009. Strengthening International Regulation through Transnational New Governance: Overcoming the Orchestration Deficit. Working paper. Accessed March 2015 at http://works.bepress.com/kenneth_abbott/2.

Abbott, Kenneth W., Philipp Genschel, Duncan Snidal and Bernhard Zangl, eds. 2015. *International Organizations as Orchestrators*. Cambridge, UK: Cambridge University Press.

Abbott, Kenneth W., Jessica F. Green and Robert O. Keohane. 2016. Organizational Ecology and Institutional Change in Global Governance. *International Organization*, 70:2, 247–277.

Adebajo, Adekeye. 2007. Pope, Pharaoh, or Prophet? The Secretary-General After the Cold War. In Chesterman, Simon, ed. *Secretary or General? The UN Secretary-General in World Politics*. Cambridge, UK: Cambridge University Press. 139–158.

Alchian, Armon A. and Harold Demsetz. 1972. Production, Information Costs and Economic Organization. *The American Economic Review*, 62:5, 777–795.

Allison, Graham T. 1969. Conceptual Models and the Cuban Missile Crisis. *The American Political Science Review*, 63:3, 689–718.

Aloisi de Larderel, Jacqueline. 1995. Sustainable Development: The Role of Business. *Public Administration and Public Policy*, 2, 1–21.

Anadon, Laura D., Gabriel Chan, Alicia G. Harley, Kira Matus, Suerie Moon, Sharmila L. Murthy and William C. Clark. 2016. Making Technological Innovation Work for Sustainable Development. *Proceedings of the National Academy of Sciences (PNAS)*, 113:35, 9692–9690.

Andonova, Liliana B. 2003. *Transnational Politics of the Environment: The European Union and Environmental Policy in Central and Eastern Europe*. Cambridge, MA: MIT Press.

2006. *Globalization, Agency, and Institutional Innovation: The Rise of Public–Private Partnerships in Global Governance*. Goldfarb Center Working Paper 2006–004. Waterville, ME: Goldfarb Center for Public Affairs and Civic Engagement.

Andonova, Liliana B. 2009. Networks, Club Goods, and Partnerships for Sustainability: The Green Power Market Development Group. In Vollmer, Derek, ed. *Enhancing the Effectiveness of Sustainability Partnerships*. Washington, DC: The National Academies Press. 65–95.

Andonova Liliana B. 2010. Public–Private Partnerships for the Earth: Politics and Patterns of Hybrid Authority in the Multilateral System. *Global Environmental Politics*, 10:2, 25–53.

2014. Boomerangs to Partnerships? Explaining State Participation in Transnational Partnerships for Sustainability. *Comparative Political Studies*, 47:3, 481–515.

Andonova, Liliana B. and Ioana A. Tuta. 2014. Transnational Networks and Paths to EU Environmental Compliance: Evidence from New Member States. *Journal of Common Market Studies*, 52:4, 775–793.

Andonova, Liliana B., and Manoela Assayag. 2015. Partnerships. In Morin, Jean Frédéric and Amandine Orsini, eds. *Essential Concepts of Global Environmental Governance*. Abingdon, UK: Routledge, pp. 146–150.

Andonova, Liliana B., Michele Betsill and Harriet Bulkeley. 2009. Transnational Climate Governance. *Global Environmental Politics*, 9:2, 52–73.

Andonova, Liliana B. and Gilles Carbonnier. 2014. Business–Humanitarian Partnerships: Processes of Normative Legitimation. *Globalizations*, 11:3, 349–367.

Andonova, Liliana B. and Marc A. Levy. 2003. Franchising Global Governance: Making Sense of the Johannesburg Type II Partnerships. In *Yearbook of International Cooperation on Environment and Development*. New York: Earthscan. 19–31.

Andonova, Liliana B. and Ronald Mitchell. 2010. The Rescaling of Global Environmental Politics. *Annual Review of Environment and Resources*, 35, 255–282.

Andonova, Liliana B. and Thomas Hale, guest editors. 2017. The Comparative Politics of Transnational Climate Governance. Special issue of *International Interactions*, 43:11.

Andonova, Liliana B. Thomas N. Hale and Charles B. Roger. 2017. National Policy and Transnational Governance of Climate Change: Substitutes or Complements? *International Studies Quarterly*, https://doi.org/10.1093/isq/sqx014.

Andresen, Steinar. 2007. The Effectiveness of UN Environmental Institutions. International Environmental Agreements: Politics, *Law and Economics*, 7:4, 317–336.

Asante, Augustine D. and Anthony B. Zwi. 2007. Public–Private Partnerships and Global Health Equity: Prospects and Challenges. *Indian Journal of Medical Ethics*, 4:4, 176–180.

Austin, James E. and M. May Seitanidi. 2012. Collaborative Value Creation: A Review of Partnering Between Non-Profits and Businesses: Part I:

Value Creation Spectrum and Collaboration Stages. *Non-Profit and Voluntary Sector Quarterly*, 41:5, 726–758.

2014. *Creating Value in Nonprofit–Business Collaborations: New Thinking and Practice*. San Francisco, CA: Jossey-Bass.

Avant, Deborah D., Martha Finnemore and Susan K. Sell. 2010. *Who Governs the Globe?* Cambridge, UK: Cambridge University Press.

Avant, Deborah and Oliver Westerwinter, eds. 2016. *The New Power Politics: Networks and Transnational Security Governance*. Oxford, UK: Oxford University Press.

Bäckstrand, Karin. 2006. Multi-Stakeholder Partnerships for Sustainable Development: Rethinking Legitimacy, Accountability and Effectiveness. *European Environment*, 16:5, 290–306.

2008. Accountability of Networked Climate Governance: The Rise of Transnational Climate Partnerships. *Global Environmental Politics*, 8:3, 74–104.

2010. From Rhetoric to Practice: The Legitimacy of Global Public–Private Partnerships for Sustainable Development. In Bexell, Magdalena and Ulrika Mörth, eds. *Democracy and Public–Private Partnerships in Global Governance*. Basingstoke, UK: Palgrave MacMillan. 145–166.

Bäckstrand, Karin and Mikael Kylsäter. 2014. Old Wine in New Bottles? The Legitimation and Delegitimation of UN Public–Private Partnerships for Sustainable Development from the Johannesburg Summit to the Rio +20 Summit. *Globalizations*, 1:3, 331–347.

Barnett, Michael and Martha Finnemore. 2004. *Rules for the World: International Organizations in Global Politics*. Ithaca, NY: Cornell University Press.

Barrett, Diana, James E. Austin and Sheila McCarthy. 2002. Cross-Sector Collaboration: Lessons from the International Trachoma Initiative. In Reich, Michael R., ed. *Public–Private Partnerships for Public Health*. Cambridge, MA: Harvard University Press. 41–67.

Bartlett, Christopher A., Vincent Marie Dessain and Anders Sjoman. 2006. Ikea's Global Sourcing Challenge: Indian Rugs and Child Labor (A). *Harvard Business School Case*, 906–414.

Bartsch, Sonja. 2007. The Global Fund to Fight AIDS, Tuberculosis and Malaria. In Hein, Wolfgang, Sonja Bartsch and Lars Kohlmorgen, eds. *Global Health Governance and the Fight against HIV/AIDS*. Basingstoke, UK: Palgrave McMillan. 146–172.

Bartsch, Sonja and Lars Kohlmorgen. 2007. The Role of Civil Society Organizations in Global Health Governance. In Hein, Wolfgang, Sonja Bartsch and Lars Kohlmorgen, eds. *Global Health Governance and the Fight against HIV/AIDS*. Basingstoke, UK: Palgrave McMillan. 92–119.

Bawn, Kathleen. 1995. Political Control versus Expertise: Congressional Choices about Administrative Procedures. *American Political Science Review*, 89:1, 62–73.

Beisheim, Marianne, Sabine Campe and Marco Schäferhoff. 2010. Global Governance through Public–Private Partnerships. In Enderlein, Henrik, Sonja Wälti and Michael Zürn, eds. *Handbook on Multi-Level Governance*. Cheltenham, UK: Edward Elgar Publishing, pp. 370–382.

Beisheim, Marianne and Andrea Liese, eds. 2014. *Transnational Partnerships: Effectively Providing for Sustainable Development?* Basingstoke, UK: Palgrave Macmillan.

Beisheim, Marianne, Andrea Liese, Hannah Janetschek and Johanna Sarre. 2014. Transnational Partnerships: Conditions for Successful Service Provision in Areas of Limited Statehood. *Governance*, 27:4, 655–673.

Bendell, Jem. 2004. Flags of Inconvenience? The Global Compact and the Future of the United Nations. *International Centre for Corporate Social Responsibility Research Paper Series*, No. 22. Nottingham, UK: International Centre for Corporate Social Responsibility.

Bendell Jem, Eva Collins, and Juliet Roper. 2010. Beyond Partnerism: Toward a More Expansive Research Agenda on Multi-Stakeholder Collaboration for Responsible Business. *Business Strategy and the Environment*, 19: 6, 351–355.

Benner, Thorsten, Charlotte Streck and Jan Martin Witte, eds. 2003. *Progress or Peril? Networks and Partnerships in Global Environmental Governance. The Post-Johannesburg Agenda*. Berlin: Global Public Policy Institute.

Bernauer, Thomas, Tobias Böhmelt and Vally Koubi. 2013. Is There a Democracy–Civil Society Paradox in Global Environmental Governance? *Global Environmental Politics*, 13:1, 88–107.

Berliner, Daniel and Aseem Prakash. 2012. From Norms to Programs: The United Nations Global Compact and Global Governance. *Regulation & Governance*, 6:2, 149–166.

    2014. The United Nations Global Compact: An Institutionalist Perspective. *Journal of Business Ethics*, 122:2, 217–223.

    2015. "Bluewashing" the Firm? Voluntary Regulations, Program Design, and Member Compliance with the United Nations Global Compact. *Policy Studies Journal*, 43:1, 115–138.

Bernhagen, Patrick and Neil J. Mitchell. 2010. The Private Provision of Public Goods: Corporate Commitments and the United Nations Global Compact. *International Studies Quarterly*, 54:4, 1175–1187.

Bernstein, Steven. 2005. Legitimacy in Global Environmental Governance. *Journal of International Law and International Relations*, 1:1–2, 139–166.

2011. Legitimacy in Intergovernmental and Non-State Global Govern-ance. *Review of International Political Economy*, 18:1, 17–51.

Betsill, Michele M. and Elisabeth Corell. 2008. *NGO Diplomacy: The Influ-ence of Non-Governmental Organizations in International Environ-mental Negotiations*. Cambridge, MA: MIT Press.

Bexell, Magdalena, guest editor. 2014. *Global Governance, Legitimacy and Legitimation*. Globalizations, special issue 11:3.

Bexell, Magdalena and Ulrika Mörth, eds. 2010. *Democracy and Public–Private Partnerships in Global Governance*. London, UK: Palgrave Macmillan.

Biermann, Frank and Bernd Siebenhüner, eds. 2009. *Managers of Global Change: The Influence of International Environmental Bureaucracies*. Cambridge, MA: MIT Press.

Biermann, Frank, Man-san Chan, Aysem Mert and Philipp Pattberg. 2007. Multi-Stakeholder Partnerships for Sustainable Development: Does the Promise Hold? In Glasbergen, Pieter, Frank Biermann and Arthur P. J. Mol, eds. *Partnerships, Governance and Sustainable Development: Reflections on Theory and Practice*. Cheltenham, UK: Edward Elgar Publishing. 239–260.

Biermann, Frank, Philipp Pattberg, Harro van Asselt and Fariborz Zelli. 2009. The Fragmentation of Global Governance Architectures: A Framework for Analysis. *Global Environmental Politics*, 9:4, 14–40.

Biersteker, Thomas J. 2017. Global Security Governance. In Cavelty, Myr-iam Dunn and Thierry Balzaco, eds. *Routledge Handbook of Security Studies*. London, UK: Routledge Publishers, pp. 425–435.

Birn, Anne-Emanuelle. 2014. Backstage: The Relationship between the Rockefeller Foundation and the World Health Organization, Part I: 1940s–1960s. *Public Health*, 128:2, 129–140.

Bissel, Richard E. 2001. A Participatory Approach to Strategic Planning: Dams and Development: A New Framework for Decision-Making. *Environment*, 43:7, 37–40.

Black, Maggie. 1986. *The Children and the Nations: The Story of UNICEF*. New York: United Nations Children's Fund (UNICEF).

1996. *Children First: The Story of UNICEF, Past and Present*. Oxford, UK: Oxford University Press.

Boisson de Chazournes, Laurence. 2009. Changing Roles of International Organizations: Global Administrative Law and the Interplay of Legit-imacies. *International Organizations Law Review*, 6:2, 655–666.

Boisson de Chazournes, Laurence and Emmanuelle Mazuyer. 2011. *The Global Compact of the United Nations 10 Years After*. Brussels: Bruylant.

Boli, John and George M. Thomas. 1999. *Constructing World Culture. International Nongovernmental Organizations since 1875.* Stanford, CA: Stanford University Press.

Bond, Alison. 2012. U.S. Funding of the United Nations: Arrears Payments as an Indicator of Multilateralism. *Berkeley Journal of International Law,* 21:3, 703–714.

Börzel, Tanja A. and Thomas Risse. 2005. Public–Private Partnerships: Effective and Legitimate Tools of International Governance? In Grande, Edgar and Louis W. Pauly, eds. *Complex Sovereignty: Reconstituting Political Authority in the Twenty-First Century.* Toronto: University of Toronto Press. 195–216.

Bremer, Jennifer Ann. 2008. How Global Is the Global Compact? *Business Ethics: A European Review,* 17:3, 227–244.

Bradley, Curtis A. and Judith G. Kelley. 2008. The Concept of International Delegation. *Law and Contemporary Problems,* 71:1, 1–36.

Brown, Theodore M., Marcos Cueto and Elizabeth Fee. 2006. The World Health Organization and the Transition from "International" to "Global" Public Health. *American Journal of Public Health,* 96:1, 62–72.

Brown, Halina S., Martin de Jong and David Levy. 2009. Building Institutions Based on Information Disclosure: Lessons from the GRI's Sustainability Reporting. *Journal of Cleaner Production,* 17:6, 571–580.

Brown, Halina S., Martin de Jong and Teodorina Lissidrenska. 2009. The Rise of the Global Reporting Initiative as a Case of Institutional Entrepreneurship. *Environmental Politics,* 18:2, 182–200.

Brugger, Ernst A. and Peter Maurer. 2010. Concluding Remarks: From Alleviating the Negative Impacts of Globalization to Transforming Markets. In Rasche, Andreas and Georg Kell, eds. *The United Nations Global Compact: Achievements, Trends and Challenges.* Cambridge, UK: Cambridge University Press. 386–396.

Brühl, Tanja and Volker Rittberger. 2001. From International to Global Governance: Actors, Collective Decision-Making, and the United Nations in the World of the Twenty-First Century. In Rittberger, Volker, ed. *Global Governance and the United Nations System.* Tokyo: United Nations University Press. 1–47.

Bruszt, Laszlo and Gerald A. McDermott, eds. 2014. *Leveling the Playing Field: Transnational Regulatory Integration and Development.* Oxford, UK: Oxford University Press.

Buchanan, Allen and Robert O. Keohane. 2006. The Legitimacy of Global Governance Institutions. *Ethics and International Affairs,* 20:4, 405–437.

Bulkeley, Harriet, Liliana B. Andonova, Michele Betsill, Daniel Compagnon, Thomas Hale, Matthew J. Hoffmann, Peter Newell, Matthew Paterson, Charles Roger and Stacy D. VanDeveer. 2014. *Transnational Climate Change Governance.* Cambridge, UK: Cambridge University Press.

Bull, Benedicte and Desmond McNeill. 2007. *Development Issues in Global Governance. Public–Private Partnerships and Market Multilateralism.* London, UK: Routledge Publishers.

Burci, Gian Luca. 2009. Public/Private Partnerships in the Public Health Sector. *International Organizations Law Review*, 6:2, 359–382.

Busby, Joshua W. 2010. *Moral Movements and Foreign Policy.* Cambridge, UK: Cambridge University Press.

Buse, Kent. 2004. Governing Public–Private Infectious Disease Partnerships. *Brown Journal of World Affairs*, 10:2, 225–242.

Buse, Kent and Andrew Harmer. 2004. Power to the Partners? *The Politics of Public–Private Health Partnerships. Development*, 47:22, 49–56.

Buse, Kent, Wolfgang Hein and Nick Drager, eds. 2009. *Making Sense of Global Health Governance: A Policy Perspective.* London, UK: Palgrave Macmillan.

Buse, Kent and Sonja Tanaka. 2011. Global Public–Private Health Partnerships: Lessons Learned from Ten Years of Experience and Evaluation. *International Dental Journal*, 61:2, 2–10.

Buse, Kent and Gill Walt. 2002. The World Health Organization and Global Public–Private Health Partnerships: In Search of "Good" Global Governance. In Reich, Michael R., ed. *Public–Private Partnerships for Public Health.* Cambridge, MA: Harvard University Press. 169–197.

Büthe, Tim and Walter Mattli. 2011. *The New Global Rulers: The Privatization of Regulation in the World Economy.* Princeton, NJ: Princeton University Press.

Cashore, Benjamin, Graeme Auld and Deanna Newsom. 2004. *Governing through Markets: Forest Certification and the Emergency of Non-State Authority.* New Haven, CT: Yale University Press.

Cassels, Andrew, Ian Smith and Gian Luca Burci. 2014. Reforming WHO: The Art of the Possible. *Public Health*, 128:2, 202–204.

Castells, Manuel. 1996 [2000]. *The Rise of the Network Society: The Information Age: Economy, Society and Culture, Vol. I.* Oxford, UK: Blackwell Publishers.

    2005. Global Governance and Global Politics. *PS: Political Science and Politics*, 38:1, 9–16.

Chayes, Abram and Antonia Handler Chayes. 1995. *The New Sovereignty: Compliance with International Regulating Agreements.* Cambridge, MA: Harvard University Press.

Chen, Lincoln C., Mary Oakes Smith and Franklin A. Thomas. 2006. *Public–Private Partnerships at the United Nations: UNF/UNFIP: A Story of Generosity, Thoughtfulness and Accomplishment.* New York: United Nations Publishing. Accessed July 2014 at www.un.org/partner ships/YLatestUpdate2006.htm.

Chesterman, Simon, ed. 2007. *Secretary or General? The UN Secretary-General in World Politics.* Cambridge, UK: Cambridge University Press.

Chorev, Nitsan. 2012. *The World Health Organization between North and South.* Ithaca, NY: Cornell University Press.

Clapham, Andrew. 2006. *Human Rights Obligations of Non-State Actors.* Oxford, UK: Oxford University Press.

Clapham, Andrew, Mary Robinson, Claire Mahon and Scott Jerbi, eds. 2009. *Realizing the Right to Health.* Zürich: Rüffer & Rub.

Clapp, Jennifer. 2005. The Privatization of Global Environmental Governance: ISO 14000 and the Developing World. In Levy, David L. and Peter J. Newell, eds. *The Business of Global Environmental Governance.* Cambridge, MA: MIT Press. 223–248.

Clark, William C., Thomas P. Tomich, Meine van Noordwijk, David Guston, Delia Catacutan, Nancy M. Dickson and Elizabeth McNie. 2016. Boundary Work for Sustainable Development: Natural Resource Management at the Consultative Group on International Agricultural Research (CGIAR). *Proceedings of the National Academy of Sciences of the United States of America*, 113:17, 4615–4622.

Clinton, Chelsea and Devi Sridhar. 2017. *Governing Global Health. Who Runs the World and Why?* Oxford: Oxford University Press.

Cohen, Michael D., James G. March and Johan P. Olsen. 1972. A Garbage Can Model of Organizational Choice. *Administrative Science Quarterly*, 17:1, 1–25.

Colgan, Jeff D., Robert O. Keohane and Thijs Van de Graaf. 2011. Punctuated Equilibrium in the Energy Regime Complex. *Review of International Organizations*, 7, 117–143.

Compagnon, Daniel. 2012. Africa's Involvement in Partnerships for Sustainable Development: Holy Grail or Business as Usual? In Pattberg, Philipp, Frank Biermann, Sander Chan and Aysem Mert, eds. *Public–Private Partnerships for Sustainable Development. Emergence, Influence and Legitimacy.* Cheltenham, UK: Edward Elgar. 137–164.

Conca, Ken. 1995. Greening the United Nations: Environmental Organizations and the UN System. *Third World Quarterly*, 16:3, 441–457.

2015. *An Unfinished Foundation: The United Nations and Global Environmental Governance.* Oxford, UK: Oxford University Press.

Cooper, Richard N. 1989. International Cooperation in Public Health as a Prologue to Macroeconomics Cooperation. In Cooper, Richard N., Barry Eichengreen, Gerald Holtham, Robert D. Putman and C. Randall Henning, eds. *Can Nations Agree? Issues in International Economic Cooperation*. Washington, DC; The Brookings Institution. 178–254.

Cutler, Claire A., Virginia Haufler and Tony Porter, eds. 1999. *Private Authority and International Affairs*. Albany, NY: State University of New York Press.

Dallaire, Roméo and Brent Beardsley. 2003. *Shake Hands with the Devil: The Failure of Humanity in Rwanda*. Toronto: Random House.

Della Porta, Donatella and Sidney Tarrow, eds. 2005. *Transnational Protest and Global Activism*. Lanham, MD: Rowman and Littlefield Publishers, Ltd.

DiMaggio, Paul J. and Walter W. Powell. 1983. The Iron Cage Revisited: Institutional Isomorphism and Collective Rationality in Organizational Fields. *American Sociological Review*, 48:2, 147–160.

Dingwerth, Klaus. 2005. The Democratic Legitimacy of Public–Private Rule Making: What Can We Learn from the World Commission on Dams? *Global Governance*, 11:2, 65–83.

Dingwerth, Klaus and Margot Eichinger. 2010. Tamed Transparency: How Information Disclosure under the Global Reporting Initiative Fails to Empower. *Global Environmental Politics*, 10:3, 74–96.

Drezner, Daniel W. 2004. The Global Governance of the Internet: Bringing the State Back In. *Political Science Quarterly*, 119:3, 477–498.

Easterly, William. 2006. *The White Man's Burden: Why the West's Efforts to Aid the Rest Have Done So Much Ill and So Little Good*. New York: The Penguin Press.

Economist. 2015. Eradicating Disease. October 15, 2015. Accessed August 2016 at www.economist.com/news/leaders/21672213-viral-and-para sitic-diseases-are-not-only-worth-killing-they-are-also-increasingly.

Eggenberger, Markus. 2011. The Global Compact: Which Role for Governments? In Boisson de Chazournes, Laurence and Emmanuelle Mazuyer, eds. *The Global Compact of the United Nations 10 Years After*. Brussels: Bruylant. 54–68.

Elsig, Manfred and Franck Amalric. 2008. Business and Public–Private Partnerships for Sustainability: Beyond Corporate Social Responsibility? *Global Society*, 22:3, 387–404.

Fakuda-Parr, Sakiko and David Hulme. 2011. International Norm Dynamics and "The End of Poverty." *Global Governance*, 17:1, 17–36.

Fall, Papa Louis and Mohamed Mounir Zahran. 2010. *United Nations Corporate Partnerships: The Role and Functioning of the Global*

Compact. United Nations Joint Inspection Unit. Geneva, Switzerland: United Nations.

Farrell, Henry and Adrienne Héritier. 2007. Contested Competences in Europe: Incomplete Contracts and Interstitial Institutional Change. *West European Politics*, 30:2, 227–243.

Farrell, Henry and Abraham L. Newman. 2014. Domestic Institutions beyond the Nation-State: Charting the New Interdependence Approach. *World Politics*, 66:2, 331–363.

Faul, Moira V. 2016. Networks and Power: Why Networks Are Hierarchical Not Flat and What Can Be Done About It, *Global Policy Journal*, 7:2, 185–197.

Finnemore, Martha. 1996. *National Interests in International Society*. Ithaca, NY: Cornell University Press.

Finnemore, Martha and Kathryn Sikkink. 1998. International Norm Dynamics and Political Change. *International Organization*, 52:4, 887–917.

    2001. Taking Stock: The Constructivist Research Program in International Relations and Comparative Politics. *Annual Review of Political Science*, 4, 391–416.

Fox, Jonathan A. and L. David Brown. 1998. *The Struggle for Accountability: The World Bank, NGOs, and Grassroots Movements*. Cambridge, MA: MIT Press.

Freestone, David. 2003. The Instrument Establishing the World Bank Prototype Carbon Fund (PCF) and the First PCF Emission Reductions Purchase Agreement. *The World Bank Legal Review*, 1, 433–524.

Fuertes, Flavio and Nicolás Liarte-Vejrup. 2010. Building Corporate Citizenship through the United Nations Global Compact: Contributions and Lessons Learned from the Argentinean Local Network. In Rasche, Andreas and Georg Kell, eds. *The United Nations Global Compact: Achievements, Trends and Challenges*. Cambridge, UK: Cambridge University Press. 370–386.

Garcia-Johnson, Ronie. 2000. *Exporting Environmentalism: U.S. Multinational Chemical Corporations in Brazil and Mexico*. Cambridge, MA: MIT Press.

Gereffi, Gary, Ronie Garcia-Johnson and Erica Sasser. 2001. The NGO-Industrial Complex. *Foreign Policy*, 125, 56–65.

Gilbert, Dirk U. 2010. The United Nations Global Compact as a Network of Networks. In Rasche, Andreas and Georg Kell, eds. *The United Nations Global Compact: Achievements, Trends and Challenges*. Cambridge, UK: Cambridge University Press. 340–355.

Glasbergen, Pieter, Frank Biermann and Arthur P. J. Mol, eds. 2007. *Partnerships, Governance and Sustainable Development: Reflections on Theory and Practice*. Cheltenham, UK: Edward Elgar Publishing.

Global Partnerships Database. 2016. Graduate Institute for International and Development Studies: Geneva.

Godlee, Fiona. 1994. The World Health Organisation: WHO in Crisis. *BMJ: British Medical Journal*, 309:6966, 1424–1428.

    1995. The World Health Organisation: Interview with the Director General. *BMJ: British Medical Journal*, 310:6979, 583–588.

Goldstein, Judith L. and Robert O. Keohane, eds. 1993. *Ideas and Foreign Policy: Beliefs, Institutions, and Political Change*. Ithaca, NY: Cornell University Press.

Goldstein, Judith L., Miles Kahler, Robert O. Keohane and Anne-Marie Slaughter. 2001. *Legalization and World Politics*. Cambridge, MA: MIT Press.

Grande, Edgar and Louis W. Pauly, eds. 2005. *Complex Sovereignty: Reconstituting Political Authority in the Twenty-First Century*. Toronto: University of Toronto Press.

Grant, Ruth W. and Robert O. Keohane. 2005. Accountability and Abuses of Power in World Politics. *American Political Science Review*, 99:1, 29–43.

Green, Jessica F. 2013. *Rethinking Private Authority: Agents and Entrepreneurs in Global Environmental Governance*. Princeton, NJ: Princeton University Press.

Gutner, Tamar. 2002. *Banking on the Environment: Multilateral Development Banks and their Environmental Performance in Central and Eastern Europe*. Cambridge, MA: MIT Press.

    2005. Explaining the Gaps between Mandate and Performance: Agency Theory and World Bank Environmental Reform. *Global Environmental Politics*, 5:2, 10–37.

Gutner, Tamar and Alexander Thompson. 2010. The Politics of IO Performance: A Framework. *Review of International Organizations*, 5:3, 227–248.

Haas, Ernst B. 1990. *When Knowledge Is Power: Three Models of Change in International Organizations*. Berkeley: University of California Press.

Haas, Peter M. 1989. Do Regimes Matter? Epistemic Communities and Mediterranean Pollution Control. *International Organization*, 43:3, 377–403.

    1990. *Saving the Mediterranean: The Politics of International Environmental Cooperation*. New York: Columbia University Press.

Hale, Thomas and David Held, eds. 2011. *The Handbook of Transnational Governance: Institutions and Innovations*. Cambridge: Polity Press.

    2012. Gridlock and Innovation in Global Governance: The Partial Transnational Solution. *Global Policy*, 3:2, 169–181.

Hale, Thomas, David Held and Kevin Young. 2013. *Gridlock: Why Global Cooperation Is Failing When We Need It Most.* Stafford, AU: Polity Press.

Hale, Thomas and Denise L. Mauzerall. 2004. Thinking Globally and Acting Locally: Can the Johannesburg Partnerships Coordinate Action on Sustainable Development? *Journal of Environment and Development*, 13:3, 220–239.

Hale, Thomas and Charles B. Roger. 2014. Orchestration and Transnational Climate Governance. *Review of International Organizations*, 9:1, 59–82.

Hall, Rodney Brice and Thomas J. Biersteker. 2002. *The Emergence of Private Authority in Global Governance.* Cambridge, UK: Cambridge University Press.

Hannan, Michal T. and John Freeman. 1989. *Organizational Ecology.* Cambridge, MA: Harvard University Press.

Hanrieder, Tine. 2015. WHO Orchestrates? Coping with Competitors in Global Health. In Abbott, Kenneth W., Philipp Genschel, Duncan Snidal and Bernhard Zangl, eds. *International Organizations as Orchestrators.* Cambridge, UK: Cambridge University Press. 191–213.

Haufler, Virginia. 2001. *A Public Role for the Private Sector: Industry Self-Regulation in a Global Economy.* Washington, DC: Carnegie Endowment for International Peace.

Hawkins, Darren G., David A. Lake, Daniel L. Nielson and Michael J. Tierney, eds. 2006. *Delegation and Agency in International Organizations.* Cambridge, UK: Cambridge University Press.

Hawkins, Darren G. and Wade Jacoby. 2006. How Agents Matter. In Hawkins, Darren G., David A. Lake, Daniel L. Nielson and Michael J. Tierney, eds. *Delegation and Agency in International Organizations.* Cambridge, UK: Cambridge University Press. 199–228.

Heimer, Matt. 1998. The UN Environment Programme: Thinking Globally, Retreating Locally. *Yale Human Rights and Development Journal*, 1:1, Article 6.

Hein, Wolfgang, Sonja Bartsch and Lars Kohlmorgen, eds. 2007. *Global Health Governance and the Fight against HIV/AIDS.* London, UK: Palgrave Macmillan.

Hein, Wolfgang and Suerie Moon. 2013. *Informal Norms in Global Governance: Human Rights, Intellectual Property Rules and Access to Medicines.* Surrey, UK: Ashgate.

Held, David and Anthony McGrew, eds. 2002. *Governing Globalization: Power, Authority and Global Governance.* Cambridge, UK: Polity Press.

Héritier, Adrienne, ed. 2002. *Common Goods: Reinventing European and International Governance.* Lanham, MD: Rowman and Littlefield Publishers, Inc.

Hirschman, Albert O. 1970. *Exit, Voice, and Loyalty: Responses to Decline in Firms, Organizations, and States.* Cambridge, MA: Harvard University Press.

Hoffmann, Matthew J. 2011. *Climate Governance at the Crossroads: Experimenting with a Global Respnse After Kyoto.* Oxford: Oxford University Press.

Hoffman Steven J. and John-Arne Roettingen. 2014. Split WHO in Two: Strengthening Political Decision-Making and Securing Independent Scientific Advice. *Public Health,* 128:2, 188–194.

Holzscheiter, Anna. 2010. *Children's Rights in International Politics: The Transformative Power of Discourse.* Basingstoke, UK: Palgrave McMillan.

Hurd, Ian. 1999. Legitimacy and Authority in International Politics. *International Organization,* 53:2, 379–408.

Hurrell, Andrew. 2007. *On Global Order: Power, Values, and the Constitution of International Society.* Oxford, UK: Oxford University Press.

Ivanova, Maria. 2007. Designing the United Nations Environment Programme: A Story of Compromise and Confrontation. *International Environmental Agreements: Politics, Law and Economics,* 7, 337–361.

Johnson, Tana. 2014. *Organizational Progeny: Why Governments Are Losing Control over Proliferating Structures of Global Governance.* Oxford, UK: Oxford University Press.

Johnstone, Ian. 2007. The Secretary-General as Norm Entrepreneur. In Chesterman, Simon, ed. *Secretary or General? The UN Secretary-General in World Politics.* Cambridge, UK: Cambridge University Press. 123–138.

Jolly, Richard. 2014. *UNICEF (United Nations Children's Fund): Global Governance that Works.* New York: Routledge.

Jolly, Richard, Louis Emmerij and Thomas G. Weiss. 2009. *UN Ideas That Changed the World.* Bloomington: Indiana University Press.

Jönsson, Christer. 2013. The John Holmes Memorial Lecture: International Organizations at the Moving Public–Private Borderline. *Global Governance,* 19:1, 1–18.

Jönsson, Christer and Jonas Tallberg, eds. 2010. *Transnational Actors in Global Governance: Patterns, Explanations, and Implications.* Basingstoke, UK: Palgrave Macmillan.

2010. Coordinating Actors in the Fight against HIV/AIDS: From "Lead Agency" to Public–Private Partnerships. In Bexell, Magdalena and Ulrika Mörth, eds. *Democracy and Public–Private Partnerships in Global Governance.* Basingstoke, UK: Palgrave Macmillan. 167–189.

Jönsson, Kristina. 2014. Legitimation Challenges in Global Health Governance: The Case of Non-Communicable Diseases. *Globalizations,* 11:3, 301–314.

Jordan, Andrew and Dave Huitema. 2014. Innovations in Climate Policy: the Politics of Invention, Diffusion, and Evaluation. *Environmental Politics*, 23:5, 715-734.

Juma, Calestous. 2000. Stunting Green Progress. *Financial Times*, July 5.

Kahler, Miles. 2009. *Networked Politics: Agency, Power and Governance.* Ithaca, NY: Cornell University Press.

Kaul, Inge. 2005. Exploring the Policy Space between Markets and States: Global Public–Private Partnerships. In Kaul, Inge and Pedro Conceicao, eds. *The New Public Finance: Responding to Global Challenges.* Oxford, UK: Oxford University Press. 91–134.

Kaul, Inge, Isabelle Grunberg and Marc A. Stern, eds. 1999. *Global Public Goods: International Cooperation in the 21st Century.* Oxford, UK: Oxford University Press.

Kaul, Inge and Pedro Conceicao, eds. 2005. *The New Public Finance: Responding to Global Challenges.* Oxford, UK: Oxford University Press.

Keck, Margaret E. and Kathryn Sikkink. 1998. *Activists beyond Borders: Advocacy Networks in International Politics.* Ithaca, NY: Cornell University Press.

Kell, Georg. 2012. 12 Years Later: Reflections on the Growth of the UN Global Compact. *Business & Society*, 52:1, 31–52.

Kell, Georg and David Levin. 2003. The Global Compact Network: An Historic Experiment in Learning and Action. *Business and Society Review*, 108:2, 151–181.

Kell, Georg, Anne-Marie Slaughter and Thomas Hale. 2007. Silent Reform through the Global Compact. *UN Chronicle*, 44:1, 26–31.

Kelly, Laurent and Jeffery Jordan. 2004. *The Prototype Carbon Fund: Addressing Challenges of Globalization – An Independent Evaluation of the World Bank's Approach to Global Programs.* Washington, DC: The World Bank.

Kennedy, Paul. 2007. *The Parliament of Man: The Past, Present, and the Future of the United Nations.* New York: Vintage Books.

Keohane, Robert O. 1984. *After Hegemony: Cooperation and Discord in the World Political Economy.* Princeton, NJ: Princeton University Press.

2001. Governance in a Partially Globalized World: Presidential Address, American Political Science Association, 2000. *American Political Science Review*, 95:1, 1–13.

2011. Global Governance and Legitimacy. *Review of International Political Economy*, 18:1, 99–109.

Keohane, Robert O. and Joseph S. Nye. 1971. *Transnational Relations and World Politics.* Harvard University Press: Cambridge, MA.

2000. Introduction. In Nye, Joseph S. and John D. Donahue, eds. *Governance in a Globalizing World*. Washington, DC: Brookings Institution Press, pp. 1–44.

Keohane, Robert O. and Elinor Ostrom, eds. 1995. *Local Commons and Global Independence: Heterogeneity and Cooperation in Two Domains*. London, UK: Sage Publications Ltd.

Keohane, Robert O. and David G. Victor. 2011. The Regime Complex for Climate Change. *Perspectives on Politics*, 9:1, 7–23.

Kickbusch, Ilona. 2009. Moving Global Health Governance Forward. In Buse, Kent, Wolfgang Hein and Nick Drager, eds. 2009. *Making Sense of Global Health Governance: A Policy Perspective*. Basingstoke, UK: Palgrave Macmillan. 320–340.

Kickbusch, Ilona and Evelyne de Leeuw. 1999. Global Public Health: Revisiting Healthy Public Policy at the Global Level. *Health Promotion International*, 14:4, 285–288.

Kiewiet, D. Roderick and Mathew D. McCubbins. 1991. *The Logic of Delegation: Congressional Parties and the Appropriations Process*. Chicago: University of Chicago Press.

King, Betty. 2001. The UN Global Compact: Responsibility for Human Rights, Labor Relations, and the Environment in Developing Nations. *Cornell International Law Journal*, 34:3, 481–485.

Kingdon, John W. 1984. *Agendas, Alternatives, and Public Policies*. Boston: Little, Brown.

KPMG. 2005. KPMG International Survey of Corporate Responsibility Reporting 2005. Accessed August 2016 at www.greenbiz.com/research/report/2005/08/17/kpmg-international-survey-corporate-responsibility-reporting-2005.

2011. International Survey of Corporate Responsibility Reporting 2011. Accessed August 2016 at www.kpmg.com/PT/pt/IssuesAndInsights/Documents/corporate-responsibility2011.pdf.

Krasner, Stephen D., ed. 1983. *International Regimes*. Ithaca, NY: Cornell University Press.

1991. Global Communications and National Power: Life on the Pareto Frontier. *World Politics*, 43:3, 336–366.

2003. The State Is Alive and Well. In Art, Robert J. and Robert Jervis, eds. *International Politics: Enduring Concepts and Contemporary Issues*, 6th edn. New York: Longman. 551–556.

Krehbiel, Keith. 1992. *Information and Legislative Organization*. Ann Arbor: University of Michigan Press.

Kuyama, Sumihiro and Michael Ross Fowler, eds. 2009. *Envisioning Reform: Enhancing UN Accountability in the Twenty-First Century*. Tokyo: United Nations University Press.

Lee, Kelley, ed. 2003. *Health Impact of Globalization: Towards Global Governance*. New York: Palgrave Macmillan.

Lee, Kelley, Kent Buse and Suzanne Fustukian, eds. 2002. *Health Policy in a Globalizing World*. Cambridge, UK: Cambridge University Press.

Left, Sara. 2002. Bush Pulls Plug on UN Family Planning Funds. *The Guardian*, 23 July 2002, accessed November 2016 via https://www.theguardian.com/world/2002/jul/23/usa.sarahleft

Levy, David L. and Peter J. Newell, eds. 2005. *The Business of Global Environmental Governance*. Cambridge, MA: MIT Press.

Lidén, Jon. 2013. *The Grand Decade for Global Health: 1998–2008*. Working Group on Governance, paper 2. Centre on Global Health Security Working Group Papers. London, UK: Chatham House.

Littoz-Monnet, Annabelle, ed. 2017. *The Politics of Expertise in International Organizations: How International Bureaucracies Produce and Mobilize Knowledge*. Abingdon, UK: Routledge.

Lucas, Adetokunbo O. 2002. Public–Private Partnerships: Illustrative Examples. In Reich, Michael R., ed. *Public–Private Partnerships for Public Health*. Cambridge, MA: Harvard University Press. 19–41.

Majone, Giandomenico. 1996. *Regulating Europe*. New York: Routledge.

March, James G. 1965. *Handbook on Organizations*. Chicago: Rand McNally.

   1991. Exploration and Exploitation in Organization Learning. *Organization Science*, 2:1, 71–87.

March, James G. and Johan P. Olsen. 1983. The New Institutionalism: Organizational Factors in Political Life. *The American Political Science Review*, 78:3, 734–749.

   1998. The Institutional Dynamics of International Political Orders. *International Organization*, 52:4, 943–969.

Martens, Jens. 2007. *Multistakeholder Partnerships – Future Models of Multilateralism?* Occasional Paper no. 29. Berlin: Friedrich Ebert Stiftung.

Martin, Lisa. 1992. Interests, Power, and Multilateralism. *International Organization*, 46:4, 765–792.

Mathews, Jessica Tuchman. 1997. Power Shift: The Rise of Global Civil Society. *Foreign Affairs*, 76:1, 50–66.

Mathiason, John. 2007. *Invisible Governance: International Secretariats and Global Politics*. Sterling, VA: Kumarin Press.

Matiru, Robert and Timothy Ryan. 2007. The Global Drug Facility: A Unique, Holistic and Pioneering Approach to Drug Procurement and Management. *Bulletin of the World Health Organization*, 85:5, 348–353.

Matson, Pamela, William C. Clark and Krister Andersson. 2016. *Pursuing Sustainability: A Guide the Science and Practice*. Princeton, NJ: Princeton University Press.

Mattli, Walter and Ngaire Woods, eds. 2009. *The Politics of Global Regulation*. Princeton, NJ: Princeton University Press.

McCoy, David and Margaret Hilson. 2009. Civil Society, its Organizations and Global Health Governance. In Buse, Kent, Wolfgang Hein and Nick Drager, eds. 2009. *Making Sense of Global Health Governance: A Policy Perspective*. Basingstoke, UK: Palgrave Macmillan. 209–232.

McCubbins, Mathew, Roger G. Noll and Barry R. Weingast. 1987. Administrative Procedures as Instruments of Political Control. *Journal of Law, Economics, and Organization*, 3:2, 243–279.

McCubbins, Mathew, Roger G. Noll, and Barry R. Weingast. 1989. Structure and Process, Politics and Policy: Administrative Arrangements and the Political Control of Agencies. *Virginia Law Review*, 75: 431–482.

McCubbins, Mathew and Thomas Schwartz. 1984. Congressional Oversight Overlooked: Police Patrols versus Fire Alarms. *American Journal of Political Science*, 28:1, 165–179.

McInnes, Colin and Kelley Lee. 2012. *Global Health and International Relations*. Cambridge, UK: Polity Press.

McIntosh, Malcolm, Sandra Waddock and Georg Kell, eds. 2004. *Learning to Talk: Corporate Citizenship and the Development of the UN Global Compact*. Sheffield, UK: Greenleaf Publishing.

Mee, Laurence D. 2005. The Role of UNEP and UNDP in Multilateral Environmental Agreements. *International Environmental Agreements: Politics, Law and Economics*, 5:3, 227–263.

Mert, Aysem. 2015. *Environmental Governance through Partnerships: A Discourse Theoretical Study*. Cheltenham, UK: Edward Elgar Publishing.

Michaelowa, Axel and Katharina Michaelowa. 2011. Climate Business for Poverty Reduction? The Role of the World Bank. *The Review of International Organizations*, 6:3, 259–286.

Milner, Helen. 2006. Why Multilateralism? Foreign Aid and Domestic Principal–Agent Problems. In Hawkins, Darren G., David A. Lake, Daniel L. Nielson and Michael J. Tierney, eds. *Delegation and Agency in International Organizations*. Cambridge, UK: Cambridge University Press. 107–139.

Mintrom, Michael. 1997. Policy Entrepreneurs and the Diffusion of Innovation. *American Journal of Political Science*, 41:3, 738–770.

Mitchell, Ronald B. 2003. International Environmental Agreements: A Survey of their Features, Formation and Effects. *Annual Review of Environment and Resources*, 28, 429–461.

Mitchell, Ronald B., William C. Clark, David W. Cash and Nancy M. Dickson, eds. 2006. *Global Environmental Assessments: Information and Influence*. Cambridge, MA: MIT Press.

Moe, Terry. 1984. The New Economics of Organization. *American Journal of Political Science*, 28:4, 739–777.

1990. The Politics of Structural Choice: Toward a Theory of Public Bureaucracy. In Williamson, Oliver E., ed. *Organization Theory: From Chester Barnard to the Present and Beyond*. Oxford, UK: Oxford University Press. 116–153.

Moon, Suerie. 2013. WHO's Role in the Global Health System: What Can be Learned from Global R&D Debates? *Public Health*. 128:2, 168–172.

Moon, Suerie, Nicole A. Szlezák, Catherine M. Michaud, Dean T. Jamison, Gerald T. Keusch, William C. Clark and Barry R. Bloom. 2010. The Global Health System: Lessons for a Stronger Institutional Framework. *PLOS Medicine*, 7:1.

Morgenthau, Hans. 1966. *Politics Among Nations*. New York: Knopf.

Morin, Jean-Frederic. 2011. The Life-Cycle of Transnational Issues: Lessons from the Access to Medicines Controversy. *Global Society*, 25:2, 228–247.

Morrow, James, D. 1994. Modeling the Forms of International Cooperation: Distribution versus Information. *International Organization*, 48:3, 387–423.

Morse, Julia C. and Robert O. Keohane. 2014. Contested Multilateralism. *The Review of International Organizations*, 9:4, 385–412.

Muraskin, William. 1998. *The Children's Vaccine Initiative and the Struggle to Develop Vaccines for the Third World*. Albany: State University of New York Press.

2002. The Last Years of the CVI and the Birth of the GAVI. In Reich, Michael R., ed. *Public–Private Partnerships for Public Health*. Cambridge, MA: Harvard University Press. 115–169.

Murphy, Craig. N. 2006. *The United Nations Development Programme: A Better Way?* Cambridge, UK: Cambridge University Press.

Mwangi, Wagaki, Lothar Rieth and Hans P. Schmitz. 2013. Encouraging Greater Compliance: Local Networks and the United Nations Global Compact. In Risse, Thomas, Stephen C. Ropp and Kathryn Sikkink, eds. *The Persistent Power of Human Rights: From Commitment to Compliance*. Cambridge: Cambridge University Press, 203–221.

Najam, Adil. 2003. The Case against a New International Environmental Organization. *Global Governance*, 9:3, 367–384.

Nakhooda, Smita. 2008. *Correcting the World's Greatest Market Failure: Climate Change and the Multilateral Development Banks*. Washington DC: World Resources Institute.

2011. Asia, the Multilateral Development Banks and Energy Governance. *Global Policy*, 2:s1, 120–132.

Nakhooda, Smita and Athena Ballesteros. 2009. *Investing in Sustainable Futures: Multilateral Development Banks Investments in Energy Policy*. Washington DC: World Resources Institute and International Institute for Sustainable Development.

Nelson, Jane. 2002. *Building Partnerships: Cooperation between the United Nations System and the Private Sector*. New York: United Nations Publications.

—— 2004. *The Public Role of Private Enterprise, Risks, Opportunities and New Models of Engagement*. Working Paper for the Corporate Social Responsibility Initiative. Cambridge, MA: Center for Business and Government, Harvard University.

New York Times. 2012. NYT Archive, Accessed January 2012 at http://query.nytimes.com/search/sitesearch.

Newcombe, Ken. 2001. *The Prototype Carbon Fund: Mobilizing Private and Public Resources to Combat Climate Change. In World Bank Operations Evaluation Department*. Global Public Policies and Programs: Implications for Financing and Evaluation, Proceedings from a World Bank Workshop. Washington, DC: World Bank. 71–78.

Newell, Peter. 2012. *Globalization and the Environment: Capitalism, Ecology and Power*. Cambridge, UK: Polity Press.

Newell, Peter and Matthew Paterson. 2011. *Climate Capitalism. Global Warming and the Transformation of the Global Economy*. Cambridge, UK: Cambridge University Press.

Newman, Abraham, L. 2010. International Organization Control under Conditions of Dual Delegation: A Transgovernmental Politics Approach. In Avant, Deborah D., Martha Finnemore and Susan K. Sell. *Who Governs the Globe?* Cambridge, UK: Cambridge University Press, pp. 131–152.

Nielson, Daniel L. and Michael J. Tierney. 2003. Delegation to International Organizations: Agency Theory and World Bank Environmental Reform. *International Organization*, 57:2, 241–276.

North, Douglass. 1990. *Institutions, Institutional Change and Economic Performance*. Cambridge, UK: Cambridge University Press.

Olson, Mancur. 1971. *The Logic of Collective Action: Public Goods and the Theory of Groups*. Cambridge, MA: Harvard University Press.

Ostrom, Elinor. 1990. *Governing the Commons: The Evolution of Institutions for Collective Action*. Cambridge, UK: Cambridge University Press.

Ottaway, Marina. 2001. Corporatism Goes Global: International Organizations, Non-governmental Organization Networks, and Transnational Business. *Global Governance*, 3:3, 265–292.

Owen, John W., Graham Lister and Sally Stansfield. 2009. The Role of Foundations in Global Governance for Health. In Buse, Kent, Wolfgang Hein and Nick Drager, eds. *Making Sense of Global Health Governance: A Policy Perspective*. Basingstoke, UK: Palgrave Macmillan. 232–245.

Oye, Kenneth A. and James H. Maxwell. 1995. Self-Interest and Environmental Management. In Keohane, Robert O. and Elinor Ostrom, eds. *Local Commons and Global Independence: Heterogeneity and Cooperation in Two Domains*. London, UK: Sage Publications Ltd., pp. 191–221.

Paine, Ellen. 2000. *The Road to the Global Compact: Corporate Power and the Battle over the Global Public Policy at the United Nations*. New York: Global Policy Forum.

Park, Susan. 2007. *Greening Up: The World Bank Group in Global Environmental Governance*. 48th Annual International Studies Association Convention 2007. Tucson, AZ: International Studies Association.

2010. *World Bank Group Interactions with Environmentalists: Changing International Organization Identities*. Manchester, UK: University of Manchester Press.

Parson, Edward A. 2003. *Protecting the Ozone Layer: Science and Strategy*. New York: Oxford University Press.

Pattberg, Philipp H. 2007. *Private Institutions and Global Governance: The New Politics of Environmental Sustainability*. Cheltenham, UK: Edward Elgar Publishing.

Pattberg, Philipp H. and Johannes Stipple. 2008. Beyond the Public and Private Divide: Remapping Transnational Climate Governance in the 21st Century. *International Environmental Agreements: Politics Law and Economics*, 8:4, 367–388.

Pattberg, Philipp, Frank Biermann, Sander Chan and Aysem Mert. 2012. *Public–Private Partnerships for Sustainable Development: Emergence, Influence and Legitimacy*. Cheltenham, UK: Edward Elgar Publishing.

Pauwelyn, Joost, Ramses Wessel and Jan Wouters, eds. 2012. *Informal International Lawmaking*. Oxford, UK: Oxford University Press.

Perkins, Richard and Eric Neumayer. 2010. Geographic Variations in the Early Diffusion of Corporate Voluntary Standards: Comparing ISO 14001 and the Global Compact. *Environment and Planning A*, 42:2, 347–365.

Piercy, Jan. 2001. *The World Bank and Global Public Goods. In World Bank Operations Evaluation Department. Global Public Policies and Programs: Implications for Financing and Evaluation*. Proceedings from a World Bank Workshop. Washington, DC: World Bank. 1–6.

Pollack, Mark A. 1997. Delegation, Agency, and Agenda Setting in the European Community. *International Organization*, 51:1, 99–134.

2003. *The Engines of European Integration: Delegation, Agency and Agenda Setting in the EU.* New York: Oxford University Press.

Polsby, Nelson W. 1984. *Political Innovation in America: The Politics of Policy Initiation.* New Haven, CT: Yale University Press.

Porter, Michael E. and Mark R. Kramer. 2006. Strategy and Society. The Link between Competitive Advantage and Corporate Social Responsibility. *Harvard Business Review*, December, 78–92.

Potoski, Matthew and Aseem Prakash. 2005. Green Clubs and Voluntary Governance: ISO 14001 and Firms' Regulatory Compliance. *American Journal of Political Science*, 49:2, 235–248.

Powell, Walter W. and Paul J. DiMaggio. 1991. *The New Institutionalism in Organizational Analysis.* London, UK: The University of Chicago Press.

Power, Samantha. 2002. *A Problem from Hell: America and the Age of Genocide.* New York: Basic Books.

Prakash, Aseem and Matthew Potoski. 2006a. Racing to the Bottom? Trade, Environmental Governance, and ISO 14001. *American Journal of Political Science*, 50:2, 350–364.

2006b. *The Voluntary Environmentalists: Green Clubs, ISO 14001, and Voluntary Environmental Regulations.* Cambridge, UK: Cambridge University Press.

Price, Richard. 1998. Reversing the Gun Sights: Transnational Civil Society Targets Land Mines. *International Organization*, 52:3, 613–644.

Princen, Thomas and Matthias Finger. 1994. *Environmental NGOs in World Politics: Linking the Local and the Global.* New York: Routledge.

Prügl, Elisabeth and Jacqui True. 2014. Equality means business? Governing gender through transnational public-private partnerships. *Review of International Political Economy*, 21:6, 1137-1169.

Rasche, Andreas and Georg Kell, eds. 2010. *The United Nations Global Compact: Achievements, Trends and Challenges.* Cambridge, UK: Cambridge University Press.

Raustiala, Kal. 1997. States, NGOs, and International Environmental Institutions. *International Studies Quarterly*, 41:4, 719–740.

2002. The Architecture of International Cooperation: Transgovernmental Networks and the Future of International Law. *Virginia Journal of International Law*, 43:1, 1–92.

Reich, Michael R., ed. 2002. *Public–Private Partnerships for Public Health.* Cambridge, MA: Harvard University Press.

Reinicke, Wolfgang H. 1999. The Other World Wide Web: Global Public Policy Networks. *Foreign Policy*, 117, 44–57.

Reinicke, Wolfgang H. and Francis M. Deng, eds. 2000. *Critical Choices: The United Nations, Networks, and the Future of Global Governance.* Washington, DC: International Development Research Center (IDRC).

Rich, Bruce. 1994. *Mortgaging the Earth: The World Bank, Environmental Impoverishment, and the Crisis of Development.* Boston: Beacon Press.

Richter, Judith. 2004. Public–Private Partnerships for Health: A Trend with No Alternatives? *Development*, 47:2, 43–48.

Risse, Thomas, ed. 2011. *Governance Without a State?: Policies and Politics in Areas of Limited Statehood.* New York: Columbia University Press.

Roberts, Marc J., A. G. Breitenstein and Clement S. Roberts. 2002. The Ethics of Public–Private Partnerships. In Reich, Michael R., ed. *Public–Private Partnerships for Public Health.* Cambridge, MA: Harvard University Press. 67–87.

Roger, Charles B. and Peter Dauvergne. 2016. The Rise of Transnational Governance as a Field of Study. *International Studies Review.* 18:3, 415-437.

Rosenau, James. 1992. *Governance without Government.* Cambridge, UK: Cambridge University Press.

Rosenberg, Mark L., Elisabeth S. Hayes, Margaret H. McIntyre and Nancy Neill. 2010. *Real Collaboration: What It Takes for Global Health to Succeed.* Berkeley: University of California Press.

Ruggie, John G. 1982. International Regimes, Transactions and Change: Embedded Liberalism in the Postwar Economic Order. *International Organization*, 36:2, 379–415.

  1992. Multilateralism: The Anatomy of an Institution. *International Organization*, 46:3, 561–598.

  1998. *Constructing the World Polity: Essays on International Institutionalization.* New York: Routledge.

  2000. Response from John G. Ruggie, Assistant Secretary-General United Nations to CorpWatch Coalition Letter to Kofi Annan on the Global Compact. Accessed March 2015 at www.corpwatch.org/article.php?id=96.

  2002. The Theory and Practice of Learning Networks: Corporate Social Responsibility and the Global Compact. *The Journal of Corporate Citizenship*, 5, 28–36.

  2003a. The United Nations and Globalization: Patterns and Limits of Institutional Adaptation. *Global Governance*, 9:3, 301–321.

  2003b. Taking Embedded Liberalism Global: The Corporate Connection. In Held, David and Mathias Koenig-Archibugi, eds. *Taming*

Globalization: Frontiers of Governance. Cambridge, UK: Polity Press, pp. 93–129.

2004. Reconstituting the Global Public Domain: Issues, Actors and Practices. *European Journal of International Relations*, 10:4, 499–531.

2013. *Just Business: Multinational Corporations and Human Rights.* New York: W. W. Norton & Company.

Sabatier, Paul A. and Hank C. Jenkins-Smith. 1993. *Policy Change and Learning: An Advocacy Coalition Approach.* Boulder, CO: Westview Press.

Sachs, Jeffrey D. 2005. *The End of Poverty: Economic Possibilities of Our Time.* New York: Penguin Books.

Schäferhoff, Marco. 2014. Partnerships for Health – Special Focus: Service Provision. In Beisheim, Marianne and Andrea Liese, eds. *Transnational Partnerships: Effectively Providing for Sustainable Development?* London, UK: Palgrave Macmillan. 45–62.

Schäferhoff Marco, Sabine Campe and Christopher Kaan. 2009. Transnational Public–Private Partnerships in International Relations: Making Sense of Concepts, Research Frameworks, and Results. *International Studies Review*, 11:3, 451–474.

Schepsle, Kenneth A. and Barry R. Weingast. 1987. The Institutional Foundations of Committee Power. *American Political Science Review*, 81:1, 85–104.

1994. Positive Theories of Congressional Institutions. *Legislative Studies Quarterly*, 19, 145–179.

Scholte, Jan A. 2010. Civil Society in Multi-Level Governance. In Enderlein, Henrik, Sonja Wälti and Michael Zürn, eds. *Handbook on Multi-Level Governance.* Cheltenham, UK: Edward Elgar Publishing. 383–397.

Selin, Henrik and Stacy D. VanDeveer, eds. 2009. *Changing Climates in North American Politics: Institutions, Policymaking and Multilevel Governance.* Cambridge, MA: MIT Press.

Sell, Susan K. 2003. *Private Power, Public Law: The Globalization of Intellectual Property Rights.* Cambridge, UK: Cambridge University Press.

Sell, Susan K. and Aseem Prakash. 2004. Using Ideas Strategically: The Contest Between Business and NGO Networks in Intellectual Property Rights. *International Studies Quarterly*, 48, 143–175.

Sethi, S. Prakash and Donald H. Schepers. 2014. United Nations Global Compact: The Promise-Performance Gap. *Journal of Business Ethics*, 122:2, 193–208.

Sikkink, Kathryn. 1986. Codes of Conduct for Transnational Corporations: The Case of the WHO/UNICEF Code. *International Organization*, 40:4, 815–840.

2005. Patterns of Dynamic Multilevel Governance and the Insider–Outsider Coalition. In della Porta, Donatella and Sidney Tarrow, eds. *Transnational Protest and Global Activism*. Lanham, MD: Rowman and Littlefield Publishers, Ltd. 151–173.

Sil, Rudra and Peter J. Katzenstein. 2010. Analytic Eclecticism in the Study of World Politics: Reconfiguring Problems and Mechanisms across Research Traditions. *Perspectives on Politics*, 8:2, 411–431.

Simmons, Beth A. 1993. Why Innovate? Founding the Bank for International Settlements. *World Politics*, 45:3, 361–405.

Slaughter, Anne-Marie. 2004. *A New World Order*. Princeton, NJ: Princeton University Press.

Social Accountability Accreditation Service. 2012. Summary Statistics. Accessed March 2015 at www.saasaccreditation.org/certfacilitieslist .htm.

Stadelmann, Martin and Paula Castro. 2014. Climate Policy Innovation in the South – Domestic and International Determinants of Renewable Energy Policies in Developing and Emerging Countries. *Global Environmental Change*, 29, 413–423.

Stadtler, Lea. 2011. Aligning a Company's Social and Economic Interests in Partnerships for Development. *Journal of Corporate Citizenship*, 44, 85–106.

Stadtler, Lea and Gilbert Probst. 2012. How Broker Organizations Can Facilitate Public–Private Partnerships for Development. *European Management Journal*, 30:1, 32–46.

Steets, Julia. 2010. *Accountability in Public Policy Partnerships*. Basingstoke, UK: Palgrave Macmillan.

Steets, Julia and Kristina Thomsen. 2009. Global Landscape: A Review of International Partnership Trends. An Input for UNICEF's Strategic Framework for Partnerships. GPPI Report. Accessed February 2015 at www.gppi.net/fileadmin/gppi/Steets_Thomsen_Global_Landscape_2009.pdf.

Stiglitz, Joseph E. 2002. *Globalization and its Discontents*. New York: W. W. Norton & Company.

Stone, Randall W. 2011. *Controlling Institutions: International Organizations and the Global Economy*. Cambridge, UK: Cambridge University Press.

Storeng, Katerini T. 2014. The GAVI Alliance and the Gates Approach to Health System Strengthening. *Global Public Health*, 9:8, 865–879.

Szlezák, Nicole A. 2012. *The Making of Global Health Governance: China and the Global Fund to Fight AIDS, Tuberculosis and Malaria*. New York: Palgrave Macmillan.

Szlezák, Nicole A., Barry R. Bloom, Dean T. Jamison, Gerald T. Keusch, Catherine M. Michaud, Suerie Moon and William C. Clark. 2010. The

Global Health System: Actors, Norms, and Expectations in Transition. *PLOS Medicine*, 7:1, http://journals.plos.org/plosmedicine/article/file?id=10.1371/journal.pmed.1000183&type=printable

Szulecki, Kacper, Philipp Pattberg and Frank Biermann. 2011. Explaining Variation in the Effectiveness of Transnational Energy Partnerships. *Governance*, 24:4, 713–736.

Tallberg, Jonas, Thomas Sommerer, Theresa Swuatrito and Christer Jönsson. 2013. *The Opening Up of International Organizations: Transnational Access in Global Governance.* Cambridge, UK: Cambridge University Press.

Tarrow, Sidney. 2001. Transnational Politics: Contention and Institutions in International Politics. *Annual Review of Political Science*, 4, 1–20.

   2005. *The New Transnational Activism.* Cambridge, UK: Cambridge University Press.

Tharoor, Shashi. 2007. "The Most Impossible Job" Description. In Chesterman, Simon, ed. *Secretary or General? The UN Secretary-General in World Politics.* Cambridge, UK: Cambridge University Press. 33–47.

Thérien, Jean-Philippe and Vincent Pouliot. 2006. The Global Compact: Shifting the Politics of International Development? *Global Governance*, 12:1, 55–75.

Thomas, Anisya and Lynn Fritz. 2006. Disaster Relief Inc. *Harvard Business Review*, November, 1–11.

Transnational Resource & Action Center. 2000. *Tangled Up in Blue: Corporate Partnerships at the United Nations.* San Francisco: Transnational Resource & Action Center.

Traub, James. 2006. *The Best Intentions: Kofi Annan and the UN in the Era of American World Power.* United Kingdom: Picador Press.

   2007. The Secretary-General's Political Space. In Chesterman, Simon, ed. *Secretary or General? The UN Secretary-General in World Politics.* Cambridge, UK: Cambridge University Press. 185–202.

Union of International Associations. 2011. *Yearbook of International Organizations 2010/2011: Guide to Global and Civil Society Organizations.* Brussels: Union of International Associations.

   2013. *Historical Overview of Number of International Organizations by Type 1909–2013.* Accessed March 2017 at www.uia.org/sites/uia.org/files/misc_pdfs/stat/Historical_overview_of_number_of_international_organizations_by_type_1909-2013 .pdf.

United Nations Department of Economic and Social Affairs NGO Branch. 2016. *Reports of the Committee on NGOs.* Accessed March 2017 at http://csonet.org/index.php?menu=93.

Urpelainen, Johannes. 2013. Unilateral Influence on International Bureau-
    crats: An International Delegation Problem. *Journal of Conflict Reso-
    lution*, 56:4, 701–732.
Utting, Peter. 2002. Regulating Business via Multistakeholder Initiatives: A
    Preliminary Assessment. In Utting, Peter, ed. *Voluntary Approaches to
    Corporate Responsibility*. Geneva, Switzerland: United Nations Non-
    Governmental Liaison Service. 61–130.
Utting, Peter and Ann Zammit. 2006. *Beyond Pragmatism: Appraising UN-
    Business Partnerships*. Markets, Business and Regulation Programme
    Paper, No. 1. Geneva, Switzerland: United Nations Research Institute
    for Social Development.
    2009. United Nations-Business Partnerships: Good Intentions and Con-
    tradictory Agendas. *Journal of Business Ethics*, 90:s1, 39–56.
Vabulas, Felicity and Duncan Snidal. 2013. Organization without Delega-
    tion: Informal Intergovernmental Organizations (IIGOs) and the Spec-
    trum of Intergovernmental Arrangements. *The Review of International
    Organizations*, 8:2, 193–220.
Van de Pas, Remco and Louise G. van Schaik. 2014. Democratizing the
    World Health Organization. *Public Health*, 128:2, 195–201.
Van Der Lugt, Cornis and Klaus Dingwerth. 2015. WHO Orchestrates?
    Coping with Competitors in Global Health. In Abbott, Kenneth W.,
    Philipp Genschel, Duncan Snidal and Bernhard Zangl, eds. 2015. *Inter-
    national Organizations as Orchestrators*. Cambridge, UK: Cambridge
    University Press. 237–262.
Vaubel, Roland. 2006. Principal-Agent Problems in International Organiza-
    tions. *Review of International Organizations*, 1, 125–138.
Viñuales, Jorge. 2013. The Rise and Fall of Sustainable Development.
    *Review of European, Comparative and International Environmental
    Law*, 22:1, 3–13.
Vogel, David. 2005. *The Market for Virtue: The Potential and Limits of Cor-
    porate Social Responsibility*. Washington, DC: Brookings Institution Press.
    2008. Private Global Business Regulation. *Annual Review of Political
    Science*, 11, 261–82.
Vollmer, Derek, ed. 2009. *Enhancing the Effectiveness of Sustainability
    Partnerships: Summary of a Workshop*. Washington, DC: The National
    Academies Press.
Wade, Robert H. 1997. Greening the Bank: The Struggle over the Environ-
    ment, 1970–1995. In Kapur, Devesh, John P. Lewis and Richard Webb.
    The World Bank: Its First Half Century, Vol. 2. Washington, DC: The
    Brookings Institution. 611–736.
Waddock, Sandra. 1988. Building Successful Social Partnerships. *Sloan
    Management Review*, 29:4, 17.

2008. *The Difference Makers: How Social and Institutional Entrepreneurs Created the Corporate Responsibility Movement*. United Kingdom: Greenleaf Publishing.

Waltz, Kenneth N. 1999. Globalization and Governance. *PS: Political Science and Politics*, 32:4, 693–700.

Washington Post. 2012. *Washington Post* Archive. Accessed January 2012 at www.washingtonpost.com/wp-adv/archives/advanced.htm.

Weaver, Catherine. 2009. *Hypocrisy Trap: The World Bank and the Poverty of Reform*. Princeton, NJ: Princeton University Press.

Weber, Max. 1964, c1947. *The Theory of Social and Economic Organization*. Translation. New York: Free Press.

Weingast, Barry and Mark J. Moran. 1983. Bureaucratic Discretion or Congressional Control? Regulatory Policymaking by the Federal Trade Commission. *Journal of Political Economy*, 91:5, 765–800.

Weiss, Thomas G. 2009. *What's Wrong with the United Nations and How to Fix It*. Cambridge: Polity Press.

Weiss, Thomas G. and Leon Gordenker, eds. 1996. *NGOs, the UN, and Global Governance*. Boulder, CO: Lynne Rienner Publishers.

Weissbrodt, David. 2008. International Standard-Setting on the Human Rights Responsibilities of Businesses. *Berkeley Journal of International Law*, 26:2, 373–391.

Weissert, Carol S. 1991. Policy Entrepreneurs, Policy Opportunists, and Legislative Effectiveness. *American Politics Quarterly*, 19:2, 262–74.

Welsh, Jennifer M. and Maria Banda. 2010. International Law and the Responsibility to Protect: Clarifying or Expanding States' Responsibilities? *Global Responsibility to Protect*, 2:3, 213 – 231.

Whelan, Nessa. 2010. Building the United Nations Global Compact Local Network Model: History and Highlights. In Rasche, Andreas and Georg Kell, eds. *The United Nations Global Compact: Achievements, Trends and Challenges*. Cambridge, UK: Cambridge University Press. 317–340.

Whitfield, Teresa. 2007. Good Offices and "Group of Friends." In Chesterman, Simon, ed. *Secretary or General? The UN Secretary-General in World Politics*. Cambridge, UK: Cambridge University Press. 86–101.

Widdus, Roy. 2001. Public–Private Partnerships for Health: Their Main Targets, Their Diversity, and Their Future Directions. *Bulletin of the World Health Organization*, 79:8, 713–720.

Willetts, Peter, ed. 1996. *The Conscience of the World: The Influence of Non-Governmental Organizations in the UN System*. United Kingdom: C. Hurst & Co. Publishers.

Williams, Oliver F. 2004. The UN Global Compact: The Challenge and the Promise. *Business Ethics Quarterly*, 14:4, 755–774.

Williamson, Oliver E. 1985. *The Economic Institutions of Capitalism: Firms, Markets, Relational Contracting*. New York: Free Press.

Witte, Jan Martin and Wolfgang Reinicke. 2005. *Business Unusual: Facilitating United Nations Reform through Partnerships*. New York: Global Public Policy Institute, UN Global Compact Office.

Woods, Ngaire. 2002. Global Governance and the Role of Institutions. In Held, David and Anthony McGrew, eds. *Governing Globalization. Power, Authority and Global Governance Policy*. Cambridge, UK: Polity Press, pp. 25–44.

2006. *The Globalizers: The IMF, the World Bank and Their Borrowers*. Ithaca, NY: Cornell University Press.

World Bank Operations Evaluation Department. 2001. *Global Public Policies and Programs: Implications for Financing and Evaluation. Proceedings from a World Bank Workshop*. Washington, DC: World Bank.

World Economic Forum. 2005. *Partnering for Success: Business Perspectives on Multistakeholder Partnerships*. Geneva, Switzerland: World Economic Forum.

Yamey, Gavin. 2002a. WHO in 2002: WHO's Management: Struggling to Transform a "Fossilised Bureaucracy." *British Medical Journal*, 325:7373, 1170–1173.

2002b. WHO in 2002: Faltering Steps towards Partnerships. *British Medical Journal*, 325:7374, 1236–1240.

2004. Roll Back Malaria: A Failing Global Health Campaign. *British Medical Journal*, 328:7448, 1086–1087.

Yasui, Yuki, 2011. Leveraging Strengths: An Analysis of the Partners and Partnership of the United Nations Environment Programme's Finance Initiative. *Journal of Environmental Investing*, 2:1, 19–31.

Youde, Jeremy. 2012. *Global Health Governance*. Cambridge, UK: Polity Press.

Young, Oran R. 2010. *Institutional Dynamics: Emergent Patterns in International Environmental Governance*. Cambridge, MA: MIT Press.

Zelli, Fariborz and Harro van Asselt. 2013. Introduction: The Institutional Fragmentation of Global Environmental Governance: Causes, Consequences and Responses. *Global Environmental Politics*, 13:3, 1–13.

Index